Early Biblical Interpretation

Library of Early Christianity
Wayne A. Meeks, General Editor

Early Biblical Interpretation

James L. Kugel
and Rowan A. Greer

The Westminster Press
Philadelphia

Scripture quotations from the Revised Standard Version of the Bible are copyrighted 1946, 1952, © 1971, 1973 by the Division of Christian Education of the National Council of the Churches of Christ in the U.S.A. and are used by permission.

Book design by Gene Harris

First edition

Published by The Westminster Press®
Philadelphia, Pennsylvania

PRINTED IN THE UNITED STATES OF AMERICA

9 8 7 6 5 4 3 2 1

Library of Congress Cataloging-in-Publication Data

Kugel, James L.
    Early biblical interpretation.

    (Library of early Christianity ; vol. 3)
    Bibliography: p.
    Includes index.
    1. Bible—Criticism, interpretation, etc.—History—
Early church, ca. 30–600—Addresses, essays, lectures.
I. Greer, Rowan A.   II. Title   III. Series: Library
of early Christianity ; 3.
BS500.K84 1986   220.6   85–26397
ISBN 0–664–21907–1

Contents

Foreword to Early Biblical Interpretation: Two Studies of Exegetical Origins

In recent years, disciplines once held to be quite separate have increasingly been studied conjointly, and modern scholarship has witnessed a convergence of interests and, in some instances, real collaboration by investigators working across several academic boundaries: between Roman historians and historians of Christianity, between New Testament scholars and church historians, between historians of Judaism and of Christianity, between biblical and postbiblical scholars, and between historians and literary critics. The present series of books is a continuation of that effort, an exercise in moving across chronological and disciplinary boundaries in order to identify broader patterns and congruences in certain areas.

Early Biblical Interpretation focuses on one such area: the interpretation of Scripture as practiced in early Judaism and Christianity. We have come to understand that the interpretation—and reinterpretation—of texts treated as sacred lies at the very heart of the way in which each of the varieties of Judaism in antiquity understood and expressed its identity, its way of being in the world. In this respect, Christianity was no different from the other Jewish movements. How very different it did become is one of the historical puzzles, and part of the evidence is to be found in *how* it sought to read Scripture, both in its continuation of earlier tendencies and in the modifications it introduced.

The two essays contained in this volume are an attempt to clarify the subject of early biblical interpretation by focusing in on two crucial phases of its history, the closing centuries before the common era, when the main lines of later approaches to Scripture were being established, and the early centuries of Christianity, when the Christian Bible and its specific traditions of interpretation took their definitive shape. While the first essay provides a clear (and long

needed) introduction to the entire subject of early biblical interpretation, demonstrating both its deep historical roots and its extraordinary diversity at the turn of the era, the second explores how the
inheritance of Jewish Scripture and its traditions of interpretation
were further developed within one particular context, early Christianity. Both essays will no doubt be of use to students and scholars
of early Christianity, but it is hoped that they will guide others as
well: students of Second Temple Judaism, of church history, and
most of all, students of the Bible itself and its history of interpretation.

James Kugel and Rowan Greer are admirable guides into the
thickly tangled groves of ancient interpretation. Professor Kugel is
not only a biblical scholar but also a historian of biblical exegesis,
the author of, among other things, a provocative and widely ranging
analysis of biblical poetry and of the way people have imagined it.
Professor Greer has published standard works on the way Theodore
of Mopsuestia read Scripture and the way many church fathers read
the Epistle to the Hebrews. They have both, in their different styles,
written of complex matters with an honest simplicity: that is, a
simplicity that does not conceal how much there is to be learned in
this area. They entice the reader to begin that learning and to
continue.

WAYNE A. MEEKS
General Editor

PART ONE

Early Interpretation:
The Common Background
of Later Forms of Biblical Exegesis

by James L. Kugel

Preface

The following essay is an attempt to review in concentrated form the main events of Jewish history from the sixth century B.C.E. to around the turn of the era, and to reconstruct from within them some of the elements that might have shaped Jewish interest in, and approaches to, sacred texts. In this task, the present work makes no pretense to completeness and very little to originality. It seeks simply to present readers with an overview and to focus on the three or four major factors that, it is maintained, molded Jewish exegesis during the period covered and, to a surprising degree, ever after.

Given these limited goals, I have refrained from detailed examination of individual sources or texts, save for the last chapter. I have also, because of the requirements of the series, written these chapters without footnotes along the way and have thus been unable to acknowledge those treatments of various aspects of my subject which have been helpful to me in the preparation of individual chapters. The final section of suggestions for further reading does, however, contain among its entries some of the works to which I am indebted and to whose authors I should like to express my gratitude. In addition to such written aid from previous and contemporary scholars, I wish to take this opportunity to acknowledge the aid of two who have been kind enough to read through my manuscript and offer suggestions, Profs. Michael Fishbane and Bernard Septimus.

In conclusion I should say that it is a source of some personal satisfaction that this essay appear in tandem with that of my friend and former colleague, Prof. Rowan Greer, and that the two essays be destined especially for use by undergraduates and seminary students. It is only relatively recently that the richness and deep roots of what might be called the exegetical movement of the closing centuries before the common era have been properly exposed—

roots that extend still earlier than the return from the Babylonian exile, where my essay begins. And even today, this long movement remains somewhat neglected, especially, though paradoxically, by biblicists. In university and seminary introductions to the Hebrew Bible, where early exegetical traditions ought logically to receive wide exposure, what the Bible *has meant* (even, in some cases, well before the close of the biblical period proper) is largely passed over in favor of what the Bible "really means," the later being identified with the (often all too hypothetical and elusive) "original" meaning of the text. It is my hope that the present essay, however brief and schematic, may in this format further somewhat the prominence given this exegetical movement and help to impress on some readers its importance not only as a precursor of later developments in rabbinic Judaism and Christianity but as an aspect of biblical history proper.

J.L.K.

N.B. I have generally followed the biblical translations of the Revised Standard Version (RSV), deviating at times for the sake of clarity or emphasis.

1

The Rise of Scripture

The Hebrew Bible is not a single book but a collection of writings, a sacred library composed over a period of many centuries. Even before the last parts of it were written, earlier parts were being written *about,* analyzed as to their true meaning and their applicability in changed circumstances—in a word, interpreted. This process of interpretation, fostered by forces we shall examine below, grew more and more elaborate by the end of the biblical period. In the centuries just before and after the turn of the common era, the Jewish people pored over their sacred texts with a single-minded intensity, seeking in them not only a history of their ancestors and the glories of days gone by but a corpus of divine instructions, a guide to proper conduct, and perhaps, as well, some clue to God's future plans for his people. The unfolding of these various aspects of Scripture was the product of many hands; the names of the Hebrew Bible's first interpreters are by and large not known to us. But the work they performed was of immense significance, not only for the career of Scripture itself but for the beliefs and attitudes of all who held that Scripture sacred. They established the basic patterns by which the Bible was to be read and understood for centuries to come (in truth, up until the present day), and, what is more, they turned interpretation into a central and fundamental religious activity.

I

The story of this great movement begins, logically enough, in the biblical period itself. From earliest times, Israel had conceived of what might be called an ongoing "discourse" between itself and its God, a discourse that was embodied in various forms. Perhaps the most prominent of these was the institution of the sacrificial cult. At various sacred spots ("sanctuaries"), and notably in the great Temple of Jerusalem, the people of Israel made offerings to their God: sacrificial animals, meal offerings, incense, and songs of praise. Israel "spoke" to God through these offerings and the words that accompanied them (though of course individual Israelites might, if we can judge by various biblical narratives, also "speak" to God in noncultic ways, particularly in prayers and vows uttered in times of need anywhere). God spoke to Israel as well. Of old, he had appeared to individual Israelites, the founders of the nation, and had established himself as their God, theirs and their descendants'. The laws by which Israel lived had been promulgated in God's name— not only civil statutes but laws governing what Israel owed to God, in obedience, in tithes, and in sacred ceremony. This too was part of the divine side of divine-human discourse. And perhaps the most forceful form of divine speech was simply "how things came out." For did not a good harvest or a poor one; a benign and predictable year with the natural elements, or the opposite; health and personal weal, or woe; external peace and internal calm, or the threat of strife; indeed, military victory and conquest, or military catastrophe —did not all of these represent a judgment, a sentence passed by the God who controlled Israel's fortunes?

Such divine speech, an everyday reality for the ancient Israelite, was not, however, usually direct and unmediated. God's words and deeds were transmitted and interpreted by a variety of human beings. Sages and elders knew the clipped sentences that told of God's deeds in times gone by—"Ask your father to recount to you, your elders that they might say" (Deut. 32:7). Priests and Temple personnel could divine the future or diagnose a disease. Judges and wise men knew the law, gave counsel to the king, quoted the wise sayings whose wisdom belonged to the underlying divine order of things. All such persons no doubt also knew how to see God's hand in the events of the world, great and small. But there had also developed in Israel a particular office, or amalgam of offices, specially associated with such acts of interpretation: that of the prophet.

Present-day biblical scholarship is aware of the complex and diverse origins of the institution of prophecy in biblical Israel and of the various sorts of functions that prophets might perform. But in general we can say that a prophet was conceived as a *spokesman* of God, a message-bearer from God to the king or other individuals, to Israel or to other nations. As such, he was sometimes held to have extraordinary powers; in the north, in particular, is evidenced the belief in the prophet's ability to perform miracles and intervene with God on the people's behalf. But everywhere, his speech—that is, *divine* speech—was powerful, effective; it might be said of him what was said of the Eastern soothsayer Balaam: "Those whom you bless are blessed and those whom you curse are accursed" (Num. 22:6). Our Bible contains in particularly rich effusion the words of prophets from the eighth century on—leading down through the catastrophic conquest of Jerusalem by the Babylonians and the destruction of the great Temple in 587 B.C.E.—and their resonance is still powerful today: words of reproach and words of comfort; counsel to kings, and to the nation; warnings of oncoming disaster, oracles of consolation and ultimate hope. It may be that we sometimes tend to make too much of the uniqueness of the prophet; to the ancient Israelite, the distinction between these "men of God" and some of the other figures cited was probably far less clear, or significant, than it seems to us, and in daily life many of these others may have played a far more visible and prominent role. Yet whatever the historical reality, what is important to grasp is the idea with which we began, that a divine-human *discourse* was perceived and carried on daily between Israel and her God, a discourse in which some figures, particularly the prophets, sought to announce God's judgments and desires and to explain the course of present and future events in terms of them.

This notion is important because of what happened to that discourse after the Babylonian conquest of Jerusalem and Judea in the sixth century B.C.E. The fall of Jerusalem (587 B.C.E.) was a terrible event, as upsetting to religious conceptions as it was to Jewish political existence. It brought to an end more than four centuries of rule by a single dynasty—how many of the great European monarchies can boast a comparable stability?—and crushed a state whose existence had certainly long been considered an immutable "given" in the region. The flower of Judea were deported en masse to Babylon, apparently in three waves, in 597, 587, and 582 B.C.E.; their capital and its Temple, the gathering place for priests and prophets and sages and the center of prayer and sacrifice, lay in ruins. Where was the God of Israel now that his House had been destroyed, and what hope was there for deliverance? Yet those who were exiled still clung to such hope, and to the words of the prophets who foretold it. And it did come: A scant half century after Jerusalem's fall, the upstart Persian empire, led by Cyrus, overthrew mighty Babylon, and among the results of this overthrow was the issuance of a royal decree allowing the exiled Judeans to return to their homeland (538 B.C.E.).

Quite naturally, many of those who returned sought to reestablish things as they had been before—to rebuild the Temple, to restore the Davidic dynasty, to bring back the economic prosperity and spiritual richness that had once been theirs. Our knowledge of this, the Persian, period (538–332 B.C.E.) in the history of biblical Israel is rather sketchy; historians must proceed largely by inference. But it seems clear that this program of restoration was only partially successful. The Jerusalem Temple was eventually rebuilt, but not without unnerving delays and difficulties. The rebuilt structure was apparently not particularly impressive, and this was damaging to the prestige of the Deity to whom it was dedicated, damaging in a way that is not easily grasped by modern sensibilities. The Davidic throne was revived, but only briefly: possibly Sheshbazzar, and certainly his successor, Zerubbabel, was a descendant of the house of David; both were appointed to govern the restored entity. But Zerubbabel disappears suddenly from the pages of history, and the Davidic kingship with him. Indeed, from the end of the sixth century (i.e., the time of Zerubbabel) to the middle of the fifth, there is no evidence that Judea had its own administration; some have hypothesized a collapse of the provincial government. Economic life was hard—the return from exile was not the glorious thronging some had expected—and the heirs to Israel's spiritual past struggled with one another; the new edifice shifted and creaked on its foundations.

And what became of Israel's dialogue with its God? Apparently both halves of the divine-human discourse suffered. The prophet Malachi, who belongs somewhat later in this period, paints a picture of tainted sacrifices, blind, lame, or sick animals unfit for offerings (Mal. 1), of a corrupt and partial priesthood (Mal. 2), and of moral disintegration and cultic laxity among the general populace (Mal. 3). If this represents a fair snapshot of reestablished life in Judea, things had sunk low indeed. Divine "speech," for its part, seemed hardly encouraging. The language of current events always speaks loudly, but sometimes its message is unclear: the mixture of good and bad just described, a restored Judea, but one subject to Persia, hard times and internal squabbling—this hardly constituted a ringing divine endorsement of the people's future. What was one to make of it all? Self-appointed prophets and omen seekers teemed with explanations and promises, but many were apparently disbelieved as charlatans. Some soon dreamed of a time when "every prophet will be ashamed of his vision when he prophesies; he will not put on a hairy mantle in order to deceive, but he will say, 'I am no prophet, I am a tiller of the soil' " (Zech. 13:4–5). If such self-proclaimed prophets were unreliable, then where was one to turn?

II

God's part in the divine-human discourse, it will be remembered, was not alone mediated by live human beings; it was also carried by texts. Long before the Babylonian exile, the word of God and his messengers had been committed to memory and to writing, and Israel had cherished these words; even in preexilic times, the record of ancient deeds and ancient legislation had constituted an important part of God's "speech" to humans. But as time went on, the significance of these texts increased, and with it the importance of those who copied and expounded them. This change, certainly characteristic of postexilic life, is probably not a mere reflex of events of the exile—its causes, tied up in part with the career of literacy and education in earlier times, need not detain us here. But something of the growing independent life of texts may perhaps be glimpsed even among writings that preceded the Return.

Israel's ancient laws, for example, are presented in various parts of the Pentateuch and restated or alluded to elsewhere in the Hebrew Bible. Scholars studying these texts have demonstrated that an ongoing process of explication, adaptation, and interpretation stands behind them; statutes were sometimes harmonized with one another, or rearranged in such a way as to reflect a new understanding of their purpose. The evidence of this activity makes clear the independent existence that legal texts had in preexilic times and the recognized authority that they already enjoyed, for when later writers wished to promulgate new rulings, they often proceeded by reusing or recombining older laws, sometimes in most awkward fashion, rather than starting afresh. It also demonstrates that what we might call biblical interpretation, or *exegesis,* was going on centuries before "the Bible" existed, that is, the canonical collection of texts we know by this name.

These same laws are sometimes alluded to, or commented upon, in nonlegal contexts, and such allusions further illustrate the extent to which these legal texts had a life of their own in the minds of the people. This is particularly clear in the prophetic writings composed just before, or just after, the Babylonian conquest. For example, Ezekiel's bill of particulars against his people and their leaders frequently seems to allude to written statutes: In Ezek. 22:1–16 the prophet presents a list of sins reminiscent of the Holiness Code in Leviticus 17–26. Indeed, in this instance Ezekiel seems to be thinking specifically of material now found in Leviticus 20. For example, to Leviticus' "Every one who curses his father or mother" (Lev. 20:9) corresponds Ezekiel's indictment "Father and mother have

been treated with contempt" (Ezek. 22:7); to Lev. 20:11 "The man
who lies with his father's wife has uncovered his father's nakedness"
corresponds Ezekiel's "In you, men uncover their fathers' nakedness" (Ezek. 22:10); to Lev. 20:10 "If a man commits adultery with
his neighbor's wife . . ." corresponds Ezekiel's "One man commits
abomination with his neighbor's wife" (Ezek. 22:11); to Lev. 20:17
"If a man takes his sister, his father's daughter . . ." corresponds
Ezekiel's "another man in you defiles his sister, his father's daughter" (Ezek. 22:11); and so on through a lengthy catalog of sins. It
would seem that Ezekiel was reflecting less on the reality that he had
actually seen or heard than on a particular *text* which he remembered or had before him—and which, it seems probable, he also
assumed would resonate in his hearers' memories.

Prophets also sometimes echoed their predecessors or contemporaries, or even quite consciously structured their words around
a well-known earlier message. One celebrated instance is the divine
call of Ezekiel, which echoes both Jeremiah's call (Jer. 1:9), when
God puts his "word" in the prophet's mouth, and a later saying of
Jeremiah, "Your words were found and I ate them, and your words
became to me a joy and the delight of my heart" (Jer. 15:16). Both
elements seem to come into play in part of Ezekiel's call (i.e., Ezek.
2:7–3:3); this passage is also a model, however grotesque, of what
the word of God was becoming:

> "And you [Ezekiel] shall speak my words to them [the people of
> Israel], whether they hear or refuse to hear; for they are a rebellious
> house. But you, son of man, hear what I say to you: be not rebellious
> like that rebellious house; open your mouth, and eat what I give you."
> And when I looked, behold, a hand was stretched out to me, and, lo,
> a written scroll was in it; and he spread it out before me; and it had
> writing on the front and on the back, and there were written on it
> words of lamentation and mourning and woe. And he said to me, "Son
> of man, eat what is offered to you; eat this scroll, and go, speak to the
> house of Israel." So I opened my mouth, and he gave me the scroll
> to eat. And he said to me, "Son of man, eat this scroll that I give you
> and fill your stomach with it." Then I ate it; and it was in my mouth
> as sweet as honey.

Like a child at mealtime, Ezekiel is urged to "eat what is offered"
to him, and his compliance in the face of what seems to be a
thoroughly indigestible meal makes him a model of obedience, the
very opposite of the "rebellious" subjects he is to address. But what
is so striking is the meal itself: the word of God! Already in Jeremiah's verse (Jer. 15:16), one could sense some of the diffuseness

that the prophetic scenario had taken on. God's words just appear, "were found"—words spoken of old? spoken directly to Jeremiah? —and Jeremiah does not simply pass them along, but "eats" them. They nourish him, equip him for his office ("for I am called by thy name"), and presumably they will be related to his mission only in the way our food is related to what we do and say; they will give him the force to speak and act. But how significant it is that, in Ezekiel, God's speech has already become a *text;* and the very act of eating God's word now demands impossible "obedience" and self-control, swallowing up an actual scroll, and then *not* (in both senses) "spitting it back," not just being the messenger and vehicle before the people, but, on the contrary, digesting the twice uneatable thing, a scroll, and one of lamentation and mourning and woe, to find it— how obedience pays off!—not bitter but sweeter than honey.

During the exile, and all the more so afterward, the divine word was increasingly a text and became the more hallowed the more the parchment yellowed and turned brown and cracked. Indeed, it is noteworthy that the scroll motif underwent one final, still more telling, modification:

> Again I lifted my eyes and saw, and behold, a flying scroll! And he said to me, "What do you see?" I answered, "I see a flying scroll; its length is twenty cubits, and its breadth ten cubits." Then he said to me, "This is the curse that goes out over the face of the whole land; for every one who steals shall be cut off henceforth according to it, and every one who swears falsely shall be cut off henceforth according to it. I will send it forth, says the Lord of hosts, and it shall enter the house of the thief, and the house of him who swears falsely by my name; and it shall abide in his house and consume it, both timber and stones." (Zech. 5:1–4)

Here the prophet is not even given to touch the divine word. It does not enter his mouth even in the form of food, but he sees it passing by, a giant scroll—what greater literalization of "the word of God in action"?—to which he can only bear witness: Its mission will be to destroy the house of thieves and perjurers, to avenge the transgression of that which is also, and most often, written, the Decalogue. But if this text represents in some form the disappearance, or mediation, of the prophet's own powerful speech, it also has a positive side: For here is Scripture as Actor, the written word which flies like an angel to carry out God's decrees and indeed, like the "angel of the Lord" in the Pentateuch, is even able to wreak physical destruction on those who have incurred the divine wrath.

III

At this image of the flying scroll—a symbol of the presence of texts in the minds of restored Judea as well as of the texts' growing independence and power—we ought now to pause in order to inquire into what might have been written on this scroll, or, more generally, to take stock of Israel's literary heritage at the beginning of this period. What constituted Israel's sacred writings after the return from exile? The answer to this question is far from certain, for two reasons: It is not clear what biblical books had been written (and/or compiled) by, say, the end of the sixth century B.C.E., and still less clear what status those books actually had whose existence in some form can be postulated. Did they constitute a proto-Bible? Were they regarded as sacred, and in what sense? Were there gradations in the sanctity attributed to them? Precise answers to these questions are lacking; nor does it seem likely that archaeology, or ingenious hypothesis, will supply them any time soon. Yet we are not entirely in the dark. Our biblical sources make it clear that there was among Israel's writings something (or things) called variously the *Torah* of the Lord, or of God, or alternatively the *Torah* of Moses, that occupied a central place in postexilic Judea.

In later times, this phrase was understood, and reused, to mean the Pentateuch, the first five books of the Bible, which were said to have been communicated by Moses to the people of Israel. But what Torah means in the various sources in question is another matter, for this word had undergone a complicated evolution. In our earliest biblical texts, the Hebrew word *torah* is frequently used in apposition to other words for "law," "statute," "ordinance," and the like, and seems to have exercised no particular predominance among these terms; it is, incidentally, often used in the plural, *torot*. Other relatively early texts do, however, use *torah* in a somewhat broader sense (thus, "the *torah* of your God," Hos. 4:6, perhaps meaning the totality of cultic legislation; or again in apposition to "my covenant," Hos. 8:1; cf. Amos 2:4). The characteristic, and frequent, use of this word in the Deuteronomic corpus (as, simply, "the torah" or "this torah") seems to designate a body of statutes, and this usage seems to have broadened still further in later times. Its apparent etymological sense of "teaching" now became more prominent: "Torah" was sacred lore and statute, specifically that communicated by Moses to Israel. The word thus came to mean specifically our Pentateuch (certainly by the second century B.C.E., but probably far earlier), and occasionally other parts of Scripture, or divine teaching, as well. But when we encounter the phrases cited, "the Torah of the Lord," and so forth, somewhat earlier (e.g., in biblical books such as Chronicles or Ezra-Nehemiah), it is still not indisputable that the Pentateuch as a whole is being referred to, still less that it is the Pentateuch precisely as we know it today. (Ezra 9:11 and Neh. 13:1–3, for example, contain inexact citations—if citation was intended—of Pentateuchal passages; compare with Lev. 18:24–30; Deut. 7:3; and Deut. 23:3–5.)

Whatever its precise borders, this "Torah of Moses" is clearly presented as *the* central text. Now in tracing the career of this term, we ought not to lose sight of a point more interesting than its various possible referents; for the fact is that a, or the, Torah had been, in many of the places cited, already functioning for some time *as Scripture*. It was a text, a written document (even if it was not known to all primarily in written form), by which people were to guide their own lives. Indeed, in key speeches inserted throughout the Deuteronomic history, as well as in numerous passages in Chronicles and Ezra-Nehemiah, there emerges clearly the notion that the contents of "Torah" constituted a code of behavior. Thus God's urgings to Joshua in Josh. 1:2–9, or David's last words to his son Solomon (1 Kings 2:2–9), contain exhortations to "keep," "observe," and so forth, God's commandments "as it is written in the *torah* of Moses." That body of commandments was to govern thoroughly each minute of daily life: "This book of the Torah shall not depart out of your mouth, but you shall meditate on it day and night, that you may be careful to do according to all that is written in it" (Josh. 1:8). So later kings and officials were judged by the degree of their adherence to "the Lord's Torah" or "the book of Moses' Torah" (see, for example, 2 Kings 10:31; 14:6; or 2 Chron. 12:1; 23:18; 31:3–4). The frequency of reference to this Torah especially in Ezra-Nehemiah is indicative of the importance that the author or authors of these accounts felt could, and should, be attached to the written word.

Some of this mentality may be discerned in the description of a public reading of the Torah contained in the Book of Nehemiah. Ezra the scribe, "skilled in the Torah of Moses which the Lord the God of Israel had given" (Ezra 7:6), was dispatched in the seventh year of the Persian king Artaxerxes (apparently Artaxerxes I, hence in the year 458 B.C.E.) to join the inhabitants of Judea in order to "appoint magistrates and judges who may judge all the people." His mission may have been self-generated, or it may have come in response to reports of unrest or sad tidings from the Jewish settlement. At any rate, he went and soon we find him addressing a public gathering of the people:

> And all the people gathered as one man into the open space before the Water Gate; and they told Ezra the scribe to bring the book of the Torah of Moses which the Lord had commanded to Israel. And Ezra the priest brought the Torah before the assembly, both men and women and all who could hear with understanding, on the first day of the seventh month. And he read from it facing the open space before the Water Gate from daybreak until midday, in the presence of the men and women and the interpreters; and the ears of all the people were attentive to the book of the Torah. (Neh. 8:1–3)

Scholars have often suggested that this passage marks a particular "moment" in history, the beginning of the religion-of-Torah which is Judaism. This is to overstate matters. Torah, as Scripture, was, as we have just seen, a long time in the making, and Ezra's public reading is simply one milestone along the way. (Its purpose, some have suggested, was to create a climate favorable to his—and his supporters'—program of wide-ranging religious reforms.) But the incident does provide a useful index for the growing role of Scripture in this community. For it is noteworthy that this Torah is not a text for rulers or community leaders alone; its statutes are not meant even to provide only the operative legal framework for community life, as for example our legal systems do. It is most significant that both men and women are present, for this is representative of a desire to have the entire populace actively instructed (cf. Deut. 31:11–13). The Torah was to be internalized, to become a generative force at the level of each individual community member, written, as in Jeremiah's "new covenant" (Jer. 31:33), "upon their hearts." Indeed, a cryptic passage (which will be of some interest to us presently) even lists a group of individuals who, during this reading or just afterward, "helped the people to understand the Torah, while the people remained in their places. And they read from the book, from the Torah of God, interpreted; and they gave the meaning, so that the people might understand the reading" (Neh. 8:7–8). The message is unmistakable: The Torah, if it is to function as the central text for the community, must truly be their common property, and be properly understood by everyone.

IV

Before leaving this scene, we should note that in addition to the "book of the Torah of Moses," Israel possessed other texts that enjoyed special standing. Again, even if we knew precisely which parts of our present Bible (as well as which books not now part of it) were extant in the late sixth or mid-fifth century B.C.E., we still would not know what sort of "proto-Bible" existed in Judea, for we would not know who possessed these documents and to what purpose, nor, therefore, the extent to which they were regarded as sacred and authoritative in the manner just seen with regard to the Torah of Moses. But certainly we can inventory some of the major works in various literary genres represented among the documents likely to have existed at this time.

Historical works of various sorts had long had an honored place in Israel, and certainly an overriding interest in historiography has left its mark on our present Bible. The Pentateuch bears the outline of a history of Israel from the creation of the people's remotest ancestors until the time of Moses. Added to this history is a great historical anthology, known as the Deuteronomic history, running from the end of Moses' life through the events recounted in the books of Joshua, Judges, Samuel, and Kings. Some of the raw material edited into this history is very old, the stuff of legends (this is especially so of the Book of Judges); and other parts belong to the genre of "annals of the king" and royal record-keeping. The bulk of this material had apparently been collected and edited well before the Babylonian conquest; an earlier form had, as its original conclusion and climax, the reign of King Josiah (2 Kings 22–23). Another edition seems to have been made in exile, bringing events up to date through the conquest and, significantly, changing the focus of the book's theology to fit drastically altered circumstances. The fact that such records were preserved and edited (more than once!) is likewise indicative of the high importance attached to the enterprise of historiography. For the editors of this history it was, more precisely, a sacred task, the act of interpreting God's "speech" in the events of the past, and the lessons to be drawn from it are presented, sometimes in heavy-handed fashion, in various speeches, prayers, and transitional insertions throughout. Nor is historiography limited to this corpus. Various other writings were collected, edited, supplemented, or created whole in the postexilic period, including 1 and 2 Chronicles, another retelling of Israel's history fitted to a particular group's ideology and concerns, the books of Ezra and Nehemiah, and still others.

In addition to historical works, *prophetic writings* of various sorts were cultivated by Jews. Not only accounts of the lives and deeds of prophets and holy men existed but also collections of the sayings and speeches of prophets early and late—the actual words of Amos and Hosea, Micah, Isaiah, Jeremiah and Ezekiel, and others. Curiously, these were not only copied and reverently edited (some during the exilic period), but some of them were eventually rearranged and even supplemented with new material. Strikingly, this editorial activity was not generally of a "cosmetic" character—prophecies that had gone unrealized or that were contradicted by later events were often left to stand as they were. Instead, the additions and rearrangements reflect a multitude of possible motives—pseude- pigraphy, commentary, perhaps even a fitting of the texts in ques- tion to public recitation or liturgical use. Moreover, it is to be noted that the corpus of prophetic writings was constantly swelling. Again, it would be unwise to equate the texts in actual circulation with those in our present Bible, for there were certainly other books that did not survive. But to the Persian period belong the prophecies of Haggai, Zechariah, and Malachi, as well as parts of the Book of Isaiah and quite possibly other biblical prophecies (others came still later). These too were collected and, eventually, edited or supple- mented in similar fashion.

Lastly, we should note the presence in Israel of miscellaneous documents of a potentially sacred character. Of those which are present in our Bible, certainly one of the most significant classes is that of sacred *psalms and songs.* Psalms had played a significant role at cultic sites in Israel long before the Babylonian conquest, their recitation apparently accompanying animal sacrifices or other cultic acts. It seems likely that the role of such cultic songs and prayers expanded even before the Babylonian conquest: Moves toward the centralization of worship begun in the eighth century deprived pro- vincial sanctuaries of some of their cultic functions, perhaps leaving prayer and song in a more central role; and the eventual reduction of these centers, either through conquest or centralization, may have sent cultic singers thronging to the Jerusalem sanctuary, caus- ing psalmody there to assume a more prominent role. In any case, it seems plausible that these songs of praise and petition were among the best-known "texts" of Israel (even if known by heart and not on papyrus or parchment) even before the Babylonian con- quest. In exile, according to Psalm 137,

> We sat down weeping when we recalled Zion. On the willows in their
> midst we hung up our harps, for there our captors asked of us songs,
> and our despoilers [asked for] celebration: "Sing to us from the songs
> of Zion." (Ps. 137:1–3)

The demand of the captors may reflect something hinted at in other texts as well, a certain preeminence in music and song among the Jews; and despite their otiose instruments, the Jews most certainly must have sustained themselves in exile by the recitation of these same songs and psalms. In restored Judea, psalmody took on an even increased significance. The reinaugurated cult resounded with the songs of the Levites, whose own view of the importance (and ancient origins) of Israelite psalmody is amply represented in the Book of Chronicles. Moreover, psalms and psalm-like compositions were probably being collected (and composed) for use outside the Jerusalem cult proper, either for some liturgical purpose or instruction or private devotion. All these, then, were part of the sacred "library."

The education of future scribes, officials, and perhaps even of a good segment of the general populace, intersected with the whole world of wisdom and its accoutrements—*collections of proverbs, wise sayings, exhortations to right conduct,* and the like. Such texts had been in Israel's possession before the exile, but their very antiquity now gave them a certain stamp of approval; like the ancient legends and histories, like olden prophecies and songs, so proverbs and sayings of reputedly ancient provenance savored of the glories of days gone by, when God so directly exercised his stewardship over Israel. The very notion of wisdom, *hokhmah,* carried with it a host of associations. Wisdom was first of all a path, a way of life; it was not acquired easily, and certainly not swiftly. "Young" and "wise" were almost opposite concepts: No youth, no matter how intelligent, could pretend to *hokhmah* (though he ought certainly to have set out in its pursuit), whereas the "elder" or "old man" (*zaqen*) is synonymous with the sage. This, in turn, should be informative about how wisdom was acquired; it was the product of patience—indeed, it was the *way* of patience, a training in moderate behavior that focused the trainee's eye on the end of things, for "better is the end of a thing than its beginning" (Eccl. 7:8). Finally, the pursuit of *hokhmah* in Israel implied the existence of an underlying plan to all of reality, a plan that was not readily visible but whose workings—in the natural order as in the world of human affairs—could now and then be discerned clearly. For all these reasons, the study of wisdom texts in Judea had a connection with the world of the sacred, indeed with some of the other texts in Israel's sacred library. To the sometimes homey insights of sayings now found in the later chapters of Proverbs was appended a prefatory section (Prov. 1–9) whose theme was precisely the integration of Israelite wisdom into the world of Judean piety: "The fear of the Lord is the beginning of understanding." Other books in the Bible that bespeak the same wisdom milieu are Job (whose date is unknown), a series of wisdom dialogues of the "acceptation of comfort" (*qabbalat tanhumim*) genre written in a mock-Eastern dialect and put in the mouths of various non-Israelite sages; Ecclesiastes (Koheleth), a kind of intellectual autobiography written during the Persian period and framed with wisdom sayings; various wisdom psalms found in the Psalter; and the Song of Songs. In addition, a number of works ultimately excluded from the Jewish canon but preserved elsewhere bespeak the continued literary productivity of this same wisdom milieu, and these include not only the sorts of compositions mentioned above but tales and legends about "wise" heroes, such as the Book of Tobit.

This is probably not all there was in the growing corpus of sacred and quasi-sacred writings. We know the names of some other books that may have held a prominent place in such a library—the *Book of the Wars of the Lord,* the *Book of the Upright* (and, possibly, the "Book of Song"), the *Book of the Kings of Israel and Judah,* the *Book of Remedies,* the *Chronicles of Samuel the Seer,* and still others—but they have been lost. Yet the foregoing should provide a representative sample of what that sacred library included and, more important, of the still fluid state of things by, say, the mid-fifth century B.C.E. To recoup: There was something known as the Torah of Moses (perhaps now in the form of the Pentateuch we know today) which seems to have had an honored place as *the* text of Judea, sanctified by its provenance, its antiquity, and its function within the community. There were historical writings that recounted the glorious deeds of Israel's God on behalf of his people, as well as the catastrophic causes leading up to the Babylonian captivity. There were the writings of prophets whose words might still be scrutinized for the bearing on current events, or supplemented with interpretations or expansions touching on the present or the time to come. There were songs and prayers connected with the divine service, and others meant for recitation outside the cult. There were wisdom texts of various genres, now connected with Judean piety. And in addition to all of these, there were new texts being composed at all times for similarly devout settings and purposes.

2

The Need for Interpretation

Why did Scripture need to be interpreted? The question might appear frivolous; after all, do not all texts require interpretation? Literary criticism, legal history, linguistics, and other modern disciplines are well aware that the answer to the second question is, in their various senses, yes. But this very diversity of disciplines should remind us that interpretation itself is not a single activity, but several, and that each operates in its own peculiar set of conventions and expectations. A modern-day literary critic might hope his book's reading of Milton's *Paradise Lost* will strike readers as informative, enlightening, even inspiring—but he probably does not aim for it to be something called *the*, only *an*, interpretation; he would like to believe that *Paradise Lost*, or any work of the imagination, defies a single interpreter. Nor, among most modern-day critics, will interpretation seek specifically to arrive at a statement of the author's intention in creating each line of the work; indeed, the work is sometimes conceived to have a life independent of the wishes of its author. In certain legal systems, on the other hand, the whole act of interpretation is geared to defining without equivocation the intentions of the system's original framers, or communicators; the purpose is sometimes to extend thereby the authority of these original figures to cover new situations or applications not originally envisaged by the text. And legal interpretation generally operates under a rather more rigorous sense of responsibility; after all, a sense of the "playfulness" of the text or an openness to the infinity of possible readings will not restore the life of an accused man put to death or bring back years spent in prison or in penury. And such notions of interpretation are yet different from those of the modern linguist, who is acutely aware of each "performance" of a text as a discrete speech act; of the indeterminate state of many utterances, whose significance can be clarified only by reference to a "gram-

27

mar" of conventions not manifest in the text per se; of "reinterpretation" as a normal process of everyday speech; and so forth. So if all utterances do, in some sense, need to be interpreted, what that process of interpretation involves, what it claims to be doing, and what is considered to be an adequate realization of its aims all tend to vary depending on the conventions surrounding the act itself. Even insofar as *biblical* interpretation is concerned, there is not one set of conventions; as we shall see, interpreters had often widely divergent methods and goals, and they produced readings of the same text which were "as far as east from west" (Ps. 103:12).

But we must at least begin by mentioning a few of the factors that made Jews in the restored province of Judea acutely aware of the need for interpretation. The first of these operates at the simplest level of linguistic meaning. The language of Babylon, where the elite of Judea had been borne off as captives, was Aramaic, a language similar to Hebrew but nevertheless incomprehensible to one not trained in it (see 2 Kings 18:26). Even two generations of captivity were probably sufficient to cause Aramaic to replace Hebrew as the everyday speech of the exiles. The first, and all subsequent, waves of returnees might therefore presumably be in need of help in understanding Hebrew Scripture, as would of course Jews who did *not* return but chose to remain outside Judea—not only in Babylon but in Egypt and other centers. Moreover, even those who had stayed behind in Judea during the exile, though they continued to speak their native idiom, were not exempt from linguistic difficulties. For their spoken idiom was certainly not identical to the often elegant literary language of the Bible; moreover, it apparently became corrupted by neighboring dialects (see Neh. 13:24). For this reason, both the Judean exiles and those who had stayed behind might be in need of that most basic act of interpretation, translation into an idiom more familiar to them. This may be precisely what the "interpreters" mentioned in connection with Ezra's public reading of the Torah (Neh. 8:1–8) were engaged in doing. For it was apparently standard practice within the Persian empire to train scribes to turn, for example, a dictated Persian text into Aramaic (in quite mechanical fashion); the Aramaic could then be spontaneously retroverted into Persian, or translated into another language, by a similarly trained scribe when the text reached its destination. The Persians referred to such a text as *huzvarišn;* the Hebrew *meforaš* ("interpreted") in Neh. 8:8 is apparently used here as an equivalent (cf. Ezra 4:18).

It is also to be noted that the fortunes of Aramaic at this time were very much on the rise. Even before Cyrus had conquered Babylon,

Aramaic had become the most widespread and best-known language in the region. But with the establishment of the Persian empire, Cyrus enthroned it as the official language of diplomatic correspondence throughout his far-flung empire, "from India to Cush," as indeed epigraphic finds have confirmed. Henceforth and until after the conquests of the Greeks in the late fourth century B.C.E., Aramaic was *the* language, not only in the diplomatic sense but in regard to the whole host of activities that confer a culture's prestige. We know from more recent examples what can happen to a local language in the presence of another endowed with such cultural prestige; even though the local language persists as a spoken tongue, its use in writing is curtailed, and it acquires a homey, unofficial quality that is not always flattering. This was not quite the case for Hebrew (and decidedly not so by the end of the Persian period), precisely because it was the exalted language of ancient Jewish records. Yet one can suppose that translation or restatement of legal or historical material into Aramaic was sometimes done not solely, perhaps not even principally, for the purpose of facilitating understanding but to confer to the text an aura of "high culture" or official standing. Indeed, this factor too has been mentioned in recent discussions of the "interpreters" in Ezra's reading.

Moving across the faint and imprecise border that separates translation from interpretation proper, we can note that, even for those whose command of Hebrew was excellent, biblical texts must nevertheless have presented linguistic usages that were puzzling or unconsciously misleading. For "Hebrew" itself is a fiction; the Bible contains different Hebrews, in texts spanning a millennium of linguistic development and incorporating several distinct dialects. The fact of their all being "Hebrew" did not make them equally understandable. After all, the ordinary English speaker of today cannot be expected to understand the writings of Chaucer, who antedates him by only six hundred years (Old English writings of a few centuries earlier are so foreign that he probably would not even recognize them as being in his "language," which, in truth, they are not). The same English speaker might believe he understands the English of Shakespeare or Milton, but the fact is that he does not, for many words that he believes he recognizes are actually significantly different in meaning. Indeed, even the prose of Ruskin or Matthew Arnold will conceal similar "false friends," usages that he believes he understands but that actually have quite other significances. And so was it with biblical Hebrew; many passages in the psalms or in Genesis must have struck Judeans of the fifth century or later as very perplexing, and still more might have seemed to mean one thing whereas their original significance was quite another.

What is more, Hebrew was apparently undergoing more than run-of-the-mill historical changes in restored Judea. The evidence for this is somewhat muted in the Persian period, since *written* Hebrew often continued to imitate the style of olden texts. But the *spoken* language, traces of which begin to appear with increasing frequency in the closing centuries of the era and which eventually became a literary language of its own (that witnessed in rabbinic texts)—the spoken language was apparently strikingly different, not only in vocabulary but in grammar and syntax. To what extent this language reflects dialect differences extant even before the exile, or Aramaic influences, or still other factors is not clear, but it seems that the language of Yehud Medinta (as the Persian province of Judea was called, see Ezra 5:8) was significantly different from that preserved in most biblical texts.

This was true in all areas of the Hebrew language. In vocabulary, for example, many words common in biblical texts had been, or were in the process of being, replaced by other words; even such common ideas as "time," "much," "get," "take," "need," "want," and others were different. These differences did not always present problems of understanding, but sometimes they must have, for the processes of linguistic change inevitably create misunderstandings of old texts. To take an example from the Bible which is attested in the biblical exegesis of a later period: In the story of Cain and Abel (Gen. 4), Cain complains to God about the punishment that has been given him for murdering his brother; his words are, "Lo, my punishment is too great to bear." To a later age, however, the word used for "punishment" seemed strange, for it had long since ceased to mean punishment and now meant only sin or crime. Jewish exegetes played on this confusion in order to turn Cain into the figure of a repentant sinner, and instead of having him complain to God that his punishment is too severe, Cain is made out to be saying, "Lo, my sin is too great to forgive," quite a different sentiment! The reasons for this "interpretation" may have been ideological or theological, but it was founded on a linguistic reality, the perceived strangeness or inappropriateness of the biblical usage to later readers.

In addition to changes in vocabulary, there were numerous and significant shifts in grammar and syntax. The verbal system that underlies many biblical texts was changing. Use of the infinitive absolute was greatly reduced, for example, and there is increased evidence of previously rare verbal forms (especially, use of the "participle" to express present tense) in the Persian period, while on the other hand a falling away of some of the literary contrastive uses of the Hebrew verb's two aspects and a reduction of the *"waw* conversive." It is easy to imagine how, as these changes solidified, a Judean might be baffled by, for example, the emphatic use of an infinitive in conjunction with a finite verb, or by an old psalm whose verbal forms are sometimes in one aspect, sometimes in another (as many modern commentators have been!). Similarly, a standardization in the use of the relative *'ašer* ("that") might make older texts, in which this word is occasionally omitted, appear strange or even incomprehensible (we have evidence of this from the ancient biblical manuscripts of Qumran, copied several centuries later).

All these are purely linguistic difficulties—a rare word, a meaning no longer understood, a form or usage now outdated, or, in the extreme case, a language simply not understood by part of the community. But the need for interpretation went beyond merely linguistic difficulties; there were many things in biblical texts which, quite apart from such problems, required explanations. Indeed, this brings us to biblical interpretation of quite a different order.

II

The aim of many in restored Judea is found in the words of the Book of Nehemiah, "to walk in God's Torah which was given by Moses the servant of God, and to observe and do all the commandments of the Lord our master and his ordinances and statutes" (Neh. 10:29). But some of those ordinances and statutes posed difficulties. For example, the Bible is most emphatic about the observance of the Sabbath—this commandment is mentioned frequently in the Pentateuch and reasserted or alluded to elsewhere in Israel's sacred writings. Yet what does proper observance of the Sabbath require? On Mt. Sinai, according to Ex. 20:10, God prohibited the Israelites from doing "any work, you or your son or your daughter or your manservant or your maidservant or your cattle or the sojourner who is within your gates." But what might "any work" mean? Did it mean simply that one could not perform one's profession on the Sabbath—farmers not farm, merchants not sell, and so forth? Or was it perhaps still more stringent, prohibiting all from doing any of the work that constitutes a livelihood—for example, prohibiting a farmer from repairing his house, or even bringing up water, on the Sabbath? Many elements of detail needed to be explained. Thus, Ex. 34:21 states: "Six days shall you work, but on the seventh day you shall rest; in plowing time and in harvest time you shall rest." Is the mention of agricultural seasons merely an emphatic flourish (i.e., "no matter how pressing the need for intensive labor might be"), or is it intended to communicate something about the *kinds* of work that are forbidden? And what of Ex. 35:3, which adds the further proviso, "You shall kindle no fire in all your habitations on the Sabbath day." Did "kindle" imply not *having* fires, or just not starting them afresh—that is, was it permitted to light an oil lamp and keep it burning the whole Sabbath long, perhaps even transferring its flame to other combustibles?

These might seem like trivial or mundane concerns when it comes to so spiritual a matter as a day of "solemn rest to the Lord." But for a community that was determined "to walk in God's Torah which was given by Moses," knowing precisely *how* to observe the Sabbath was of vital importance. Indeed, the welfare of the community as a whole was dependent on divine approval, and since the community had been instructed not only to observe the Sabbath but to put to death anyone who violated the provision against work (Ex. 35:2), this was one matter that required absolute clarification. The precise meaning of "any work" needed to be *interpreted* in some definitive fashion.

One phenomenon on which interpreters might rely was that just witnessed in the case of the Sabbath; a given subject is often treated or alluded to in more than one place within the ancient books. Thus, the prohibition against kindling fires on the Sabbath might clarify the meaning of the overall prohibition against "any work," and one might look to all the other references to the Sabbath, within the Pentateuch and perhaps outside it, in order to find some basis for community norms. In the case of the Sabbath one might learn, for example, from Jer. 17:21–22 that so insignificant a form of "work" as carrying burdens was forbidden on the Sabbath: "Let them not take out a burden from their houses on the Sabbath day." Still further refinements could be learned from a cryptic pronouncement in the Book of Isaiah (Isa. 58:13–14) or elsewhere. This interpretive procedure, using one text to clarify the meaning of another on the same subject, was adopted, we know, by interpreters from a very early period.

Yet textual comparisons sometimes yielded not clarification but confusion. For example, what animal was a Jew to use for the Passover sacrifice? Exodus 12:5 is quite clear: "You shall take it from the sheep or from the goats." Yet when one looks at the Passover laws of Deuteronomy, it says (Deut. 16:2), "from the flock or the herd," the latter word implying cattle as well. And how was it to be cooked? Exodus 12:8 says "roasted," Deut. 16:7 says "boiled." Was the

Sabbath to be "remembered" (Ex. 20:8) or "kept" (Deut. 5:12), and what was the difference? How can one reconcile the fate of the Israelite slave girl as stated in Ex. 21:7—"When a man sells his daughter as a slave, she shall not go free in the same manner as male slaves"—with the law of Deut. 15:12, which treats slaves of both sexes, "a Hebrew man or a Hebrew woman," the same? These were the sorts of questions, in ritual law and in civil statute, in disputes between neighbors and in matters between man and God, that required precise and definitive interpretation.

In addition to such legal questions, there were all manner of details in the ancient books that cried out for explanation or commentary. Many of Israel's ancestors and heroes are presented in the Bible in terms that are not particularly heroic, or even ethical. Thus, in Genesis 12 we encounter Abram, God's favorite and the ancestor of all Israel (as well as of other nations), passing off his wife Sarai as his sister in order to save his own skin—and, what is worse, she is apparently allowed to cohabit with Pharaoh. Nothing in the text implies divine disapproval of Abram's behavior, nor does he suffer for it. On the contrary, he leaves Egypt a rich man. Worst of all, the same thing happens again (Gen. 20) and again (Gen. 26)! Was this the moral code God had enjoined on Israel's ancestors—and, if not, why should these things have been included in Israel's corpus of sacred annals? Similarly, Jacob and Rebecca are represented as conspiring to deceive Isaac; King David is shown as a ruthless schemer and adulterer; Judah, the man who gave his name to the tribe and territory of Judea—and thus the immediate physical and spiritual "ancestor" of the Jews—is shown as a frequenter of prostitutes; and so on. Sometimes the heroes of Scripture's narratives seem to violate specifically the laws of biblical law codes. The Book of Ruth recounts a moving tale of love between a man of Bethlehem and a lovely Moabite woman, consummated in holy matrimony. King David, God's own choice for founder of the great dynasty, is a direct descendant of that union. What, then, can Scripture mean when it says, "Let not an Ammonite *or a Moabite* enter into the congregation of the Lord; even the tenth generation from them shall not enter into the congregation of the Lord, not ever" (Deut. 23:3)? Similarly, why is it that Reuben, clearly described as Jacob's "firstborn," does not inherit the "double portion" of the firstborn as prescribed in Deut. 21:17 (the double portion seems instead to have gone to Joseph; cf. Gen. 48:22)? Did Jacob thus favor his second wife's eldest over his first wife's, in a way that this verse in Deuteronomy specifically forbids?

No doubt whenever one reads a text—a book, a letter, or even some public notice—there are questions one might be inclined to ask of the author; but since authors are often at some remove, in time or space, from readers, most such questions never get asked. When, however, a group of texts takes on the special role witnessed in Ezra 7 and elsewhere, when it becomes, or is becoming, the (it might not here be inappropriate to use the anachronism) "Bible" of the community, readers' questions take on a more urgent quality. If these texts were to play a crucial role in governing community affairs, in setting forth models of ethical behavior and educating the young, then questions such as these certainly did not die in the breasts of readers and listeners; they were asked often, and in public, and they demanded unambiguous response.

Yet even this need for interpretation, more widespread and more demanding than the mere linguistic function described above, does not touch on all, perhaps not even on the most important, of the factors that led to the rise of biblical interpretation.

III

attitude toward relat. of past to present is most impt

In order to fill out the picture, it is necessary to recapture something of the attitude toward the past, and its relationship to the present, that existed in restored Judea. It should be evident from the preceding that the inhabitants of Judea in postexilic times necessarily had an interest, perhaps a fascination, with days gone by. The very mode of "restoration" dictates such an interest; those who had returned had gone back to the ancestral homeland, the place in which patriarchs had wandered and where kings and prophets had once held sway. But if the Return constituted a physical reconnection with the past, it did not ipso facto clarify restored Judea's standing vis-à-vis that past. Was it, in its present form, simply the resumption of all that had been, indeed, the fulfillment of biblical prophecy? Or did reality still fall short of what was to be expected —and therefore could one not look forward to some further divinely directed events in the near future, in which the final unfolding of God's plan for his people would be accomplished?

exploited by NT-

Different answers to these questions are reflected in different parts of the Bible; it must have been an issue from the time of Cyrus' edict on through the period of Ezra and Nehemiah, and still later times. The prophets Haggai and Zechariah, who prophesied at the beginning of the reign of Darius (i.e., after 521 B.C.E.), felt that a "true" restoration was nearly at hand: Their interest focused on the Temple and its cult, on the people's observance—and particularly on Zerubbabel son of Shealtiel, the Davidic heir. For was it not

God's will to restore the Davidic throne to its former glory and to re-create Judea as an independent nation, indeed a world power? For a time it must have seemed so, and in the prophecies of these men we may read stirrings toward the elevation of Zerubbabel to the heights occupied by his ancestors:

> In the second year of Darius the king, in the seventh month, on the twenty-first day of the month, the word of the Lord came by Haggai the prophet, "Speak now to Zerubbabel the son of Shealtiel, governor of Judah, and to Joshua the son of Jehozadak, the high priest, and to all the remnant of the people, and say, 'Who is left among you that saw this house in its former glory? How do you see it now? Is it not in your sight as nothing? Yet now take courage, O Zerubbabel, says the Lord. . . . For thus says the Lord of hosts: Once again, in a little while, I will shake the heavens and the earth and the sea and the dry land; and I will shake all nations, so that the treasures of all nations shall come in, and I will fill this house with splendor, says the Lord of hosts.' " (Hag. 2:1-7)

> Speak to Zerubbabel, governor of Judah, saying, I am about to shake the heavens and the earth, and to overthrow the throne of kingdoms; I am about to destroy the strength of the kingdoms of the nations, and overthrow the chariots and their riders. (Hag. 2:20-22)

> This is the word of the Lord to Zerubbabel: Not by might [i.e., of the nations!], nor by power, but by my Spirit, says the Lord of hosts. What are you, O great mountain? Before Zerubbabel you shall become a plain. (Zech. 4:6-7)

Whether, as some scholars have urged, we read in these words a call to rebellion against Persian authority, it is in any case clear that some people saw in Zerubbabel the focus of imminent and drastic political change; very soon the world order was to be reorganized by the God of Israel, and Zerubbabel was to have a crucial role.

Elsewhere, and certainly in later periods, the assessment was quite different. It is striking that, in their treatment of Zerubbabel, the books of Ezra and Nehemiah omit mention of his Davidic origins; he is not presented as the heir to the throne. Did the wisdom of hindsight impose this omission, or does it reflect a rather different view of Judea's possibilities vis-à-vis its glorious past? For Ezra-Nehemiah on the whole does not look forward to a re-creation of Israel's royal glories; the house of David has no place in its world-view, which on the contrary sees in the kings of Persia the political instruments of the divine will. It is through them that Israel's God has chosen to act: "The Lord stirred up the spirit of Cyrus" (Ezra 1:1) in order to cause him to issue his Edict of Return, and Cyrus himself is made to say, "The Lord, the God of heaven, has given me all the kingdoms of the earth, and he has charged me to build him a house at Jerusalem, which is in Judah" (Ezra 1:2).

Of course it is perfectly normal that different men in the same or different times should have disagreed about Judea's present or future—either in this matter of political leadership or in the assessment of the role to be played by different subgroups and parties in the life of the state, the operation of the Temple cult, and other vital matters. But what should draw our attention is the extent to which *the past* intrudes in such questions and the issue of continuity with that past is raised again and again. When Haggai issues an oracle concerning Zerubbabel's future glory,

> on that day, says the Lord of hosts, I will take you, O Zerubbabel my servant, the son of Shealtiel, says the Lord, and make you like a signet ring; for I have chosen you, says the Lord of hosts. (Hag. 2:23)

It is probably no accident that his words echo a dire oracle of Jeremiah:

> As I live, says the Lord, though Coniah the son of Jehoiakim, king of Judah, were the signet ring on my right hand, yet I would tear you off and give you into the hand of those who seek your life. (Jer. 22:24–25)

Nor should it be surprising that the full text of the beginning of Ezra 1:1, cited above, reads:

> In the first year of Cyrus king of Persia, *in order to accomplish the word of the Lord uttered by Jeremiah*, the Lord stirred up the spirit of Cyrus king of Persia so that he made a proclamation . . . (Cf. 2 Chron. 36:20–22.)

For the past was everywhere. It was what explained the present, and was the standard by which the present was to be judged and upon which future hopes were to be based; and it was legitimacy. Recent scholarship has been particularly aware of this in regard to the Book of Chronicles, whose compilation probably dates from the Persian period. This retelling of biblical history, based in large measure on the books of Samuel and Kings and other biblical material, succeeds —through additions and omissions, small shifts in emphasis and wording—in presenting a particular orientation to the present and future, one that stresses the themes of the continuity of postexilic times with preexilic, the eternity of Israel's relationship with its God, and of its bond with the land. The book looks forward to a time when Israel will strictly adhere to God's Torah and thereby vouchsafe the continued existence of the "whole people of Israel" on its own land and under the leadership of a Davidic king. Yet how remarkable that this vision should be presented in the form of a history of Israel before the exile. It is as if the past had to be consulted—and touched up a bit—in order to find a program for Judea's future, or a legitimation for a particular outlook and approach.

The same concern with the past is reflected somewhat in the scattered findings of archaeologists from among the remains of the Persian period. While seal impressions from the early part of that period—that is, prior to the middle of the fifth century—are no different from seals used throughout the Persian empire, the later years, those from the mid-fifth century to the time of Alexander's conquest of the region in the last third of the next century, yield strikingly different evidence. Numerous and varied seal impressions suddenly appear, all with the name "Yehud" written on them, either in the (by then) standard Aramaic alphabet or, remarkably, in the old Hebrew script. Coins from the fourth century similarly bear "Yehud" in Hebrew script. There was also apparently an attempt to reinstate the system of weights that had existed before the Babylonian conquest. The extent to which these findings are connected with the political reality (and perhaps specifically with the conferring of some new status on Judea—at the time of Ezra and Nehemiah?) cannot yet be determined. But this evidence does seem to argue for a growing (or continuing) concentration on glorious bygone days. Indeed, a priori we might have expected just the reverse —that as the memory of the traumatic exile faded and as the inhabitants of restored Judea became more solidly entrenched, their dependence on all that had been before the exile would have diminished. This does not appear to have been the case. Of course there was certainly no single attitude toward the past, and interest in it must have varied within subgroups of the population and in different periods. But these findings from the material culture of Persian Judea only support the impression provided by biblical texts that the great days of the preexilic monarchy continued to serve as a model for national revival and as the focus of hopes for the future.

The significance of this interest in the past for the course of biblical interpretation should be clear. For where was the past to be found? The hills of Judea could not speak to the people and tell them how life had been lived in the time of David and Solomon, nor could they vouchsafe the continuity of the new with the old, or on the other hand prescribe the changes needed to make the Restoration a complete one. *The past was in texts,* and if the past was that to which the exiles were returning, then those texts had to be studied in their tiniest details. More than this, the texts had to be—in the broadest sense encountered in this chapter—*interpreted*. That is, the past was not approached in the spirit of antiquarianism but for what message it might yield, and this is necessarily predicated on an interpretive stance, indeed, a willingness to deviate from the texts' plain sense. The words of prophets, the accounts of ancient historians, were to be "translated" into present-day significance, referred to (and sometimes distorted) in order to support a particular view of the present, or a program for the future. The actual interpretations that we possess from this period (found within the Bible itself) run the gamut from explanations of rather narrow textual difficulties—for example, the apparent conflict mentioned earlier between the "roasting" of the paschal sacrifice in Exodus and the "boiling" of it in Deuteronomy is harmonized by the "interpretation" of 2 Chron. 35:13 (literally, "boiled in the fire"); or the status of Reuben the firstborn is clarified by the "interpretation" of 1 Chron. 5:1–2, where it is recounted that Reuben was indeed the firstborn but lost his birthright because "he polluted his father's couch" (cf. Gen. 35:22)—to interpretations in the broadest sense, the recasting of past history, as in Chronicles as a whole, in such a way as to make past events bear on present reality. But the interest in this "broad" sense of interpretation also underlies all the individual, narrow, interpretive acts, for *it was precisely the intermittent obsession with past events and the necessity of having them bear on the present that gave interpretation of all kinds its urgency.*

The methods and scope of biblical interpretation did not remain static; later ages of scholars and readers worried about questions that never troubled the inhabitants of Persian Judea and sought answers to them in ways that might have been thought strange indeed. Yet one aspect of biblical exegesis did remain a constant, and it should already be apparent in these brief remarks about Judea in the Persian period. It is precisely *the belief that sacred texts have a bearing on the present.* This may seem a natural enough state of affairs for the time—indeed, an almost unavoidable by-product, as we have seen it, of the fact of the return from exile. But it was an orientation that was to cling to these texts evermore, even to the present day. Henceforth, the history of Israel's ancestors and the records of court goings-on were to be consulted not in the spirit of historical inquiry alone but as a guide to proper conduct; the words of prophets, uttered in one particular context and to one specific audience, were now scrutinized for their possible bearing on later situations and other audiences; and laws regarding particular individuals or subgroups in Israel were soon read for their applicability to the whole community. In other words, the role of these writings was to teach not only about the past and within the framework of their original context but about the present and its new context. No doubt some of this orientation existed even before the exile; but we are probably not wrong, in judging the evidence of Haggai, Zechariah, Malachi, and other prophetic texts, or of Chronicles and Ezra-Nehemiah, to believe that the Return itself was crucial in inculcating this attitude among the Jews. The Bible as such was still centuries away, but a key element in its use and understanding was already in existence.

3

The Messiness of History

The Persian empire, swept into world power with the collapse of mighty Babylon, was overcome in its turn. Alexander III (the Great), son of Philip II of Macedon, crossed the Hellespont and with his united Greek forces crushed Darius III, the last Achaemenid king of Persia, at the Battle of Issus, which, conveniently for the memory, took place in the year 333 B.C.E. To Alexander's control soon fell all that had been Persia's, including, of course, the province of Judea. This was a seminal event in the history of the Jews in cultural as well as political terms, for the Greek conquerors brought with them a highly developed civilization which they were not reluctant to share with, indeed impose upon, newly conquered "barbarian" territories. Alexander died prematurely, in 323 B.C.E., leaving no eligible heirs to rule his empire, and his generals quickly fell to struggling for control of the captured territories. The lands that constituted biblical Israel, including Judea, were among the most hotly contested, lying as they did on an ancient and strategic trade route and military crossroads. During the struggle for succession they changed hands several times, finally ending up, at the very end of the fourth century, under the control of Ptolemy I, founder of a dynasty of rulers of Egypt. The Ptolemies ruled over the Jews for a century; then control was wrested from them by the Seleucids, masters to the north and east, whose scion, Antiochus III, defeated the Ptolemies in 198 B.C.E.

These dramatic political shifts—and still others yet to come—must have been profoundly unsettling for the Jewish people, even after the initial shock of change had worn off. Of course a century, however brief it may appear on the pages of history, is longer than most human lives, and it does not take nearly a century for the new to become the normal. Yet in surveying the period of Alexander's conquest, the hundred-odd years of Ptolemaic rule, and the tumultuous decades that followed it, one cannot escape the impression that the changes arrived in sufficient intensity and frequency to keep the population of Judea off-balance much of the time, divided as to where new trends would lead and (as always) how these might square with the vision suggested by Israel's great past. The issue was not necessarily that of foreign domination and the possibilities of political independence. It was, first of all, what to make of the status quo and how to reevaluate the past in terms of it. More concretely, to what extent might the Jews adapt themselves to the civilization of their rulers?

By at least some measurements, the answer to this last question would be: To a great extent! There is evidence of the inroads of Hellenic civilization in the material culture of Judea even before Alexander's conquest, and things of course intensified greatly after it. The conquerers were bearers of a sophisticated civilization which was soon implanted within the conquered territories, not only the Greek language but Greek temples, schools, theaters, and so on. There is little evidence concerning the extent to which this cultural invasion gained acceptance in the Jewish homeland before the beginning of the second century (though certainly we know of Hellenism's inroads in the surrounding areas); but beyond the obvious penetration occasioned by the political situation, one can divine the allurements attached to a civilization not only endowed with military might and organizational skill but one in which mastery of the language and conventions afforded access to a political, cultural, and economic continuum that stretched from India to Gaul. As elsewhere in the territories conquered by Alexander, Greek-style cities were soon founded in much of Palestine (if not in Judea proper), along the Mediterranean coast, on the far side of the Jordan River, and northward, in Samaria and Galilee. Such cities were outposts of Greek culture. Some, like Alexandria in Egypt, were to become important centers of learning; all served to hold together a vast territory and to disseminate the values of the Greek *polis* ("city") to native populations.

There were areas in which the culture of the Greeks must have seemed congruent with that of the Jews, or, more precisely, areas in which each might, without too much distortion, find in the other analogous beliefs and practices. Both had a profound respect for learning and wisdom, and both cultivated a body of texts in which that learning was conveyed. Though precise information about the extent of written education among the Jews at the beginning of this period is scarce, it seems to have been an important value, as it surely was among the Greeks; with the passage of time, the Greek model could only have stimulated or reinforced tendencies toward broad education of the young among the Jews. Moreover, the Greeks were wont to think of themselves as an upstart civilization (see Plato's *Timaeus* 21–25) whose wisdom had been acquired, through Pythagoras or other hoary figures, from the sages of Egypt or "the East"; this too might make Hellenes sympathetic to the teachings of their "Eastern," including Jewish, subjects. The Greek religion was of course polytheistic, and other conquered nations were quick to identify their own gods with various elements of the Greek pantheon. Yet the religion of the Jews was in its own way appealing to Hellenic sensibilities. As early as the sixth century B.C.E., some Greek thinkers had spoken of a single overarching divinity in the universe, and this Greek idea of the one God runs ever stronger from Diogenes of Apollonia through Plato and his school and the Stoic Cleanthes on to the theological speculations of the early Roman imperial age. Was not the "philosophy" of the Jews strikingly similar to this Greek belief? In all these respects, the champions of Greek culture might view the Jews as brethren, or at least distant cousins (to the extent that they concerned themselves with this issue at all), and Jews, for their part, might embrace aspects of the dominant culture without having to give up their (already well developed) native tradition.

Something of a cultural synthesis has been observed, for example, in the Book of Ecclesiasticus (Ben Sira). (In some Bibles this book is called The Wisdom of Jesus the Son of Sirach, or Sirach for short.) This book is a collection of wisdom that apparently was composed at the beginning of the second century B.C.E.; although it was eventually excluded from the Jewish Bible, it was preserved by Christians in translated form. (Part of the Hebrew text has since been recovered.) Ben Sira's book is in some ways a manifesto against Greek ideas and practice, fiercely nationalistic, a glorification of Israel's past and, along with it, of Israel's Scripture and sacred traditions. Much of the book is devoted to pious exhortations in language sharply reminiscent of earlier wisdom teachings. It is therefore all the more remarkable that, amid this concentration on old forms, the influence of Hellenism—and particularly of Stoic philosophy—has nonetheless been detected in places. Scholars have traced resemblances between Ben Sira's thought and Stoic presentations of monotheism, ethical conduct, identity of the cosmic and moral orders of the universe, and other themes. Perhaps even the role of "Wisdom" in Ben Sira is to be connected with Stoic and earlier ideas, a notion which, however, Ben Sira further identified with the Jewish "Torah": "All this is the book of the covenant of the Most

High God, the law *(torah)* which Moses commanded us as an inheritance for the congregations of Jacob" (Ecclus. 24:23; cf. Deut. 33:4). From a period only slightly later come works of a more obviously synthetic character, in which Jewish themes or beliefs are set forth in frankly Hellenistic garb, and sometimes written in the Greek language.

But if such instances suggest a period of gentle symbiosis between Hellenism and Judaism, this vision must be tempered by the implications of other texts, as well as by the fact of Hellenism's violent clash with Judaism shortly after the inauguration of Seleucid rule in the second century. The outline of the latter is well known. Although the transfer from Ptolemaic to Seleucid rule (after the Battle of Paneion in 198 B.C.E.) was apparently welcomed at first by the Jews, things degenerated rapidly. Antiochus III, the Seleucid ruler, was killed in 187. His son and successor, Seleucus IV, ruled for little more than a decade; he in turn was followed by his brother, Antiochus IV (Epiphanes). The latter, through his Jerusalem surrogates, promoted various Hellenistic institutions and innovations and, as resistance to these built, finally issued, in 168 B.C.E., a decree banning such central Jewish practices as circumcision, observance of the Sabbath and holidays, and the Torah. The Jerusalem Temple was converted to a pagan sanctuary, a "sacrilege of desolation" set up on its altar in 167 B.C.E. A group of Jews revolted, led by the five sons of a single priestly family who are known collectively as the Maccabees (after the byname of Judah, one of the five); they and their descendants are also referred to as the Hasmoneans, after the family name. In the succeeding years of armed struggle, the Maccabees gradually gained the upper hand, retaking the Temple Mount and reinstituting the former cult in 164 B.C.E. By 141 B.C.E., Simon, the last of the five brothers, was able to be crowned king of a politically independent Judea. His dynasty, the Hasmonean, endured until 63 B.C.E., when the Romans conquered Jerusalem and set up their own choice of rulers, who governed an occasionally restive population. (Armed revolt against the Romans broke out in 66–70 C.E., resulting in the destruction of the Jerusalem Temple, and once again in 132–135 C.E., the so-called "Bar Cochba Revolt." However, neither effort succeeded in permanently displacing Roman rule.)

Thus, the period of contact with "Western" (i.e., first Greek, then Roman) civilization brought about both profound changes in the ideas and worldview of the Jews and at the same time a mistrust, resistance, and even armed revolt against this civilization. Nor, of course, were "the Jews" a single entity with only one set of attitudes toward Greek and Roman ways. In the Jewish writings that were composed during this long period of seesawing fortunes, a host of different attitudes are represented. Scholars now theorize, furthermore, that the conflict between Judaism and Hellenism that expressed itself so clearly in the Maccabean revolt had probably gone on among Jews themselves before 168 B.C.E. Jerusalem certainly had long had its own champions of Hellenization, those who not only accepted the status quo of Ptolemaic rule but saw in the Greek culture and worldview a legitimate successor to earlier traditions, perhaps even a superior understanding and wisdom. And just as certainly these had their opponents: not only Jews who continued to champion "the Torah of Moses" but some who also believed that the status quo in no way constituted a fit fulfillment for the people whom God had chosen as his own and who looked forward to a day when history would yet be set aright.

II

Among the literary compositions of this period, two types of writing in particular should attract our attention for what they imply about changing Jewish attitudes to past and present. The first type belongs within that collectivity known as apocalyptic literature (from the Greek word *apokalypsis*, "revelation"). This term has proven somewhat unwieldy, and scholars still disagree as to which texts ought legitimately to be so labeled. In general we can say that these texts, particularly in their earlier forms, are presented as revelations to various figures from the distant past—Enoch (mentioned in Gen. 5:24), or Moses, or various biblical patriarchs. The identity of their true authors is thus masked behind these ancient personae, and for this reason such texts are described as pseudepigraphs ("falsely attributed" works). The information that is revealed is, typically, of the sort that could be known only in heaven—not only the course of history to come but secrets concerning the order of the universe, details of divine governance and the nature of the celestial realms, and information about the "time of the end." The roots of this literature go back to the period of the Babylonian exile and the Restoration; apocalyptic tendencies are discernible in parts of the books of Isaiah, Ezekiel, Zechariah, and others. But if the connection with the institution of prophecy is articulated hereby, it is also likely that apocalyptic writings were intimately tied to the pursuit of wisdom, not only in their interest in the ways of divine governance but in their occasional choice of sagelike figures as pseudepigraphic speakers and their apparent delight in underlying patterns, numerology, and other "wise" pursuits.

Some of these apocalyptic writings reflect directly on the cultural conflict we have been discussing, the struggle against Hellenism, which is represented as a foreign dominion persecuting Israel or leading her astray. Within the Jewish canon, Daniel 7–12 contains many of the elements typical of apocalyptic writings; these chapters date from the time of the persecutions of Antiochus IV, and there is veiled reference to him throughout. Later apocalypses continued to explore the mysteries of heaven and, sometimes, reveal the divine plan for the people of Israel in its latter-day history.

A second type of writing that continued to be popular was "wisdom literature"—not only collections of proverbs and wise sayings but psalms and prayers that abound in wisdom motifs, and even tales that centered on "wise" heroes or inculcated the lessons of wisdom. This ongoing interest in wisdom may be charted from the Book of Ecclesiastes (Persian period), through Ben Sira (composed, as we saw, at the beginning of the second century), and on to the Psalms of Solomon (written in the middle decades of the first century B.C.E.) and still later works. Indeed, if the pursuit of wisdom had ancient roots in Israel, it is nonetheless true that it became an ever-growing force in Jewish intellectual life during the years of direct contact with Hellenism, when its literary and ideological horizons were also greatly expanded.

The popularity of these two types of writing may tell us something about Israel's changing attitude toward its history during this period. The Great Past, we have observed, had loomed large in the imagination of restored Judea during the Persian period; there was a sense that the momentous events of destruction, deportation, and restoration bespoke the most assiduous sort of divine guidance of Israel's fortunes. God had punished the Jews, speaking loud and clear through the armies of the Babylonian invader; and lest anyone think it was Babylonian power alone that was responsible for defeat, God had rapidly humbled that empire in turn and restored Israel, just as his spokesman Jeremiah had foretold. What then remained? A people, bent on not relieving the mistakes of the past, pored over its historical records and created new ones, to extract the proper lessons. It sought to organize itself, perhaps as never before, in strict observance of divinely dictated statutes. Politically, priests and other religious figures were invested with great temporal power. Ezra and his camp even sought to undo marriages that Judeans had concluded with "foreign" women—and why? Lest the ancient sins of these other peoples again lead the Jews to destruction: "Shall we again break your commandments and intermarry with these peoples of abomination? Will you not be angry enough with us [this time] to the point of utter destruction, with no survivors or remnant left?" (Ezra 9:14). There is, in all of this, a sense of the recentness of these great events and a desire to "do it right the second time."

But as we have seen, events that followed this Restoration did not continue in any easily discernible pattern. Things were neither glorious nor terrible, and in the economic and political ups and downs that followed, the very relationship of Jews to the world of their past began subtly to shift. If, in the period of the Restoration and its immediate aftermath, we are sometimes able to discern a clear desire for continuity with the past and a feeling of connectedness with it, the literature of the later period increasingly betrays a different mood, perhaps even a different sense of history. So it is that the question with which many of the works of this period are concerned is: How can the present be brought back under the "coverage" of biblical history (from which it now seemed so removed), and the biblical sense of world events as a form of divine speech be reasserted in the present day?

Such is patently the concern of some of the "apocalyptic" writings just described. For the indisputable effect of some of this literature's concentration on impending events, cataclysm or political consummation, is the *setting aright of history:* The confusions, the seemingly patternless ups and downs of current events, will all make sense, or at least be overshadowed into insignificance, by the great "time of the end" (in Greek, *eskhaton,* hence "eschatology," the interest in "last things" that characterized some apocalyptic works). The great concern among certain late- and post-biblical writers with *time itself* is symptomatic of the same worldview. In such diverse works as the Book of Daniel and the *Book of Jubilees* (probably second century B.C.E.) we encounter the clear feeling for the time being dealt out like a hand of cards, and an interest in arranging time into subgroups and corresponding units, for such arranging of time not only made recent history more manageable ("Classify and conquer!") but made it partake of (indeed, be continuous with) that comforting world of biblical history in which events made sense.

Connected with this is the *typological* reading of Israel's history, which saw in past events patterns for present or future time, or actual foreshadowings of events to come. So, for example, even within the Bible, the latter part of the Book of Isaiah at times evokes the exodus from Egypt as a model for the return from Babylonian exile, as elsewhere Israel's wanderings in the wilderness and the heyday of King David had been held up as models for the future (see, e.g., Hos. 2:14–15; Amos 9:11). Later on, writers who were moved by a similar spirit identified various groups or individuals of their own day with biblical nations or persons, and so read the biblical figures as *types* foreshadowing things to come. Particularly evocative for apocalyptic writers was the notion that the time of the end would in some fashion partake of the beginning, and thus put its ordering stamp on the disorders of history.

There is more. To put words about the present or near-future in the mouth of an angel, or of a long-dead biblical patriarch or sage, as many second-century and later writers do, is to accomplish precisely the same extension of biblical history to the present. For in having a figure from "back then" (the God of biblical history—or his angel—who knows the arrangement of all things, or some ancient worthy solidly planted "back then" when the Divine Plan was clear) speak about current events and recent history, the author manages to make the present day too savor of the biblical world. Moreover, the cryptic representation of the passage of time (in Daniel, for example, by Daniel's vision of the four great beasts in ch. 7, representing the periods of successive dominance of world kingdoms, or indeed the dream of Nebuchadnezzar of the succession of empires in ch. 2) bespeaks a concern with finding the "hidden message" in things: It is hidden in this literature because it was indeed hidden—not apparent—in real life; but the true sage, these works maintain, can penetrate to the heart of things and understand.

There were, besides such direct attempts to bring the present and recent past under the "coverage" of biblical time, other ways to endow them with a biblical glow. The retelling of recent events in a highly biblical (i.e., archaizing) Hebrew style is characteristic not only of many post-biblical writings but even of parts of late biblical historiography. The Book of Esther, which is not directly concerned with the great theological matter we have been examining, is one such instance; it recounts the entertaining tale of a wicked courtier's overthrow and the salvation of the Jews in such a way as to make it sound like the great events of the past—and particularly the story of Joseph on Pharaoh's court, on which some of its language is modeled. Many post-biblical narratives, prayers, and songs use purposely archaic or awkward language. (Some original Greek compositions were even written in "Septuagintese": that is, modeled on the language of the Hebrew Bible in Greek translation.) By describing current events from, as it were, the Bible's perspective, or by having present-day congregations address themselves to God in the same style as biblical heroes, the present is thus encouraged to become part of biblical history.

All this may be read as symptomatic. For were not these varied attempts at "biblicizing" recent events, or revealing a divine plan not apparent in recent history, really representative of a widespread malaise, an uneasiness at the gap between the biblical ideal and the political reality? But there is another side to the writings of this post-Alexander period in their grapplings with the messiness of recent history: it is the "wisdom connection." For, as we have already seen, the Way of Wisdom was first and foremost the way of patience. Only one who had seen much of time—that is, the old sage, the *zaqen*—could rightly pretend to wisdom, for he had been alive long enough to learn the lesson of patience. Therefore, all who trod the path of wisdom knew that underneath apparent confusion lies a pattern—this is the essence of wisdom—and that with patience the pattern, or at least fragments of it, will emerge to the wise. We saw above that some scholars have connected apocalyptic writings with the milieu or wisdom, and indeed there are common points: the belief in an underlying, divinely drafted, order to apparently incomprehensible phenomena (cosmic, natural, or social) is a solid point of contact. But the Way of Wisdom does not necessarily lead to imagining an impending setting aright of history. Indeed, it was sometimes the discipline that cured one's impatience with history and the need to bring the present under the coverage of biblical history. For in wisdom, time became curiously "unbiblical."

This observation is most often connected with the biblical book of Ecclesiastes, a work probably written, as stated earlier, in the middle of the Persian period (though some have dated it still later). For its author, history itself seems scarcely to exist—he makes no mention of Israel's great past—and certainly not history as a series of unique, divinely dictated events. Instead, life just goes around and around. The sun rises because that is simply part of the ongoing cycle, ordained from time immemorial (contrast with Josh. 10:12–13); it rises only to set and travel under the earth, back to where it will rise again (Eccl. 1:5). Even the flow of a river's waters, which to other minds has presented itself as a model of an ever-changing, ever-unique universe, is to Ecclesiastes only another instance of that which is beyond change; the rivers flow as they have always flowed, and ever to the sea, for "what has been is what will be, and what has been done is what will be done again." This ahistorical sense of time, so explicit in Ecclesiastes, is nevertheless not nearly so unique as is sometimes claimed; much wisdom literature, especially that of later vintage, bears the same stamp. Even Ben Sira, with his patent interest and pride in Israel's history, has no sense of the present as a continuation of the biblical past. On the contrary, when one reads his recapitulations of biblical heroes, they emerge as "men of renown" who "left a name behind them, that their praises might be retold." This is how Ben Sira knows them, as chapters in a book, and for him Josiah and even Zerubbabel dwell in the same mythic fog as Abraham or Enoch. For these once-real people have become, essentially, *lessons*, whose importance can be captured in a line or two. It is also clear not only that Ben Sira was using biblical texts as his source material but that he intended his audience to know these and pick up his allusions, as in his reference to the story in 1 Sam. 18:6–8 with the brief "So the people honored him [David] with ten-thousands," or the description of Zerubbabel as "a signet on the right hand" (whose source in Haggai we have seen above).

The pursuit of wisdom, which was certainly a popular path during the Age of Hellenism, thus contained its own set of answers to the messiness of history. It was a way of patience, one that did not insist that the right must triumph immediately, only ultimately. It held that the world order, cosmic and political, was organized "with wisdom"—that is, according to plan—but held that that plan was not necessarily, or totally, apparent. And it belonged, moreover, to an intellectual tradition that was singularly uninterested in history's ups and downs; its focus was the system that lay beneath those ups and downs, the domain of universal and timeless truth.

III

In regard to the interpretation of Scripture, apocalyptic and wisdom writings are central concerns—first and foremost because compositions belonging to these two modes often contain interpretations of, or reflections upon, biblical texts and thus constitute an important source of information about how the ancient books were being read and interpreted from the Hellenistic period on. Wisdom writings such as Ecclesiasticus (Ben Sira) or the Wisdom of Solomon, and apocalyptic writings stretching from the Enoch literature to the *Book of Jubilees*, to various testaments (including the above-mentioned *Testaments of the Twelve Patriarchs*, the *Testament of Abraham*, the *Testament of Job*, etc.) 4 Ezra (= Second Esdras or the Apocalypse of Ezra), the *Apocalypse of Abraham*, and others—these works make up a significant part of the total of extant Jewish writings from this period. Thus the *context* of much of the biblical interpretation that has survived from the third century B.C.E. to the turn of the era and beyond is that of apocalyptic and wisdom writings; it is in such works that the processes of sifting, explaining, retelling, and expanding upon biblical texts are to be studied.

But beyond this simple factual observation, one ought to reflect on the significance of the connection between the interpretation of Israel's ancient texts and specifically these two modes, apocalyptic and wisdom. For can we not see in them two new ways (related, but nonetheless distinct) of connecting the present with these ancient documents? Some there were who wished to read these writings in a frankly apocalyptic mode—to interpret the prophecies of Isaiah or Jeremiah as if they had originally been uttered (perhaps unwittingly) with secret teachings intended for ages yet unborn, most often for the time in which the interpreter himself was living, or slightly later. (An example of this is Dan. 9:2 and 24–26, whose author seeks to read in Jeremiah's prediction that the Babylonian exile would end in seventy years a statement not about the late sixth century but about the first century B.C.E., seventy "weeks of years" later.) For others, however, the "sense of time" of ancient events had simply receded. More in a wisdom mode, these interpreters read the ancient records in such a way that they lost some of their historical connectedness to the present; the events existed "way back when," and they were thus deprived of historical reality. Instead, they were actualized and made relevant by being read in the spirit of exempla, indeed, of wisdom sayings; what happened to Abraham or David was instructive not so much about ancient history as about God's ways with man, or about ethical behavior, or the inner world of the soul.

To sum up, the period from Alexander's conquest and the rise of Hellenism in Judea to the destruction of the Jerusalem Temple in 70 C.E. was a period of crucial importance in the history of Jewish biblical interpretation, for the contact with Hellenism had proven decisive in both its positive and its negative aspects. It provided a wealth of new ideas and techniques that helped to shape Jewish attitudes toward their own ancient writings and influenced, as well, the interpretation of those writings. At the same time, resistance to Hellenization focused the gaze of some Jews squarely on the past and on the ways of their fathers, and this provided the impetus for ever greater interest in the ancient texts and their significance. Meanwhile, actual political events were not without their echo in the interpretation of those texts. The very inconclusiveness of history's ups and downs may have been what pushed some to seek (or create) hidden teachings from Israel's past, teachings that might, by means of the various strategies seen, bring the present under the "coverage" of ancient truths and so make their pages yet relevant to a later day.

We have thus charted three important elements in the emergence of biblical interpretation in postexilic Israel. The first (presented in chapter 1) was the growth, and the growing importance, of Israel's sacred library. The second (chapter 2) was the perceived necessity of *interpreting* these sacred texts, not only in the narrow sense of making linguistic and other difficulties comprehensible but more broadly so as to "perfect" them and, moreover, to make them have some bearing on the present. The third (chapter 3) was the tendency, especially pronounced after long contact with Hellenism, of interpreters of the Great Past to grapple with the "messiness of history" and the apparent absence of divine direction in Israel's current affairs—either by focusing interpretation on some hidden, underlying pattern in history (often, one just about to manifest itself dramatically) or, on the contrary, by further removing biblical events to the time "way back when," so distant from the present as to be temporally disconnected and relevant primarily not as history but as a corpus of laws and figures and events divinely intended for Israel's instruction. It remains now for our survey to look at the character of the biblical interpreter himself as he emerges through the end of this period and, in so doing, to flesh out somewhat the varied character of early Jewish interpretation.

4

Interpreters of Scripture

Who were the interpreters of Israel's ancient texts? This is another question whose answer will depend on period and circumstance. Interpretation, as we have seen, is a broad and flexible concept. Priests performed one sort of "interpretation" as they went about their duties in the sanctuary; judges and elders were interpreters of ancient statute in a rather different sense; sages who reflected on, and retold, ancient tradition interpreted in yet another way; prophets, echoing the words of predecessors or building on their messages (as well as those anonymous figures whose additions to prophetic texts have found their way into our canonical collections), fulfilled yet another interpretive function. Might the figure of the *teacher* be added to such a list? The answer certainly is yes. But it must be said at the same time that it is far from clear when the institution of schools began in Israel or when the teacher as a distinct and specialized figure first emerged. In truth, all of the above—priests, judges and elders, sages, and prophets—have been argued to have function as, among other things, teachers of the young.

Of course education, and in particular training in reading and writing, had long been a concern. Excavations within the territory of biblical Israel have turned up a number of practice alphabet texts, as well as isolated letters, or letters apparently grouped by similarity of shape, and other materials indicative of elementary instruction. These finds, unearthed at Lachish, Arad, Kuntillat-Ajrud, and other sites, suggest the existence of some form of literacy training (whether or not actual *schools*) in these locations by the eighth century B.C.E. Certainly it is difficult to imagine that the seats of government and diplomacy and other centers were without a substantial literate elite even earlier, but these "provincial" finds are perhaps more impressive because they indicate how widespread literacy training might have been by the eighth century. (Unfortunately, the climatic conditions of the Land of Israel are such that elementary exercises performed on relatively cheap materials such as stone, pottery, or plaster could survive; if more advanced education went on at the same sites, for which expensive materials such as papyrus or, later, animal hides might have been used, these exercises are most likely lost forever.) The widespread use of inscribed seals and other popular written materials also bespeaks the spread of at least elementary literacy in the preexilic period.

The Bible itself contains several indications of the existence of places of instruction, as well as of the fruits of such instruction. (Indeed, the fact that from the eighth century on the "writing prophets"—that is, those whose oracles have been preserved at length for us in written form—were active may directly reflect an increasing literacy.) Scholars have long speculated on the existence of guilds of prophets, whose members (called *benei hannebi'im*, "sons of prophets") presumably learned from a master, perhaps in school-like settings (see 2 Kings 6:1–3). Wisdom writings, by their subject matter and didactic form (the frequent use of "my son" denoting address from teacher to student, and "your father" perhaps also signifying the former), would fit in such a setting, though conventional language here proves little about lived reality. Within the writings of the latter part of Isaiah on, there are possible references to pupils and teachers.

As for the latter, prophets, Temple priests, and Levites generally (i.e., descendants of the tribe of Levi) are all presented in teacher-like roles. The connection between Levites and education (among other religious functions) is particularly to be stressed. Some scholars have proposed that the centralization of worship and the fall of certain cultic centers by conquest left at least some Levites "structurally unemployed," and the teaching of the young, if it was not a central levitical function before these changes, might certainly have become so after them. Significantly, it was the Levites whom we saw in Nehemiah 8 imparting the sense of Scripture to the people. But far earlier, the Blessings of Moses (Deut. 33:10) had described the Levites' amalgamation of functions in these terms: "Let them teach your statutes to Jacob and your law to Israel; let them place incense at your nostrils, and a whole burnt offering upon your altar."

The priesthood in particular was in a position to exercise great influence in matters of education and, later on, specifically in regard to interpretation. In restored Judea, a "temple state," various priestly figures, and notably the high priest (*kohen gadol*), not only enjoyed great political power but, through their office, promulgated interpretations and extensions of the law for the entire populace. Indeed, one can sense some wonderment at this strange state of affairs in an early account of Jewish ways by the third-century B.C.E. historian Hecataeus of Abdera, preserved now in the works of Diodorus of Sicily (*History* 40.3). There we read that Moses

> picked out the men of most refinement and with the greatest ability to head the entire nation and appointed them priests; and he ordained that they should occupy themselves with the temple and the honors and sacrifices offered to their God. These same men he appointed to be judges in all major disputes, and entrusted to them the guardianship of the laws and customs. For this reason the Jews never have a king, and authority over the people is regularly vested in whichever priest is regarded as superior to his colleagues in wisdom and virtue. They call this man the high priest and believe that he acts as a messenger to them of God's commandments. It is he, we are told, who in their assemblies and other gatherings announces what is ordained, and the Jews are so docile in such matters that straightway they fall to the ground and do reverence to the high priest when he expounds the commandments to them.

We have seen above some indications that in postexilic times books, scrolls, and other realia of literacy education seem to have exercised a wide role in the consciousness of Jews. Not only do the occasional references, metaphorical or otherwise, to the accoutrements of writing and education in later biblical books attest to this, but reflection on the political and cultural situation of the Jews in this period leads to the same conclusion. That Ezra, *priest and scribe* (the combination is surely significant, and an informative contrast to such priests-and-prophets as Jeremiah and Ezekiel), is sent on an official mission to Judea is a telling item; for the king's charge to Ezra, recorded in Ezra 7, specifies that he is being "sent by the king and his seven counselors to make inquiries about Judah and Jerusalem *according to the law of your God, which is in your hand.* . . . Whoever will not obey the law of your God and the law of the king, let judgment be strictly executed upon him" (Ezra 7:14, 26). This charge thus not only confers upon the law of Israel's God official status in Judea, side by side with the law of the king, but makes further provision for its application *and teaching:*

> And you, Ezra, according to the wisdom of your God which is in your hand, appoint magistrates and judges who may judge all the people in the province of Abar Nahara ("Beyond the River"), all such as know the laws of your God; and those who do not know them, you shall teach. (Ezra 7:25)

If the rise of the great house of David had occasioned, early on, the creation of a court bureaucracy and the educational activities needed to support it, the resurrection of Judea under Persian rule must have required something similar, though perhaps on a smaller scale; at the same time, the evidence of literacy makes it difficult to believe that education in Judea was limited just to future bureaucrats and priests. Education in the ways of wisdom may have once been intended for future courtiers, as is indicated even in the relatively late Ecclesiastes (e.g., Eccl. 8:1–5, but this may simply be part of the conventions of wisdom writing); on the other hand, the same Ecclesiastes is described in the book's epilogue (which may well be part of the original work, and in any case not much subsequent to it in time) as having "taught *the people* knowledge." The whole discussion of the career of the sage in Ecclesiastes 2 implies that pursuing higher studies and "going further in wisdom" (Eccl. 2:15) was not an issue confronted solely by an isolated few. Still more generally, we can note that the stress placed on widespread popular acquaintance with the "Torah of Moses" in Ezra, Nehemiah, and other late sources, as well as the overall interest in the ways of Israel's past observed above, made education in Israel's traditions —and perhaps, more specifically, in the means of access to the written sources of that tradition—an expected feature of life in restored Judea. Doubtless this only continued in the period of contact with Hellenism, which presented both a reinforcing model and a rival curriculum.

But what is to be stressed is that the teaching—and interpreting —of Israel's ancient texts was carried out in a variety of settings and by a multiplicity of interpreters and teachers. Children and various sorts of "trainees" and apprentices, as well as mature adults, were certainly among those instructed about the texts' significance, and those who did the teaching included wise men and scribes associated with various institutions of society (including the cult), priests, Levites, prophets, and others. To the extent that some of this teaching involved the regular and routine study of specific texts, it may not be anachronistic to ask what the various "curricula" looked like. And the answer is implicit in what has been said above: the Bible, or rather some of the constituent texts that were to make up the Bible, must have served in this capacity. It has recently been argued that this was the case even before the exile—that, indeed, many of the early biblical compositions or compilations owe their very existence to their intended use as texts for the education of future priests, scribes, courtiers, and prophets. Be that as it may, we are certainly on safe ground in believing that many parts of our present Bible might have served in this capacity at various educational levels in postexilic times. The "Torah of Moses," judging from the sources seen above, is the prime candidate for Israel's most widely studied text; indeed, pedagogical features of the language of parts of the Pentateuch have long been noted, and, more recently, resemblances between some Pentateuchal texts and children's literature have been alleged. (These might conceivably advance the use of Pentateuchal texts for elementary education to a very early period.) In regard to the term "torah," it is to be noted that, whatever its actual original significance in biblical Hebrew, it came to be understood as meaning "teaching," an etymology that may, it has been suggested, explain the preeminence of this term in Deuteronomy as well as in Joshua–2 Kings. When we encounter the "Torah of Moses" in postexilic sources, this term perhaps ought to be understood specifically as the *teaching* of Moses—that is *the thing that is taught* (to students). Other biblical texts may still have had a more limited audience—priestly writings for the education of priests, wisdom books such as Proverbs, Ecclesiastes, and Job for those who trod the "path of wisdom." Yet it is significant that Ben Sira's wisdom includes, as mentioned, a long reflection not just on the history of the people of Israel but one that is specifically tied to the language of various biblical narratives. Thus by the second century, and probably earlier, the eternal verities cultivated by wisdom teachers and their pupils included not only the wise sayings that we would recognize as the ordinary stuff of wisdom but the history of Israel too. (This further evidences the dehistoricization of that history, as discussed in the previous chapter.)

Finally, it is to be noted that the contact with Hellenism must have supplied by its example a reinforcement or inspiration for the enthronement of a central text or group of texts as a central pedagogical tool. For in the Greek world there was one such text: Homer. All who aspired to full literacy and initiation into Greek culture passed through the great poetic corpus; the *Iliad* and the *Odyssey* were the very foundation stones of the Greek *paideia*. Was it not natural for Jews to think of their texts, and perhaps specifically the "Torah of Moses," in much the same terms—employed not only as the central text of literacy education but as a model and ongoing inspiration for educated Hebrew style, as well of course as a focus of communal identity (the "myth of foundation" sociologists talk about) and a manual of social and religious law and ethical behavior? As noted, the use of at least some biblical texts in this fashion may be very early

—and it is certainly the program of Deuteronomy that "this instruction" *(hattorah hazzot)* be widely taught *(lmd)*, not only at a public assembly (e.g., Deut. 31:9–13) but from parent to child, at home or away, from dawn to dusk (Deut. 6:7). But this program, however it may have been enacted earlier, was taken to heart after the exile: the Bible-in-the-making was the ideal textbook, the "Homer of the Jews."

II

It may be appropriate here to say a word about the "canonization" of the Bible. This term has long been used by scholars to designate a moment in history when the final content of the Hebrew Bible was fixed, an act of sorting between the "ins" (books that were accepted as Scripture and are currently found in the biblical canon) and the "outs" (books such as the *Book of Jubilees* and the other pseudepigrapha mentioned earlier). But the fact is that, while there may have been a "moment" when decisions were finalized and published, canonization was a process that went on for some time. Again, if one can learn from the cultures surrounding biblical Israel, the institutions of education operated as a prime sifting mechanism in the creation and selection of the Jewish "proto-canon"; decisions were constantly being made as to which texts were to be taught and copied, and perhaps also which texts revised or combined. In the closing centuries before the common era, there probably was no "canon" in the sense in which we use the term, with clearly defined lines separating the sacred from the profane and divine revelation from mere human invention. But there surely was a (loosely defined) group of *basic texts*, whose centrality and sacredness were recognized by all, texts like the Pentateuch, which were studied with care and whose words were accepted as decisive for all of Israel. One might say that, if there was not yet a canon in our sense, there probably was at least a *curriculum*, or different curricula, studied by various groups. The gradual process of assembly and manifold decisions that stand behind such curricula—these constitute the major work of canonization; the little acts of inclusion and exclusion that come later are of a far lesser order.

III

As these texts were studied, the questions asked and answered were probably of the sort described above—questions about the proper application of biblical law, or about the meaning of a rare word or difficult turn of phrase, or about the implications of a particular narrative for one of Israel's heroes. But it would surely be wrong to suppose that the interpretations presented in such study were all of an "academic" nature, and still more misguided to imagine that biblical interpretation generally had such a character. For many of the texts being interpreted were, as we have seen, attributed in their own words to divine origin or inspiration, and even those which were not so specifically had been "hallowed by time" and belonged to the now idealized preexilic heyday of prophets and kings. Interpreting them, looking deeply into their meaning, was thus a sacred task.

It has already been suggested above that in postexilic times the sage who interpreted sacred words was something like an adjunct to the prophets; the spokesman of God who was "in thy midst" was supplemented by men who *interpreted* or found the hidden meaning in oracles delivered of old by God's chosen spokesmen. Something of this role of the prophet-as-interpreter (or sage-as-prophet) is adumbrated in the Book of Daniel, whose principal theme is interpretation. Daniel is of course a "reader" of dreams (dreams were interpreted in late antiquity in much the same way as texts), but how striking that, unlike that other biblical dream interpreter, Joseph, Daniel is required not just to interpret the meaning of the dream but to retell the dream to the dreamer in the first place (Dan. 2). Later (Dan. 5), Daniel is called upon not only to interpret the message written on the wall of Belshazzar's palace but, first and foremost, to decipher the undecipherable writing and so be able to speak the mysterious prophecy. Both features represent the same basic idea: Interpretation begins by the interpreter reproducing the *text itself*, for the latter, whether dream or scribbling, is itself a gift from God *granted afresh to the interpreter;* proper understanding is akin to prophecy itself. And so to Daniel is revealed the "correct" sense of Jeremiah's plain speaking about the endurance of exile and domination (Jer. 25:11–12; 29:10): Jeremiah's "seventy years" means seventy groups of seven years each (Dan. 9:24). Elsewhere, after interpretation is revealed, Daniel offers thanks to God—but it is a cryptographer's praising:

> Blessed be the name of God for ever and ever, to whom belong wisdom and might. He changes times and seasons; he removes kings and sets up kings; he gives wisdom to the wise and knowledge to those who have understanding; he reveals deep secrets and mysterious things; he knows what is in the darkness, and the light dwells with him. (Dan. 2:20–22)

We ought to note well the idea of God-the-revealer, and of revelation as specifically the unfolding of *secrets*, that apparently stands behind such words. A priori, there need be nothing mysterious about God's messages; on the contrary, if the divine purpose is communication, one might expect messages to be of an unparalleled clarity, able to be understood and retransmitted by anyone. And indeed, in other (especially earlier) biblical texts, this is very much the case. As Amos puts it (Amos 3:8), "If a lion roars, who is not afraid? If God speaks, who will not be a prophet?" Similarly, Isa. 6:9–10 implies that only some externally imposed obtuseness can prevent ordinary Israelites from understanding divine oracles. And when the Book of Exodus presents its explanation for the need for prophets in Israel, it does not advance the prophet (as might seem only logical to us) as that rare sage capable of penetrating the cryptic meaning of divine utterances, nor yet as a sensitive soul uniquely able to perceive divine messages overlooked by ordinary people. On the contrary. The divine roar is so powerful that ordinary people are afraid to listen to it—they fear for their lives (Ex. 20:18–20). That is why, in this view, prophets are needed, or at least why prophecy was first instituted (Deut. 18:15–18): to perform a task that ordinary mortals found too terrifying. Yet by the time these chapters of Daniel were written, such a notion of the divine word was no longer evident. God's speech was mysterious, and even when its message *seemed* obvious (e.g., "seventy years"), its true meaning might be quite otherwise (490 years). To understand properly the word of God, great care and insightfulness were required—and perhaps, as we have seen in Daniel the Interpreter, divine inspiration as well.

Some of these same phenomena are witnessed in the latest psalms included within our Psalter. Thus Psalm 111 observes, "Great are the deeds of the Lord, studied by all who have pleasure in them" (or: "in all their details"); by "deeds" the psalmist apparently means the *accounts* of God's deeds contained in old texts (as he notes two lines later, "He made an account of his miracles, [showing that] the Lord is gracious and merciful" [cf. Ex. 34:6]). The fact of the deeds themselves, the signs and wonders, has receded into the background. It is not enough merely to know that they happened; they must be scrutinized nowadays, "studied" (*drš*) by present-day interpreters. The long alphabetical Psalm 119, one of the latest psalms in the Psalter, is sometimes called a "Psalm of the Law (= Torah)" because of its exaltation of divine statutes and those who observe them. But more than this, it is a renewed litany of exhortations for help in *understanding* divine laws and therefore in properly observing them:

Blessed are you, Lord, teach me your statutes!
Open my eyes and let me behold wonders from your law.
Make me understand the way of your precepts and let me meditate on
   your wonders.
Teach me, O Lord, the way of your laws, and I will keep it to the end.
Give me understanding, that I may keep your law and observe it with
   my whole heart.
Lead me in the path of your commandments, for I delight in it.
                                          (Ps. 119:12, 18, 27, 33–35)

The "precepts," "laws," "statutes," and so forth mentioned are not
obvious or self-explanatory bits of divine legislation; if that were the
case, there would be no need for these heartfelt pleas! But the
simplest statute required study and meditation in order to be understood aright—indeed, it required, so the psalmist believed, divine
help.

   Hence, some of Israel's interpreters presented their understanding of texts as *inspired* interpretation, understandings which had
been communicated to them, or which they had arrived at, with
divine help. Again, some of the pseudepigrapha of the last two
centuries before the common era provide a reflection of this curious phenomenon. For example, the *Book of Jubilees* (which may
have been composed early in the second century B.C.E.) is essentially a retelling of the first (and nonlegal) part of the Pentateuch,
from the first chapter of Genesis to the fourteenth chapter of Exodus. What was the point of retelling, often in much the same
words, a text that presumably was already well known and revered
by Jews? But this particular retelling is full of additions, omissions,
and changes. Although the original is, as noted, not concerned
with legal matters, the retelling is at pains to derive binding norms
of behavior from narrative—to set out, for example, rules for the
observance of Israel's sacred holidays (and to root them even in
the lives of Israel's earliest ancestors). Some of its additions are
aimed at explaining things in the Genesis narrative that might otherwise strike us as mysterious or illogical, such as why God decided to test Abraham by ordering him to sacrifice his son Isaac on
an altar, or indeed why God had "chosen" Abraham in the first
place when he called to him to leave his homeland (Gen. 12:1).
And the entire sequence of events is set in a rigorous chronological framework, with key occurrences coinciding with dates from
the festive calendar. In all these respects, *Jubilees* might fairly be
described as a commentary on Genesis and Exodus 1–14. Yet it is
not just a commentary; it is an inspired commentary. It is presented in the form of a revelation: The text, so the author claims,

was transmitted by an angel to Moses on Mt. Sinai. This is doubtless part of the same urge to pseudepigraphy described above; the author wished to extend the authority of ancient figures and events to "cover" the present, including present-day practices and modes of interpretation. But it is an equally telling detail that the interpretation belongs not to Moses but to an angel (and hence to God); the proper understanding of the text was no less of divine origin than the text publicly promulgated by Moses. Other pseudepigrapha from this or a slightly later period present similar interpretations of biblical texts, either placed in the mouths of angels or spoken by biblical figures who were "there when it happened" or are of sufficient lineage, wisdom, or prophetic gifts to vouchsafe the trustworthiness of their words.

One final indication of the inspired status of early biblical interpretation comes from the collection of ancient manuscripts discovered in the Judean desert, at Khirbet Qumran and elsewhere, in the 1940s and subsequently; these are the manuscripts known as the Dead Sea Scrolls. The Jews who settled at Qumran (probably in the mid- to late-second century B.C.E.) were a religious sect, one whose concerns had a decidedly eschatological character. They regarded themselves as the true remnant of Israel, and many of their fellow Jews as misguided or worse; they looked forward to a messianic age just around the corner, when Israel's fortunes would be restored and God's covenant with his people renewed once more. A great many of the manuscript fragments found at Qumran and elsewhere are copies of parts of the Bible. Apparently, the study of these ancient and sacred writings was a crucial community concern, and what is more, these texts provided the community with its very raison d'être, for community members saw in various biblical prophecies and narratives hints about events of their own day, including the founding of their own sect.

Indeed, the leader of the sect is referred to as *moreh haṣṣedeq,* a phrase best translated as "the true (or "right") teacher." He also had another name, even more apposite: *doresh hattorah,* the "interpreter of the Torah" (the title is given to other figures as well). But not only was he an interpreter of Scripture, he was an *inspired* interpreter, "to whom God made known all the secrets of his servants the prophets" (1QpHab 7:5). It is the gift of the "spirit of knowledge" from God, or the "spirit of holiness" (*ruaḥ haqqodeš*), that allows the Qumran interpreter to penetrate the "secrets," "mysteries," or "hidden things" in ancient Scripture and read aright their message for himself and his contemporaries. The Dead Sea Scrolls in themselves provide valuable evidence about the nature of early

Jewish interpretation of the Bible, for the Qumran caves have yielded not only biblical manuscripts but a wealth of interpretive and other documents indicating some of the ways in which texts were read and explained in the second and first centuries before the common era. But they incidentally also provide information about the person of some of Scripture's interpreters during this period. Though the school was certainly now a primary place for the interpretation of texts, the interpreters were not simply schoolmasters, and their interpretations did not just savor the musty odor of the classroom. In the Qumran sect, as undoubtedly elsewhere, penetrating to the true meaning of sometimes cryptic biblical texts was the most important of tasks, entrusted to the leaders of the community. Their work was the product of long study, and they themselves are descendant from the traditional wisdom teachers of old. But, in these closing centuries, they have taken on something of the prophet too. Like prophets, they are mediators of the divine word and deliverers of divine messages of contemporary significance, whether eschatological revelations of the "true sense" of oracles delivered of old or simply proper interpretations of ancient laws whose sense or full application might not be apparent from the ancient texts themselves. In presenting these interpretations, the interpreters sometimes cloaked their words with the mantle of ancient authority and sometimes presented them in their own names. In either case, the interpretation itself might not be merely the result of careful study and meditation, it could come, directly or indirectly, from God or the angels.

IV

Many of these tendencies are summed up in Ben Sira's famous description of the sage; written in the early second century B.C.E., it presents a composite of most of the elements seen thus far:

> He who devotes himself to studying the law of the Most High interprets the wisdom of the ancients and studies prophecies. He observes the words of men of renown, and penetrates the depths of proverbs. He interprets hidden meanings, and is familiar with parables. He serves among princes, and appears before the mighty. He travels to foreign nations, weighing good and evil among men. He rises early to worship his Maker, and pray to the Most High, opening his mouth in prayer and making supplication for his sins. If the Most High God so will, he will be filled with the spirit of understanding: he will utter words of wisdom, and give thanks to the Lord in prayer. (Ecclus. 39:1–6)

Here is the theme of the inspired interpreter ("If the Most High God so will, he will be filled . . ."), and the sacred writings that he interprets (not only the "law of the Most High," i.e., Torah, but also "prophecies" and the "words of men of renown") have become the natural focus of a sage's wisdom; he is an interpreter. Hidden meanings, finding the secrets of old texts, are his stock-in-trade. Yet, far from being a mystic recluse, such a sage is ipso facto a leader of men, adviser to princes and emissary to foreign lands. His wisdom assures him fame and honor above all his contemporaries.

From such early teachers stemmed the great early works of biblical commentary, retelling, and expansion, as well as myriads of little insights into the significance of individual verses within the Bible. Many of these teachers are anonymous. We do not know the name of the author of the aforementioned *Book of Jubilees,* for example, or the author of the *Testaments of the Twelve Patriarchs* (possibly second or first century B.C.E.); like many writers from this period, these authors chose to hide behind biblical personae. We do not know the name of the author of the *Genesis Apocryphon,* a fragmentary retelling and expansion of parts of Genesis found at Qumran—but this may be an accident of history. We *do* know the name of Joshua (or Jesus) Ben Sira (second century B.C.E.), the author of Ecclesiasticus cited above, and he was doubtless a respected teacher and sage in his own day. From a slightly later period, we know the names and even the life history of some interpreters: In particular, two Jews who wrote in Greek, Philo of Alexandria (ca. 10 B.C.E.–ca. 45 C.E.) and Josephus (37/8–ca. 100 C.E.), not only have left behind voluminous retellings and interpretations of biblical texts but have given us a valuable glimpse of their own training, ideas, and accomplishments. (Both were active in political life.) Yet even after the first century C.E., the authors of many documents embodying the early interpretation of Scripture are unknown to us. Moreover, as noted earlier, "interpretation" was not a single activity, but many, performed by the broadest variety of figures in postexilic times; most of these persons are perforce anonymous.

V

Our focus throughout has been upon the earliest beginnings of Jewish biblical exegesis. Yet before we leave this somewhat heterogeneous crowd of early interpreters, it may be well to locate within their midst the direct ancestor of a somewhat later figure, a brand of interpreter who ultimately would produce an enormous corpus of biblical commentary and, what is more, whose activity would serve to crystallize Jewish practice in a form still recognizable to us today. This interpreter is known by various names. From the first century C.E. onward, he is often called by the honorific title "Rabbi" ("my master" or "teacher")—hence his religion is sometimes styled "rabbinic Judaism" to distinguish it from the Judaism practiced or urged by other interpreters. Before the introduction of this title, this brand of interpreter is referred to variously as "sage," "elder," *sofer* ("bookman" or scribe), Pharisee, and yet others. The question of names is a difficult one, as we shall see, but, as to his personal and intellectual characteristics, he is very much at home in the collection of interests and traits enumerated above; indeed, *all* the aspects of the interpreter outlined earlier can be seen to figure in his particular genealogy. He has a lively interest in the priesthood and the Temple ritual (though he may or may not himself be of priestly family); he is an expert in the law, perhaps himself a judge; he is, most characteristically, a teacher; yet he is also something of a holy man, a selfless benefactor, sometimes even a miracle-worker, and one whose wise insights and personal piety make him a leader of his community.

As noted, the title "Rabbi" only makes its appearance in the first century C.E., but the rabbinic sage certainly goes back to an earlier date. Indeed, he is descended from an ongoing group of teachers or sages of a particular orientation whose origins reach far back into the history of postexilic Judaism. Unfortunately, the details of this spiritual ancestry are unclear, for the lines separating the "proto-rabbinic" sage from other sages grow fainter the farther back into history one searches. The Rabbis themselves traced the origin of their teachings ("Torah"—i.e., not only Scripture but its interpretation and application to daily life) back to Moses; according to one celebrated statement, Moses orally transmitted his teachings to Joshua, and Joshua on to a subsequent chain of prophets and wise men, culminating in various named sages from the second century B.C.E. to the first century C.E. which the Rabbis knew as their immediate ancestors. In this chain, a significant if somewhat hazy link are the members of an institution known as the Great Assembly (or Great Synagogue), an entity whose founding is perhaps to be located in the Persian period. Rabbinic literature depicts the members of this body in what we might call proto-rabbinical roles, not only in the study of Scripture (they are, in fact, attributed a role in determining what texts were suitable for inclusion within the sacred corpus) and the transmission of scriptural interpretation and Jewish law but in the enactment of religious decrees, specifically the institution of certain regular prayers and liturgical practices. These details may, of course, be retrojections from a later period. But there is broad consensus that the existence of the Great Assembly is not a fabrication, and the fact that the Rabbis claimed it as a link in their tradition may indicate that the Assembly's jurisdiction did include the interpretation and practical application of sacred statutes. This would certainly be consistent with the role of biblical texts as we have depicted it in the restored community of Judah.

In considering the antecedents of the later, rabbinic interpreter's approach to his own task, we must bear in mind one fact: early interpretation was an activity with great political consequences. Probably from the very moment of the return from exile, Judea had been a place of internal strife and factionalism. As we have seen, Jews disagreed among themselves over such fundamentals as the acceptance of foreign domination versus strivings for political independence; the leadership role to be played in society by various groups; the very composition of the new society (who was to be included, and who not), and the related issue of their attitude toward surrounding peoples and cultures (what is sometimes described as the conflict between "assimilation" and "exclusiveness"); and, of course, the relationship of the new society to its Great Past and, specifically, to the laws and beliefs that existed before the exile. These were issues on which Israel's sacred writings were held to have direct bearing, and people looked to the interpreters of these texts to provide the basis, or at least support, for various opposing positions on these issues.

In seeking out the roots or origins of rabbinic Judaism, therefore, scholars not only have looked to institutions such as the Great Assembly, cited by the Rabbis themselves and attributed certain proto-rabbinical functions, they have also considered what can be reconstructed of the political situation, the factions and political "parties" whose existence can be divined from historical records, in order to seek out spiritual ancestors. Thus, for example, in the conflict with Hellenism, it has been supposed that the spectrum of Jewish attitudes described earlier was actually represented by different organized groups or parties. It has thus been convincingly argued that the Maccabean revolt was virtually a civil war (rather than the revolt of an oppressed, united populace against its foreign rulers) and that, indeed, the program of Antiochus IV was neither of his own invention nor a simpleminded attempt to impose Greek religion upon Judea. Rather, it was more likely the program of a native "reform party" bent on striking a cosmopolitan balance between old and new, Jewish tradition and Greek culture. "Let us go," these reformers were reported to say in 1 Macc. 1:11, "and make a covenant with the Gentiles round about us, for *since we separated from them* many evils have come upon us." To them, apparently, there was an earlier time when "separation" had not been the norm; for them, the message of the Great Past was one of tolerance, openness to common, philosophical truths, perhaps even assimilation.

The "party" that opposed this position (and within which some have sought the Rabbis' spiritual forebears) is even known by name. They were called in Hebrew the *Ḥasidim* ("pious ones," sometimes also called by the hybrid English form "Hasideans"), a name first found in historical literature at the time of the Maccabean revolt. Here they are referred to as if already a well-established entity (1 Macc. 2:42), and it has thus been conjectured that their existence can be traced to an earlier period; some have argued that their founding goes back to Simeon the Just (ca. 200 B.C.E.), a high priest and political leader known to us from various sources. (In the rabbinic chain of ancestors described above, Simeon is mentioned by name; he is said to be one of those "left over" from the members of the Great Assembly.) But it is impossible to know whence the Hasidim spring, or even how formal a group is intended; perhaps a coalition of interests corresponding to those of the Hasidim goes back still earlier. In any event, one thing that stands behind the attempt to trace the beginnings of "rabbinism" back to the emergence of the Hasidim is the belief that it was in the caldron of politics that attitudes were fixed and coalitions formed—that schools of interpretation formed around the great issues of the day and coalesced into ongoing entities.

From the late second century B.C.E. onward, the groups and parties known to us take on a more definite outline. Two groups familiar from the writings of the Jewish historian Josephus as well as from the New Testament can be traced back to this period: the Pharisees and the Sadducees. Josephus first speaks of them in connection with the reign of John Hyrcanus I (134–104 B.C.E.) during the Hasmonean period. (Apparently the Hasmoneans had previously been well disposed toward the Pharisees, but a dispute now led the king to favor the aristocratic Sadducees. How early, therefore, they go back can only be conjectured; nor is it known whether the Pharisees are a continuation of, or an offshoot from, the Hasidim mentioned above.) The Essenes, also known to us from Josephus and other writers, were a third group; quite possibly the founders of the "retreat" community at Qumran (the sect of the Dead Sea Scrolls) were Essenes.

The Pharisaic interpreters are the immediate ancestors of rabbinic Judaism. We hear of them through the turn of the era and into the first century, after which their students and successors, now no longer identified as Pharisees, survive and consolidate in the traumatic period following the disasters of 70 and 135 C.E. The Pharisees of the New Testament are petty, heartless, and immoral, but this surely arises out of polemic; modern scholars, Jewish and Christian, have been at pains to right this picture and show these saintly scholars in a truer light. Yet the precise nature of the Pharisees' standing in the larger community, and of their origins, remains disputed. Were they, as some scholars claim, originally a political party, with a national program and agenda that only later took on the character known to us from rabbinic writings? Was their approach a reflex of society as a whole, rooted in class and occupational differences in the population of Judea? Or were they, in yet another view, very much of a mainstream phenomenon, a group whose basic orientation and teachings may be traced back through the whole history of Judah from the Persian period, and perhaps even earlier? At issue is not only the character of the Pharisees as a group, or more generally of rabbinic Judaism, but the standing of that Judaism vis-à-vis the tradition: Was it a radical departure, the idiosyncratic program of one sect or party among many, or was it (as the Rabbis claimed) *the* tradition, a collection of practices and biblical interpretations sanctified by an unbroken chain of authority? We cannot, in the present format, seek to answer these questions, but we can take a closer look at the characteristic interests of these sages, and at their writings.

VI

The activities of the Rabbis and their forebears were multifarious. They themselves were, as stated, teachers and preachers, judges and priests, holy men and communal leaders. But surely interpretation itself leads the list of their concerns. *Midrash*, a Hebrew term that means "interpretation" or "textual study," was an all-consuming activity, and the *beit midrash* ("study house") came to be a prime rabbinic institution, meeting place of sages and training ground for successive generations of scholars.

We have seen earlier that one of the pressing concerns of the Jews who returned to their homeland after the Babylonian exile was the proper observance of divine law; we have also seen that the sacred texts themselves are not always explicit about how laws are to be observed—what, for example, the prohibition against "work" on the Sabbath may or may not involve—and that, indeed, some biblical texts even seem to contradict others. The need to pin things down, especially in matters of everyday behavior, was thus crucial. This domain came to be called *halakha*, a word that might be translated as "rule of conduct" or "established practice (of divine law)" but whose meaning was connected by popular etymology to its root sense in Hebrew, "to walk." Halakha was the path on which one walked, the way of proper observance; it was, in the broadest sense, the *legal* part of Jewish study, the part connected with actual rules of behavior in daily life. (This is "walking" par excellence; recall the phrase in Neh. 10:29 cited above, "to walk in God's Torah which was given by Moses the servant of God, and to observe and do all the commandments of the Lord our master and his ordinances and statutes.") No doubt from an early period, questions of how biblical laws were to be interpreted, fleshed out, and even supplemented were the subject of discussion and textual scrutiny, out of which emerged a living, vibrant halakha.

When did this halakha begin to emerge? As noted, this question is hotly disputed even today, and the debate is due in part to a curious circumstance. For reasons that are not entirely clear, halakhic traditions of the Rabbis and their forebears were, at least for a long time, not transmitted in writing; they were passed down orally, from teacher to pupil, learned by heart. At the end of the second century of the common era, some of these traditions were codified as the Mishna, a topical compendium of halakha on such diverse subjects as agricultural law, the observance of Sabbath and holidays, civil and criminal law, laws of the Temple and all that affects it, laws concerning man and wife and family life, and so forth. This compendium (the size of a large book) was held to be simply that, a compendium of earlier material (indeed, of earlier compendia), so that the ultimate origins of its prescriptions and derivations remain obscure. But what is more, even after its definitive compilation, the Mishna (as well as a great deal more interpretive material of the Rabbis) continued to be passed on primarily by rote for centuries to come. Because of this salient characteristic, these rabbinic materials acquired the general name of Oral Torah (*torah shebbe'al peh*). "Torah" here has the general meaning of "divine teaching," and this body of divine teaching, transmitted orally, was implicitly counterposed to the Written Torah—that is, the Bible—which it interpreted and supplemented.

As noted, rabbinic tradition traces its "Torah" back through various named sages to the time of the Great Assembly and still farther, through prophets, sages, and biblical figures, back to Moses himself. This of course does not mean that they claimed that *all* of the Oral Torah originated in hoary antiquity (an absurdity), but that the *institution* of it began back then and that it was transmitted and supplemented through a chain of authorities, with each generation adding new interpretations, as well as decisions and decrees necessitated by changing circumstances. Though this general notion of the growth of the rabbinic tradition is quite plausible, some modern scholars, working from the other extreme and seeking simply to eliminate all unproven hypotheses, have been reluctant to date the rabbinic traditions much earlier than the end of the second century C.E. (the editing of the Mishna). But most contemporary scholars would probably be dissatisfied with this overly cautious approach. Fortunately, although the bearers of the Oral Torah were reluctant to write things down, others were not, and we have a number of indications from the time of the turn of the era, and even earlier, that point to the existence of an already highly developed "proto-rabbinical" exegetical tradition. Scholars have found traces of ideas and interpretations later embodied in the Mishna in far earlier works—for example, in the Old Greek translation of the Pentateuch (the Septuagint, begun in the third century B.C.E.). Moreover, halakha itself was not the exclusive domain of a single group; rival traditions of what constituted the proper practice and application of biblical statute coexisted, and written, nonrabbinic sources from this period sometimes bear witness to the centrality of this concern. Above we saw in passing that the *Book of Jubilees* (second century B.C.E.) was concerned with connecting legal (i.e., halakhic) concerns to narratives in Genesis. It seems probable that the author of *Jubilees* was, by his writing, seeking to modify or protest against halakhic norms already in existence and sanctioned by authority—that, in other words, the transmission of halakha deemed authoritative was already well established. From a somewhat later period come documents of a halakhic character belonging to the Qumran sect; these attest to exegetical concerns, methods, and even terminology held in common with the Rabbis. In view of the Qumran group's opposition to the "proto-rabbinic school," the fact of these instances of a common approach and language again argues the existence of an authoritative ancestor still earlier. Of course, "How much how early?" is a question that is doubtless not susceptible to precise answer; but certainly it is plausible to imagine a continuous tradition of interpretation and practical application of divine statutes going back to the Great Assembly and still earlier, a tradition ever enriched and modified to fit new circumstances and insights.

We have stressed halakha in the foregoing because it *was* stressed—to act in accordance with sacred statute was not only to "obey the law," it was a continual form of devotion, an ever-

renewed offering up of one's behavior—hence of one's daily existence—to God. The more precisely particular acts and forms
could be connected to the sacred prescriptions, the more precisely
could one's everyday actions be shaped in obedience to God. As a
later sage, R. Hananiah b. Aqashia, was to put it (creatively interpreting the words of Isa. 42:21), "It was because God wished to
make Israel meritorious that he gave them so many commandments"—that is, the more statutes there were to be observed, the
more fully might Israel seek to align its daily life with God's word.
But besides the interpreting and supplementing of scriptural commandments, there was a growing and soon enormous body of
scriptural interpretation of a nonpractical sort, aimed at solving
potential dilemmas posed especially by scriptural narrative (of the
kind seen above: difficult or rare Hebrew words, potential contradictions or unexplained details; biblical heroes that act in unseemly ways, and so forth) or simply bringing out little details in
the text that might normally be missed—indeed, elaborating biblical narratives and other texts with details or entire incidents "deduced" from the slightest particularity in the original. This
sophisticated and often humorous (though at the same time highly
moralistic) body of rabbinic exegesis is sometimes referred to as
aggadah ("narrative"). Aggadah is the complement of halakha: it
covers the "nonlegal" part of rabbinic exegesis. (The term also
embraces material that is not, strictly speaking, exegetical at all,
such as tales from the lives of famous rabbis.) The other Hebrew
term mentioned above, *midrash* ("study" or "interpretation"), although it includes both halakha and aggadah, is sometimes used
inexactly by modern scholars to refer especially to the latter.

How does biblical interpretation preserved for us in rabbinic
literature differ from other, nonrabbinic, early interpretation? We
might say, from a modern vantage point: strikingly little. Of course
the Rabbis themselves were highly conscious of the doctrinal and
practical issues that separated their spiritual ancestors the Pharisees
from various other groups active before the destruction of the
Jerusalem Temple in 70 c.e.; on disagreements about a single word
in the Pentateuch, or about the propriety of observances not specifically mentioned in Israel's festive calendar, had hung disputes and
communal divisions as bitter as can be found to afflict any society.
Yet if an observer were to take a step backward and examine the
assumptions and even the methodology of our entire corpus of
biblical interpretations from, say, the second century B.C.E. to the
second century C.E., he would find the quantity of congruences and
agreements strikingly high. This should seem to us only natural in

the light of what was seen above: that certain broad assumptions of biblical interpretation were shaped by events and circumstances of a still earlier period and that, by 200 B.C.E., it is probable that a large body of actual interpretations of individual biblical verses was in wide circulation among the Jews, either in oral or written form. In its *conclusions*, the halakha of the Qumran sect was not only different from that developed in rabbinic writings but irreconcilably so; yet, as noted, the language in which it is presented, and the manner in which it is related to Scripture, is at times uncannily similar. Philo of Alexandria, the Egyptian Jew of the turn of the era who wrote an imposing series of commentaries on the Pentateuch, at first seems light-years away from rabbinic midrash expounding the same passages; there is all the difference in the world between the Rabbis' terse, often cryptically phrased, insights and Philo's expansive and sweet-flowing Greek prose, and the same distance separates Philo's highly allegorical style of reading (wherein biblical persons and events become transported into the world of the soul and of abstract virtues and vices) from the Rabbis' utterly nonallegorical, yet equally imaginative and creative, exegesis. Nevertheless, even between these two a basic kinship is observable. Both bodies of exegesis stay remarkably close to the text, seeking to explicate any peculiarity in its manner of expression—indeed, using such peculiarities as the springboard to some larger, often moralizing, point. Both are concerned with extracting teachings from the text relevant to their contemporaries. Both are bent on bringing out the essential perfection of the text, its worthiness as a divine teaching given to man (in which not a little element of apologetic is to be identified in each). Both believe the exegete's job is to reveal things not immediately apparent, and both see this "hidden" layer of meaning as an expression of the text's greatness. What is more, apart from such methodological and ideological similarities, it is simply true that there is a certain amount of overlap in actual interpretations and motifs found in these various interpretive works. Understandings of a particular verse in Genesis found in *Jubilees*, or underlying the Old Greek translation of the Pentateuch, can be found later on in Philo's works, in New Testament explanations of biblical verses, or in rabbinic collections. Did the later sources consult the earlier ones? In some cases, direct influence can be posited, but in others it is more reasonable to suppose that the interpretations belonged to a common store of midrash that circulated in various forms in Jewish communities within Palestine and, as well, in the great Jewish communities beyond its borders, in Egypt or Babylon.

VII

If we have singled out for special comment the Rabbi and his prototype, it is not only because he is the founder of rabbinic Judaism and, hence, the subject of much scrutiny by scholars past and present. It is because he is, as well, the transmitter of an enormous body of exegetical material, halakhic and aggadic, some of it of undoubted antiquity. The rabbinic teachers who flourished up to the end of the second century or so (referred to as *tanna'im* to distinguish them from the post-200 teachers, called *amora'im*) are the authoritative teachers and transmitters cited not only in the Mishna, and in the far longer Tosefta, a work that parallels and supplements the Mishna, but in a series of exegetical commentaries on the books of Exodus, Leviticus, Numbers, and Deuteronomy. (These commentaries, called tannaitic midrashim, were presumably compiled shortly after 200 C.E.; because their focus is primarily halakhic exegesis, Genesis—a book of narrative—is not included.) From their circle also emanated Aramaic translations of the Bible (called targums), which apparently accompanied public readings of Scripture as well as its study; these too constitute a large body of scriptural interpretation, not only because every translation is ipso facto an interpretation but because these in particular aimed at more than mechanical duplication. Their teachings are further cited, interpreted, and elaborated upon in the still more voluminous works of the amora'im and *their* successors, most notably in the Jerusalem and Babylonian Talmuds and the aggadic interpretations grouped in such collections as *Midrash Rabba*. The tannaitic corpus in itself constitutes a small library of biblical interpretation, and the amoraic corpus a large one. Nor did Jewish exegesis end there. For in truth what the Rabbis had founded was a religion of interpretation, a tradition of studying Scripture and putting it into practice that touched every member of the community and that elevated these activities to the very highest level. If the Rabbi's earliest origins are held in common with those of other interpreters, he is unique not only because the tradition that he founded took shape as a body of early interpretation of imposing dimension but because that tradition was a dynamic one, engendering new generations of teacher-interpreters and thus new works of transmission and synthesis, a monumental tradition of study and piety that stretches from late antiquity to the great Jewish exegetes of medieval Spain and on even to the present day.

5

A Look at Some Texts

Having viewed some of the currents that shaped Israel's interest in, and approaches to, Scripture from the Persian period onward, and having examined the diversity of interpreters that existed in the closing centuries before the common era, we may now examine some actual interpretive texts from the end of that period in order to see how they embody the various trends and tendencies described. At the outset, however, it will be well to survey briefly the sorts of materials that might be used in such a sampling. This is no simple task, since biblical "interpretation" can range from the most casual allusion to a biblical text (or even to a subject treated in such a text) to detailed retellings or even meticulous exegetical dissections of each word; given a generous definition of interpretation, such a survey would be ponderous indeed. But here, at least, are some of the obvious places to which one might turn in order to assemble such a sampling.

The Hebrew Bible itself (by which is meant here the canon of Scripture that ultimately became normative for rabbinic Judaism) contains, as we have seen all too briefly, a great deal of interpretation. Among the many forms that this intrabiblical interpretation can take are: the interpretation of earlier historical texts in later retellings (such as Chronicles); the interpretation of legal material through reordering, rewording, expansion, and harmonization, as well as allusions to laws and their application found outside legal corpora proper (as in prophetic oracles); prophetic reuse or reinterpretation of earlier prophetic sayings, as well as those anonymous expansions to prophetic collections, many of which build new material around a saying or theme of the original prophet; reinterpretation by reuse of linguistic formulae, liturgical motifs, proverbs and sayings, and so on; and (to the extent that the foregoing does not encompass it) the whole area of "editorial interpretation"—that is, the interpretive act embodied in the ordering of earlier material, arrangement and splicing of fragments, as well as actual excisions, headings (such as those that now precede many of the psalms), chronological notes, glosses of rare or technical terms, and so forth. This multifarious activity corresponds, as we have seen, to the various sorts of figures in ancient Israel who initiated it, wise men and scribes connected with various institutions (including the Temple), priests, Levites, judges and cultic prophets, interpreters who were inspired and quasi-prophetic, or more humdrum, highly political, or quite above the vulgar fray.

This intrabiblical interpretive material is by and large older than the interpretive material outside the Hebrew Bible. In part, it seems, this is because at least some would-be interpreters were, at an earlier date, still free to tack on their interpretations or expansions to the actual biblical text. Such are, for example, some of the later additions to prophets like Isaiah or Joel; while these collections were still in a relatively fluid state, interpolations explaining or expanding the prophet's utterances in a certain direction could simply be attached to the text itself. But precisely because they are older and their sense of the status of Scripture is less rigid, these intrabiblical interpretations often stand in a class by themselves. While of course overlapping exists (there is not an enormous difference, for example, between some of the prophetic expansions just described and the style of separate prophetic commentaries known from the Dead Sea Scrolls), extrabiblical interpretation is frequently of a different order, one more recognizably exegetical. What forms does this (generally later) material take?

One might begin by mentioning various extant translations of biblical texts. Among the most important of these is the Greek translation of the Hebrew Bible popularly known as the Septuagint ("seventy," because it is said to have been accomplished by seventy, or seventy-two, translators; it is sometimes abbreviated LXX). This is actually a collection of translations probably begun in the early third century B.C.E. and continuing for the next few centuries. The translation of the Pentateuch and other early parts thus provides an important source of information about how the Bible was understood in the third and second centuries B.C.E. It should be mentioned that this translation also provided the basis for various secondary translations. For example, the Old Latin translation (called the *vetus Latina*) was based on the LXX. Another Latin translation, undertaken by Jerome (ca. 342–420), ultimately supplanted the Old Latin; it became known as the Vulgate and is also a valuable source of interpretive traditions.

Various translations of the Hebrew Bible into Aramaic (called targums) also bear witness to early interpretation, but the process of their compilation and editing makes it difficult to date them with any certainty. Targum Onkelos, an Aramaic translation of the Pentateuch, ought perhaps to be dated to the second or third century c.e., at least in its final form. Apparently it had previously been put together and shaped for use in rabbinic circles within the Land of Israel; quite conceivably it contains Aramaic translation traditions that go back to a much earlier period. (We have even seen above that Jewish tradition associates the start of targum with Ezra's public reading.) Subsequently this translation was probably brought to Babylon and adapted to the Aramaic dialect in use by Jews there. A fairly close translation, Onkelos is nonetheless hardly "literal" (as it is sometimes described); it often deviates (for reasons of doctrine, clarity, polemic, and so on) from the words of the Hebrew text.

Still freer is the targum tradition represented by the "Palestinian" or "Jerusalem" targums, including Targum Pseudo-Jonathan, the "Fragment Targums," and Targum Neophyti (all of the Pentateuch), which are often closer to retellings than translations and contain frequent interpolations, sometimes whole sentences or more, that do not appear in the Hebrew. The dating of this material is equally problematic; some of it is indisputably of ancient origin, but this ancient material is sometimes jumbled together with material from much later periods. These targums, as well as targums for the rest of Scripture, constitute a rich source of midrashic material. Also worthy of mention are various versions of the Samaritan targum of the Pentateuch (the earliest of which have been dated to before the fourth century c.e.), and the Peshitta, a Syriac targum with ancient roots. Beyond these, there are translations of the Bible into other ancient languages—Coptic, Ethiopic, Armenian, Old Church Slavonic, and others.

A related and highly popular form in which early biblical interpretation has been preserved is that of actual retellings or paraphrases of biblical material. (This, as will be seen, is at times indistinguishable from what might be called biblical commentary proper.) We have already seen a form of this in the book of Ben Sira (Ecclesiasticus), written in the early second century b.c.e., which summarizes biblical narratives, comments upon or reworks biblical sayings or themes, and in other ways seeks to interpret Scripture (see especially chs. 44–49). The *Book of Jubilees* (second century B.C.E.), discussed above, is another rich retelling and an important source of early exegesis. Much of its version of Genesis and the beginning of Exodus was done in the Bible's own words but supplemented at every turn with calendric and chronological interpolations as well as with bits of explanation or additions intended to account for apparent difficulties in the text, or to harmonize discordant elements, or to meet any of the other goals of early exegesis outlined above.

The Dead Sea Scrolls from the caves of Qumran have provided a striking example of biblical retelling in the document known as the *Genesis Apocryphon*. Written in Aramaic, this fragmentary text consists in part of a lengthy retelling of the story of Abraham and Sarah in Egypt (Gen. 12), narrated by Abraham in the first person. Like other works of this genre, it seeks to touch up a bit the biblical account, which does not, to our eyes at least, seem to portray its protagonists in a very flattering light. In the *Genesis Apocryphon* account, on the contrary, Abraham receives a divine warning that his life is in danger (thus justifying somewhat more his subsequent conduct); his "lie" about Sarah is both justified and harmonized with Genesis 20; we are specifically told that Sarah, though she was taken to the house of Pharaoh, did not compromise her honor; and so forth. In addition to such apologetic elements, there are many details that simply flesh out the narrative, identify anonymous characters and places, and illustrate other concerns typical of rabbinic midrash—indeed, there are many points that connect this text with later midrashic material. The *Genesis Apocryphon* has been dated to the time of the turn of the era.

We have also seen briefly that the spiritual "last will and testament" form, in which some character from hoary antiquity sets down his reflections before death, was a popular literary genre both before and after the beginning of the common era. These testaments were attributed to various biblical figures and therefore often contain, among other things, material that parallels and supplements biblical texts. Above we have seen that the *Testaments of the Twelve Patriarchs* may have existed, in primitive form, in the second century B.C.E. (though some scholars deny this possibility); it certainly embodies an impressive corpus of early exegesis/expansion, especially in regard to the person and story of Joseph. The *Testament of Moses* (also called the *Apocalypse of Moses*), though revised at the beginning of the common era, goes back to a second century B.C.E. original; it is framed around the end of the book of Deuteronomy (chs. 31–34). Other testaments, though somewhat later, also include retellings of biblical events or present evidence about the exposition of sacred Scripture.

The Qumran caves have provided other documents of early biblical interpretation, some of them belonging to the genre of biblical commentaries proper. Particularly striking is the genre (or genres) known as *pesher* ("interpretation"). Most of our examples of this form consist of verse-by-verse explanations of passages from various prophets and the psalms, which typically seek to connect the passages with events in the future, events touching on the Qumran community itself or its enemies. These texts thus represent the eschatological interest of much early exegesis (see above, chapter 3), but in form they are also somewhat reminiscent of the verse-by-verse format that was to be exemplified in later Jewish and Christian homilies and scriptural expositions. That this was an old and widespread form of interpretation is hardly to be doubted—indeed, as noted earlier, some have connected the later additions incorporated in such biblical books as Joel to this particular genre. The Qumran pesher material has largely been dated to the latter half of the first century B.C.E. (A wealth of interpretive material comes to us from the Qumran community in other forms—in the *Temple Scroll,* the *Rule of the Community,* and still other works.)

Combining both retellings of the Bible and detailed biblical commentary proper are the great exegetical works of two Jews who wrote in Greek, Philo of Alexandria and Flavius Josephus. Philo was heir to an earlier tradition of Hellenistic-Jewish biblical exegesis, represented in such works as the pseudepigraphic *Letter of Aristeas* or the allegorical interpretations of Aristobulus of Paneas. (Incidentally, a book long attributed to Philo, the *Liber antiquitatum biblicarum,* or *Book of Biblical Antiquities,* is actually the work of an anonymous author or authors, a midrashic retelling of biblical history from Genesis to 1 Samuel. Probably compiled in the first century C.E., it too is a valuable witness to early exegesis; it belongs to the "Retold Bible" genre.) Josephus, a colorful figure descended from a distinguished priestly family, was well acquainted with various groups within the Land of Israel (it is to him that we owe much of our knowledge of first-century Jewish groups) and was a self-proclaimed student of the Pharisees. His multivolume *Jewish Antiquities* (completed in 93–94 C.E.) begins with a retelling of biblical history and contains a wealth of interpretive material, much of it otherwise attested or paralleled in the *Book of Jubilees* or other early sources. These are only two among many Jews and, later, Christians who wrote in Greek and whose works (sometimes not directly concerned with Scripture at all) bear traces of early exegetical traditions.

The great corpus of rabbinic expositions of Scripture, as mentioned earlier, belongs to a period subsequent to those included in our survey; nonetheless, students of early exegesis have found myriad parallels between these rabbinic interpretations and datably earlier material. It is obvious that not only the Mishna, Tosefta, and other tannaitic compilations but also the Jerusalem and Babylonian Talmuds, various midrashic collections, and still later works are likely to contain much that originated in an earlier period. The same is of course true of much of the exegetical material found in the New Testament and other early Christian writings, which in themselves embody diverse trends in the exposition and adaptation of Hebrew Scripture as pursued in late antiquity.

Nor do the groups of works alluded to above constitute the whole corpus of exegesis—far from it! For since the most casual allusion to a biblical figure or event can sometimes reveal much about how one part of the Bible was being weighed and studied at a particular time, our corpus of early "interpreters" must also include almost all writers in late antiquity, Jews and Gentiles, who make even the slightest mention of the Bible, biblical figures, or the Jews and their history. Moreover, early interpretation can sometimes be found, or elucidated, in works from a far later period—not only rabbinic and medieval Jewish writings of the most varied character but the writings of early Christian apologists, of the Church Fathers, and indeed of all of early and medieval Christendom. We must also include the sermons, liturgical poetry, and scriptural expositions preserved by Eastern churches; long-lost treatises by Gnostic writers, Jewish and Christian; Samaritan writings about Scripture, including early sermonic and liturgical compositions; Moslem retellings of biblical history, both within the Qur'an and among later Arabic writers; and still others. Given this great diversity, one can hardly undertake to list individually all the materials that may be of use in reconstructing the early history of biblical exegesis. Indeed, seen from this perspective, the study of "early" exegesis is hardly to be separated from that of later material; nor, as we have seen above, is the growth of this movement separable from the biblical text itself or the history of Israel in the biblical period. The truth is that this literature is both vast and a continuum, stretching from the earliest reworkings of biblical traditions within the Hebrew Bible through the translations, retellings, and commentaries of early Judaism and Christianity, and on to the Middle Ages and still more recent times.

II

Let us now look at a few of the sources mentioned and so glimpse, however briefly, the early interpretation of Scripture as it has been preserved for us. Our first example is of the pesher type of interpretation practiced at Qumran. As noted, these commentaries, which take various forms, often seek to connect the words of the text not with the historical situation of the actual biblical author (as a modern critic might do) but with events connected to the time of the Qumran community itself. Here, for example, is how two lines from the seventh-century B.C.E. prophet Nahum (3:6–7) were interpreted at Qumran:

> And I [the Lord] shall cast abominations upon you [Nineveh], and make you contemptible and vilified, so that all who behold you will recoil from you. (Nah. 3:6)—
>
> This refers [lit., "its interpretation," pesher, is] to the false interpreters who, at the end of the present time, will have their evil deeds exposed to all of Israel, and many will perceive their [the interpreters'] errors and despise them and vilify them for their willful wickedness. And when the glory of Judah is revealed, the simple folk of Ephraim will recoil from amidst their assembly and abandon those who have led them astray and will join together with Israel and will say—
>
> Wasted is Nineveh, who will bemoan her? Whence may I seek comforters for you? (Nah. 3:7)—
>
> This refers [pesher] to the false interpreters, whose counsel shall perish and whose company will be cut off, that they may no more lead the assembly astray, and that simple folk may no more embrace their counsel.

Nahum's original words, of course, applied to the historical Nineveh (which fell in 612 B.C.E.) and its Assyrian rulers who had so long embittered Judean life. His oracle thus belonged to the distant past and was hardly relevant to political life in Judah in the first century B.C.E.; yet it was the pleasure of the author of this pesher to read these verses in Nahum as if they referred to people known to him in his own time. Thus "Nineveh" is here equated with the "false interpreters" (literally, the "interpreters of smooth things"; the latter word, *halaqot*, sounds suspiciously like *halakhot*, the plural of *halakha;* the interpreters in question have been identified by some modern scholars as none other than the Pharisees). Nahum's prophecy thus "becomes" a foretelling of the downfall of this group of interpreters and its followers. Note that, beyond the identification of Nineveh with this group, the Qumran pesher goes on to reuse

Nahum's own words in its restatement: "vilified" in Nahum yields "despise them and vilify them" in the pesher; "recoil from you" in Nahum yields "will recoil from amidst their assembly" in the pesher; and so forth. All this, the interpreter says, will be happening "at the end of the present time."

It is to be noted that Qumran pesher, like other bits of early exegesis, is fond of "biblicizing" current events. Thus in the cited passage, "Judah" seems to mean specifically the Qumran community and "Ephraim" perhaps the followers of the Pharisees; elsewhere the Romans are referred to as the biblical *Kittim*, the Sadducees as "Manasseh," and so on. One might associate this tendency with the typological reading of Scripture (mentioned in chapter 3), which sees earlier people and things as foreshadowings of later ones.

Here it might well be asked: Can one properly call our pesher a form of "interpretation"? That is, was the author of this pesher (or those of similar passages) actually seeking to understand the meaning of a biblical text, or was he simply *using* that text to give authority to one particular view of things? This is a question well worth asking, but its answer is far from simple. Certainly it would be disingenuous to claim that this pesher is a dispassionate attempt to arrive at the "original meaning" of the biblical text—but then, such a description would not fit very much of the early exegesis we have been discussing. On the contrary, we have seen that *actualizing* Scripture, making it relevant in one way or another to the interpreter's own present time, had probably characterized exegesis from the time of the return from exile. Moreover, both the sacred provenance of ancient prophecies and the interpreter's own status as one possessed of great wisdom or even divine inspiration must have seemed to vouchsafe the effort to find "secrets," "hidden meaning," and the like in the ancient words—including references to the interpreter's own day or to things destined shortly to come. We have above identified this attitude in the biblical book of Daniel itself, whose interpretation of Jeremiah's "seventy years" is indeed quite close in spirit to Qumran pesher. And, on the other hand, pesher is to be compared to developments and forms familiar from later biblical exegesis. It is only a short hop from Qumran to the sort of typological interpretation known from the New Testament and other early Christian writings, whereby parts of the Hebrew Bible are read as a foreshadowing and prediction of the events of the Gospels; nor is this interpretive posture utterly foreign to rabbinic exegesis. Interestingly, the form of pesher represented in this extract has also been connected with an exegetical mode familiar in rabbinic literature, in which consecutive phrases of a biblical passage are read as if referring to a single biblical figure or event quite remote from the passage's (often vague or general) subject.

III

The allegorical approach to Scripture, whereby biblical persons and incidents become representative of abstract virtues or doctrines or incidents in the life of the soul, is attested in Hellenistic Jewish writings as early as the second century B.C.E. This approach to interpreting Scripture was modeled on a far older phenomenon, the allegorical reading of Homer and other Greek texts, which had long been a standard literary procedure in the Hellenistic world. There its purpose frequently was to identify philosophical doctrines or proper teachings in texts where such teachings were often none too apparent. The presence of some "underlying sense" in a literary text soon became thereby a mark of distinction, and it was probably inevitable that Jews under the spell of Hellenic culture (especially those in the large Hellenistic center of Alexandria, Egypt) should seek to read their "Homer" (i.e., Moses, author of the Pentateuch) in the same fashion. This was particularly the case when it came to seemingly petty *details*—the names of unfamiliar persons or places, narratives that seemed to have no overriding theme or message, or laws that were entirely too occupied with mundane matters. These cried out (at least to readers with Greek sensibilities) for some additional, overarching significance or simply seemed to suggest, in view of both their curious details and the lofty provenance attributed to them, that some *other meaning* beyond the obvious one had been the author's intention. The following excerpt from the so-called *Letter of Aristeas* (probably written in the latter part of the second century B.C.E.) is an early instance of this approach. In it, the author seeks to explain the (to a Greek mind) apparently irrational distinction in the Torah (see Lev. 11; Deut. 14:3–21) between "clean" and "unclean" birds and animals:

All the regulations concerning what is permissible with reference to these and other creatures, then, he [Moses] has set forth by way of allegory. For "the parting of the hoof" and the "cloven foot" are a symbol to discriminate in each of our actions with a view to what is right; for the strength of the whole body and its energy depend upon the shoulders and the legs. He constrains us, by taking note of these symbols, to do all things with discrimination and with a view to righteousness. . . . Furthermore . . . "whatsoever parteth the hoof and cheweth the cud" clearly signifies memory to thinking men. For chew-

ing the cud is nothing else than recalling life and its subsistence, since
it appears to subsist through the taking of food. (*Letter of Aristeas*
150–154)

The Pentateuch's prohibition of eating certain animals might, on
the face of it, appear quite irrational or superstitious. To make
matters worse, its list of prohibited species is preceded by the statement of the general principle that only an animal that "parts the
hoof and is cloven-footed and chews the cud" (Lev. 11:3) is to be
considered edible; for however much such a statement may simplify
the task of identifying the permitted and the forbidden, a reflective
temper must of necessity wonder why it is that the divine legislator
has chosen precisely these characteristics. It is to such musings that
the above excerpt is addressed. "Parting the hoof" and the "cloven
foot" both suggest to Pseudo-Aristeas the act of dividing and (especially the former in Greek) *discriminating*, sorting the good from the
bad; as for the hoof or the foot, these body parts *support* the entire
structure. To insist, then, that only animals with such characteristics
be considered fit for consumption is not irrational at all but is an
attempt to keep the people mindful of the crucial role that rational
discrimination is to play in directing, supporting, their lives. To add
to this the stipulation that the animal also chew the cud is to call to
mind the role of rumination, "chewing over" one's past deeds, in
the proper management of one's life.

Philo of Alexandria, mentioned above, lived two centuries or so
later, at a time when this approach to Scripture was doubtless a
commonplace among his fellow Alexandrian Jews. In his voluminous writings he shows himself a master at combining the allegorical method with his own gifts as a close reader of biblical texts, as
a philosopher, and as a profound religious thinker. While insisting
on the truth of the "literal and evident" meaning of the text (i.e.,
the validity of the Pentateuch as a historical account and the necessity of observing its laws—such as those of pure and impure animals
just seen—regardless of their higher meaning), he set out to explore
the deeper significance of the text, "according to the laws of allegory." Biblical characters became representative of abstract virtues
or else of the soul in its journey of life; names were explored for
their hidden significance on the basis of etymologies, real or imagi-
nary; and numbers, measurements, and other seemingly mundane
details were given cosmic or mystical significance.

This side of Philo is well known. What is also to be stressed,
however, is the extent to which he illustrates an approach to Scripture still broader than these celebrated aspects of his allegorizing.

For Philo did not write in isolation. Many of his explanations of Scripture parallel, in their general assumptions and in specific details, treatments of the same passages known to us from other sources, frequently from rabbinic midrash; and he shares with the latter, and with other early interpreters, a meticulous and inventive approach to the text, especially an interest in accounting for its little anomalies and details. Representative of this particular side of Philo is the following, his retelling of the "call of Moses" in Ex. 3:1–10:

> Now, as he [Moses] was leading the flock to a place where the water and the grass were abundant, and where there happened to be plentiful growth of herbage for the sheep, he found himself at a glen where he saw a most astonishing sight. There was a bramble-bush, a thorny sort of plant, and of the most weakly kind, which, without anyone's setting it alight, suddenly took fire; and though enveloped from root to twigs in a mass of fire, which looked as though it were spouted up from a fountain, yet remained whole, and, instead of being consumed, seemed to be a substance impervious to attack; and instead of serving as fuel to the fire, actually fed on it. In the midst of the flame was a form of the fairest beauty, unlike any visible object, an image supremely divine in appearance, refulgent with a light brighter than the light of fire. It might be supposed that this was the image of Him that is; but let us rather call it an angel or herald, since, with a silence that spoke more clearly than speech, it employed as it were the miracle of sight to herald future events. (*Life of Moses* 1.65–66; tr. by F. H. Colson in *Philo*, Vol. 6 [London, 1935], p. 311)

At first glance, no doubt, this may simply seem like a wordy, and even somewhat inflated, attempt to put the Exodus narrative in smooth-running form, but closer inspection will reveal Philo's desire throughout to provide an explanation for every detail in the biblical text that might otherwise trouble a reader. Thus, in the first sentence he offers an explanation (much in the manner of later rabbinic exegetes) for the text's specifically mentioning the fact that, on the day in question, Moses had led his flocks near the wilderness. In the Bible, this detail is there to tell us that Moses had gone "off the beaten track," to a place he did not normally frequent; but Philo, sensing that the mention of the "wilderness" might make readers wonder what was on Moses' mind, specifies that the place was one of lush greenery to which a good shepherd like Moses would naturally wish to bring his many sheep. In the biblical account, the burning bush burns primarily to attract Moses' attention, to bring him to where God is; and what is noteworthy about it in the Bible is not so much the fact that the bush is on fire—biblical bushes seem to catch fire easily (see Judg. 9:15)—but that it *keeps on burning*. As

Moses says, "Let me turn aside now and see this great sight, why the bush is not burnt up" (Ex. 3:3). For Philo, however, the vision of the bush takes on quite a different aspect. It is, first of all, a major conflagration, covered with flame as if "spouted from a fountain" —a most supernatural sort of sight. For in Philo's version, its purpose is not simply to catch Moses' attention and bring him before God but to communicate in and of itself a message. That message is transmitted symbolically, without words. The bush, described here (but not in the Bible) as "of the most weakly kind," is representative of the people of Israel suffering under Egyptian bondage; as Philo goes on to explain, "the burning bramble was a symbol of those who suffered wrong, as the flaming fire of those who did it." The substance of the message is contained in the relationship between the bush and the fire; for the latter (representing the Egyptians) is unable to destroy the bush (i.e., the Israelites). On the contrary, the bush, "instead of serving as fuel to the fire, actually fed on it." Thus, by simply seeing the burning bush, Moses was able to grasp the message that God wished to communicate to him: that the Israelites, though weak and oppressed, would ultimately triumph over their would-be destroyers.

In reading the passage in this fashion, Philo has wonderfully transformed the text's insistence on the fact that the bush "was not consumed." For now we know that this was not simply something to excite Moses' curiosity, but a message; and thus the whole divine choice of a burning bush as the place from which to speak to Moses has been handsomely explained (cf. *Exodus Rabba* 2:5). What is more, that this divine communication be accomplished by *sight* alone (in Greek reckoning, the highest of the senses) was surely an important consideration for Philo, who is elsewhere troubled by the notion of God *speaking* to man as a human being. It remains only to notice that in his handling of the divine Presence in the burning bush, Philo has exercised further ingenuity. His description of it as "a form of the fairest beauty, unlike any visible object," places what is seen beyond the realm of ordinary experience; the Greek phrase implies, without quite saying so, that Moses *saw* in a manner different from ordinary sight. What he saw was "divine-seeming," but this may be simply reflective of its flashing brightness, greater "than the light of fire." Both these descriptions tend to remove the vision from the stark, face-to-face confrontation presented in the biblical text. Moreover, Philo manages to paper over what must have seemed like an inconsistency in the biblical narrative, which first identified the Presence in the bush as an angel (v. 2), then as the Lord himself (v. 4). Philo, having described the form in the midst of the bush as being, in any case, an image, then provides a rationale for the biblical inconsistency: Divine in appearance, the form is nonetheless properly called an "angel" (i.e., a herald, one who announces) because its very appearance announces the future, the ultimate triumph of the Israelites over the Egyptians.

IV

Let us now examine how a variety of sources may shed light on a particular interpretive motif. We have seen that one of the central concerns of early exegetes is that of explaining *problems* in the biblical text—apparent contradictions, unexplained or unseemly behavior, difficulties in vocabulary or syntax, and so forth. One such problem is to be found at the beginning of the saga of Abraham in Genesis 12. The text begins:

> And the Lord said to Abraham: Betake yourself from your homeland and your birthplace and your father's house to the land that I shall show you. And I will make you into a great nation and I will bless you; and I will make your name great and it will be a blessing. And I will bless those that bless you, but those that curse you I will execrate; and through you all the families of the land will be blessed. (Gen. 12:1–3)

Later (especially rabbinic) exegetes would be drawn to explain, among other things, the unusual wording of this passage—why, for example, the first verse contains three apparently synonymous references to Abraham's homeland, when one would have been sufficient (the economy of divine speech and the avoidance of apparent pleonasm is a frequent concern of rabbinic midrash). But the problem this passage posed to the Bible's earliest exegetes functioned less on the level of wording than on that of plot: Why does God start speaking to Abraham in this fashion? What has Abraham—who was only just introduced to the reader a few verses earlier and about whom we still know almost nothing—done to deserve the great rewards promised him in this passage? And on the other hand, why are God's first words to him a summons to leave all that is familiar and dear to him?

In seeking the answer to such questions, biblical exegetes did not deal with the above passage in isolation. They of course read it in the light of the rest of the story of Abraham: his journey to Canaan and subsequent wanderings, his "calling on the name of the Lord," his faithfulness and trust in times of adversity, and his obedience to divine command, including, of course, his willingness to sacrifice his beloved Isaac if God required it. All this bespoke in Abraham an extraordinary devotion to God, and it was only natural to read this back into the Abraham encountered in Genesis 12. But especially noteworthy in connection with this passage was another, from the Book of Joshua:

> And Joshua said to all the people, "Thus says the Lord, the God of Israel: 'Your forefathers of old had dwelt beyond the River (Euphrates): Terah, the father of Abraham and of Nahor; and they served other gods. Then I took your father Abraham from beyond the River and led him through all the land of Canaan . . .' " (Josh. 24:2–3)

These words, uttered in a context quite different from that of Genesis 12, were nonetheless understood to illuminate it. For what might have been the (otherwise unexplained) cause of God's choosing Abraham and promising him such blessings? Does not the author of Joshua hint at the cause in his words "and they served other gods"? Abraham, so reasoned the early exegetes, was unique among his family in understanding that a single Deity controlled men's fortunes, and he went on to worship that God and do his bidding with unparalleled devotion. "*They* served other gods"—but not Abraham! "Then I took your father Abraham from beyond the River" to Canaan, presumably both to reward him for his monotheistic insight and to allow him to worship the true God away from his idolatrous environment.

That this was how some early readers of the Bible understood Genesis 12 is obvious from various retellings, translations, and commentaries on the biblical tale. Thus, for example, the Book of Judith (whose origins may stretch back to the Persian period) seems to know of a tradition connecting Abraham's departure from his homeland of "Ur of the Chaldeans" (see Gen. 11:31) with the worship of the one true God. Although Abraham is not mentioned by name in Judith, his removal from Ur to Haran, and thence to Canaan, is clearly alluded to:

> This people is descended from the Chaldeans. At one time they lived in Mesopotamia, because they would not follow the gods of their fathers who were in Chaldea. For they had left the ways of their ancestors, and they worshiped the God of heaven, the God they had come to know; hence they drove them out from the presence of their gods; and they fled to Mesopotamia, and lived there for a long time. Then their God commanded them to leave the place where they were living and go to the land of Canaan. (Judith 5:6–9)

These words in Judith are not presented as "biblical interpretation" —in fact, they are part of another story and are introduced as dialogue. Yet there can be no doubt that they are based on the biblical account of Abraham just seen and that, moreover, they thus constitute a very old attempt to understand that account, for the mention of the Hebrews' worshiping "the God of heaven, the God they had come to know" is not in the Genesis 12 text itself but, as just explained, was an attempt by interpreters to account for its strange, and otherwise unaccountable, provisions.

Other early interpretations of this episode in Genesis do specifically mention Abraham and his father, Terah, as well; Terah is sometimes presented as a kind of foil to Abraham the monotheist. Thus, for example, the *Book of Jubilees* in its retelling of Genesis 12 inserts before God's call to Abraham a whole scene in which Abraham and his father discuss idolatry. Abraham reproaches Terah for his belief in mere images: "There is no spirit in them, for they are dumb forms, and a misleading of the heart. Worship them not: worship the God of Heaven." Terah, although he apparently agrees with his son, nevertheless refuses to reject idolatry for fear of incurring the wrath of the authorities and cautions Abraham: "Keep silent, my son, lest they slay thee." Abraham, however, gets up in the middle of the night and sets fire to the "house of the idols," destroying them; he and Terah then leave their homeland of Ur.

Note how well this insertion has answered the problems posed by Genesis 12. Why did God "choose" Abraham and promise him all the blessings? Because, as evidenced by the "clue" in Josh. 24:2, Abraham alone recognized God's sole authority and acted upon it, refusing to be an idol worshiper. And why then were God's first words to him "Betake yourself" or, in plain English, "Get going!"? Perhaps because, as the *Jubilees* version implies, *not* worshiping idols was a dangerous practice in Ur. In order to worship God with impunity, therefore, Abraham is forced to flee; and God promises him that, although any emigration is painful, this one will result in manifold blessings to him and his descendants. (This explanation assumes that God's words to Abraham were uttered while he was still in Ur. Other exegetes, taking Gen. 11:31 as chronologically preceding Gen. 12:1, located these words in Haran.)

A word about the "fire" motif is in order here. Elsewhere in Genesis (15:7) God says to Abraham, apparently reflecting on this incident, "I am the Lord who brought you from Ur of the Chaldeans." Now "Ur" here is a place-name, but in Hebrew the same word has another meaning: fire or flame. Thus, especially to early interpreters of the Bible, for whom the place-name Ur might no longer mean anything, the words of Gen. 15:7 would inevitably sound like "I am the Lord who brought you from the *fire* of the Chaldeans." Even if it were obvious enough to him that Ur was a place-name, a somewhat playful exegete, with that other meaning of *ur* resounding in his (and other readers') ears, might nevertheless be tempted to imagine a scene such as the one in the *Book of Jubilees*, in which the idols are set ablaze and Abraham is subsequently brought out of the "fire" of the Chaldeans.

There is more. Pseudo-Philo's *Book of Biblical Antiquities*, dated possibly to the early first century C.E., contains a further reworking of this motif which cleverly connects Genesis 12 to the account of the tower of Babel in Genesis 11. In the Bible, the would-be tower builders say, "Come, let us make bricks, and *burn them thoroughly*" (Gen. 11:3). This, and their somewhat cryptic urging, "Let us make a name for ourselves" (Gen. 11:4), suggested to Pseudo-Philo (or to an earlier, anonymous midrashist) that the builders' purpose was to write their names, and possibly thereby the names of gods, and bake them in the bricks of the tower. Although Abraham is not mentioned in the biblical story of the tower of Babel, the Pseudo-Philo account, without too much stretching, puts him there. Opponent of idolatry that he is, Abraham is then represented as refusing to participate in the making of the bricks-with-names. Well then, the builders say, if he refuses to participate, let him be put into the kiln to burn along with the bricks (much in the style of the "fiery furnace" known from Daniel 3). So it is, in this version of the tale, that Abraham is saved from the "fire of the Chaldeans"—that is, the fire that the Chaldeans had prepared for the bricks of the tower. Abraham's piety is thus both the cause of his distress and the occasion for God to save him—and, quite naturally, to urge him, "Betake yourself . . ."

As noted before, although the earliest written traces of this understanding of Genesis 12 appear only toward the end of the biblical period, that does not mean it did not originate earlier. On the contrary, there is every likelihood that the same questions had been asked about Abraham's call, and perhaps similar answers provided, for some time. Nor, of course, does our exegetical history end there. Other, often later texts contain variant versions and new ways of connecting Genesis 12 to its surroundings. Thus, for example, the *Apocalypse of Abraham* (first century C.E.) presents a slightly different Terah, a dyed-in-the-wool idolater and, in fact, an idol maker. He cannot understand his son's misgivings about idols, but Abraham, having understood that idols are merely man-made objects, feels compelled to show his father the error of his ways: "The gods are blessed in you, [Terah,] because you are a god for them, because you made them" (*Apocalypse of Abraham* 4:3). Abraham senses, without proof, that there must be a single power who controls all those earthly and heavenly bodies venerated as gods and, "in the perplexity" of his thoughts, wishes that this God might reveal himself. It is then that God appears to him as in Gen. 12:1 and instructs him: "Go out from Terah, your father, and go out of the house, that you too may not be slain in the sins of your father's house" (*Apocalypse of Abraham* 8:4).

Other texts specifically connect Abraham's insight with the legendary excellence of the Chaldeans in astronomy. It was Abraham who taught them all that they were to know about the stars, being so exceedingly wise (a version of this is attributed to the Hellenistic Jewish writer Artapanus in the second century B.C.E.); or, in a more telling version, it was Abraham who understood that the stars venerated by the Chaldeans were nothing but the tools of a single, all-powerful Deity. This is witnessed, inter alia, in Josephus' retelling of the story of Abraham, whom he describes as "the first one boldly to declare that God, the creator of the universe, is one, and that, if any other being contributed anything to man's welfare, each did so by His command not by virtue of its own inherent power." Somewhat dryly, Josephus adds, "It was in fact owing to these opinions that the Chaldaeans and the other peoples of Mesopotamia rose against him." The Chaldean connection with astronomy and star worship is also attested in various rabbinic refractions on this chapter. In one version (*Genesis Rabba* 39:1), Abraham is compared to a traveler who comes upon a building that is all lit up. Is it possible, the traveler wonders, that there should be such a building and no one inside who looks after it? Its owner then reveals himself. So, similarly, the text implies, the heavens all lit up with stars only indicated to Abraham that there must be One within who controls them; God then spoke to Abraham as in Gen. 12:1. Other rabbinic exegetes interpreted God's words to Abraham in Gen. 15:5 in connection with Chaldea and astronomy: "And he [God] brought him outside and said, 'Look toward heaven, and number the stars, if you are able to number them.'" In context, this is to be a vivid demonstration to Abraham of how numerous his descendants will be; but it was also, according to this midrashic reading, a gentle hint to Abraham to reject the astronomical calculations typical of his homeland of Chaldea (*b. Talmud Shabbat* 156a; cf. *Nedarim* 32a and *Genesis Rabba* 44:12).

This is not a complete account of how Genesis 12 and related material were interpreted by early exegetes—far from it! But it may serve at least to show how different exegetes inherited, and reworked, common traditions, sometimes using the occasion of solving a particular problem (in this case, the whys and wherefores of God's summons to Abraham) as the means of connecting one part of the Bible to another (Josh. 24:2; Gen. 15:5 and 15:7), or further buffing a particular hero's luster (Abraham becomes still more meritorious and courageous), polemicizing (against idol worship), and so forth.

V

As noted, legal exegesis played a prominent role in the early interpretation. Here is one example. A particularly perplexing complex of laws comes in Leviticus 19, part of the legal body known to biblical scholars as the Holiness Code. The chapter begins with the well-known injunction, "You shall be holy; for I the Lord your God am holy" (Lev. 19:2). There follows a miscellany of cultic, civil, and ethical injunctions—laws about sacrifices, prohibitions of stealing and other crimes, provisions for the welfare of the poor and helpless —laws whose seemingly random arrangement must have attracted the attention of exegetes from early times. In the middle of the chapter appear the following statutes:

> You shall do no injustice in judgment; you shall not be partial to the poor or defer to the rich, but in righteousness shall you judge your neighbor. You shall not go as a tale-bearer among your people. You shall not stand idly by the blood of your neighbor: I am the Lord. You shall not hate your brother in your heart; you shall surely reproach your neighbor, and you shall bear no sin because of him. You shall not take vengeance or bear any grudge against the sons of your people, and you shall love your neighbor as yourself; I am the Lord. (Lev. 19:15–18)

As a divine summons to right conduct, the passage is stirring indeed, and its concluding law was later justly celebrated as the great principle in the Torah's governance of human conduct. Yet one can imagine as well the perplexity of interpreters who sought to apply its words as the "law of the land," the halakha by which Jewish society was to regulate its internal relations. For how can one legislate human emotions? What did it mean to forbid vengeance, or even holding a grudge? What was the point of the Torah's stipulating, "You shall not hate your brother in your heart"? And, perhaps most puzzling, how did one thing connect with another?

That these were the sorts of questions that students of the Torah were wont to raise is apparent from various reflections upon this passage and specifically upon the brief prohibition, "You shall surely reproach your neighbor," on which we shall now focus. Here, to begin with, is Ecclesiasticus (Ben Sira) in an elaboration upon this verse:

> Reproach a friend, perhaps he did not do it; but if he did anything, so that he may do it no more. Reproach a neighbor, perhaps he did not say it; but if he said it, so that he not say it again. Reproach a friend, for often it is slander, so do not believe everything you hear. A person may make a slip without intending it, and who has never sinned with his tongue? Reproach your neighbor before you threaten him, and let the Torah of the Most High take its course. (Ecclus. 19:13–17)

One difficulty in interpreting the biblical law is the very meaning of the verb translated as "reproach" (*hokheaḥ*). "Reproach" is indeed one of its meanings, but it can also mean other things: "warn," "decide," "correct," "condemn," and still more. In any case, it seems that Ben Sira has constructed his exhortation as an elaboration of the different ways in which the biblical injunction can be of value, both as a means of ascertaining what has in fact occurred and as a warning against future offenses. Now this twofold aspect of reproaching (for both deeds and speech) may be no mere rhetorical flourish. For there is a peculiarity in the language of Lev. 19:17; here the verb "reproach" is emphatically "doubled" in the Hebrew text (through the prefixing of an infinitive to the finite verb), and this may have suggested to Ben Sira, or some yet earlier exegete, two different sides of this divine commandment, investigating after the fact and reproving lest the offense be committed in the future.

While reproach in Ben Sira thus has a twofold function, the establishing of the facts of the case seems paramount in our author's mind. If the slight was not actually witnessed or heard by the injured party, reproach is especially important, for "often it is slander, so do not believe everything you hear." Nor is that all. Reproach may further bring out the fact that the slight was unintentional (one may err "without intending it"), a most likely possibility if the offense was committed by words alone (for "who has never sinned with his tongue?"). Then, finally, "Reproach your neighbor before you threaten him, and let the Torah of the Most High take its course." The phrase "before you threaten him" (or possibly, "before you abuse him") has not been added by chance. It is apparently an interpretation of the last clause of Lev. 19:17, "and you shall bear no sin because of him." The precise relationship of this clause to the preceding one can be understood in various ways, as we shall see. But for Ben Sira, at any rate, "you shall bear no sin" suggests that open reproach prevents one from sinning, specifically from getting angry and threatening the offender. Indeed, it is as if Ben Sira has read all three parts of Lev. 19:17 as a single exhortation: You shall not hate your brother in your heart, *but instead* you shall surely reproach your neighbor, *so that* you shall bear no sin because of him. Open reproach heads off anger and hatred—as he later observes, "How much better it is to reproach than to be angry" (Ecclus. 20:2)—and thus protects the offended party as well. In sum, Ben Sira's message is: Reproach your fellow for all the good reasons I have stated: because reproach may prove that the offense in question never was committed, or because it may at least prevent a recurrence of the offense, or because reproach may show the offense to have been done unintentionally. And even if none of these be the case, you still ought to reproach him to avoid being guilty of sinning against him. Then, as to his offense, "Let the Torah of the Most High take its course," which may mean "Divine justice will take care of itself" (cf. Rom. 12:19), or, again as we shall see, let further legal proceedings, ordained in the Torah, then take place.

A somewhat different understanding of the same passage in Leviticus is reflected in another early source, the *Testament of Gad*, which is found within the *Testaments of the Twelve Patriarchs*. Toward the end of this spiritual "last will," Gad is made to reflect on human relations in the light of his own life's history:

> Now my children, each of you love his brother. Drive hatred out of your hearts. Love one another in deed and word and inward thoughts. For when I stood before my father I would speak peaceably about Joseph, but when I went out, the spirit of hatred darkened my mind and aroused my soul to kill him. Love one another from the heart, therefore, and if anyone sins against you, speak to him in peace. Expel the venom of hatred, and do not harbor deceit in your heart. If anyone confesses and repents, forgive him. If anyone denies his guilt, do not be contentious with him, otherwise he may start cursing, and you would be sinning doubly. (Tr. by H. C. Kee in J. H. Charlesworth, ed., *The Old Testament Pseudepigrapha*, vol. 1, p. 816)

At first this passage might seem to have nothing to do with Leviticus, and indeed it is hardly exegesis in the commonly accepted sense. But one thing should emerge upon closer inspection: The theme of this passage, and its connection of different injunctions, is not simply "natural" or random but is based on an understanding (perhaps widely known at the time this testament was written) of Lev. 19:17 and its provision for "open reproach." Here, as in Ben

Sira, the entire verse is represented: "You shall not hate your brother in your heart" becomes, in this text, "Drive hatred out of your hearts. . . . Expel the venom of hatred, and do not harbor deceit in your heart." The next clause, "You shall surely reproach your neighbor," becomes, in Gad's mouth, "And if anyone sins against you, speak to him in peace." It seems clear, from what follows, that this "speaking" is not merely friendly conversation but an attempt to confront the sin committed. If such open reproach results in the offender's regretting his deed ("If [he] confesses and repents . . ."), then it will have served both to prevent future occurrences and, what seems to be still more crucial to our author, to have expelled the "venom of hatred" from the heart of the offended party. Thus, open reproach is the *means* to avoiding hatred; like Ben Sira, our author understands the words of Leviticus as saying, "You shall not hate your brother in your heart, *but instead* you shall surely reproach your neighbor." But what of the last part of his injunction, "If anyone denies his guilt, do not be contentious with him, otherwise he may start cursing, and you would be sinning doubly"? This is merely a "translation" of the somewhat ambiguous third clause of Lev. 19:17, "and you shall bear no sin because of him." Our author reads this not as Ben Sira did—that is, as referring to the "sin" that would result from *not* openly reproaching—but as a statement *limiting the extent of the reproach.* "Do not be contentious with him" when you reproach him, "otherwise he may start cursing, and you would be sinning doubly"—both by your contentious behavior and by the act of cursing which you yourself ultimately caused. This reading of Leviticus, while it agrees with the previous reading in regard to clauses one and two, interprets the third in a new way.

But if our author had such a subtle understanding of this biblical text, why did he not make its connection to Leviticus more obvious? While we cannot say for certain, it seems entirely possible that this bit of exegesis was not tailor-made for the occasion, perhaps was not even written by the author of the *Testament of Gad.* It may have been around for some time, becoming a commonplace not only in specific attempts to explain Lev. 19:17 but in public exhortations and homilies or in courts of law and the like. If so, one can well imagine the author of the *Testament of Gad* seizing upon it as an ideal motif to put in the mouth not only of one of the brothers of Joseph who conspired to kill him but specifically of the one whom early exegetes (including our author—see *Testament of Gad* 1) held had been specifically injured by Joseph in his thoughtless conduct. It was a perfect fit! Who better than Gad could discourse on the evils worked by the "venom of hatred," and who more sincerely, or more literally, could expound on the divine injunction, "You shall not hate your brother in your heart"?

It may be interesting to note that later writings also bear witness to a struggling with the provisions of this verse. Thus, the tannaitic midrash *Sifra* on Leviticus interprets as follows:

> "You shall not hate your brother in your heart"—... And whence [do you know that] if you have reproached him even four or five times [and it has not worked], go back and reproach him further? From the [doubling of the verb] "reproach." Might you understand this to mean that you should reproach him even to the point of public embarrassment? Scripture says, "and you shall bear no sin because of him."

As perhaps in Ben Sira, so this rabbinic exegesis seeks significance in the doubling of the verb "reproach," but its solution is somewhat different; the doubled verb indicates that the act of reproaching is to be repeated as often as is necessary. But having advanced this reading for the middle clause of the verse, the text then sees (just as in the *Testament of Gad*) the final clause as stating a limitation on the act of reproach, though of a somewhat different nature: The doubled verb, however much it exhorts the offended party to be persistent, does not provide a warrant for shaming the offender—you shall not bear a sin (that of publicly putting one's fellow to shame) because of him (or, more likely, "because of it," that is, the injunction to reproach him). Quite the opposite is the reading of the Targum Pseudo-Jonathan, which translates: "Even if he is shamed, you shall not bear a sin on his [or "its"] account." This reads the third clause not in an oppositional or limiting sense but as a reassurance that respect for the offender's pride need not discourage one whose reproaches have heretofore proven ineffective. Some Jewish exegetes separate the first clause, "Do not hate your brother . . . ," from the other two. This separation is supported by the fact that the first clause speaks of "your brother" and the second "your neighbor"—the two are not necessarily synonymous. Thus separated, the first becomes a general injunction against "hidden hatred," while the second and third take on a new meaning; one who does not reproach his fellow when he sees him in danger of sinning bears part of the responsibility for his sin. Here, the would-be reproacher is not the injured party at all; he is simply a bystander who, much in the spirit of the previous injunction, "You shall not stand idly by the blood of your neighbor," is obliged to act as a policeman or bear responsibility for his fellow's crime.

A final approach to understanding the Leviticus passage is to be found among the writings of the Qumran sect. The sect's *Rule of the Community* enjoins members

> to reproach each other in truth, and humility, and in loving considera-
> tion. Let one not speak to his brother in anger or in contentiousness
> or stubbo[rnly or in] a mean spirit, and let him not hate him in . . . his
> heart but on that very day let him reproach him and not bear sin
> because of him. Moreover, let a man not bring against his fellow a
> matter before the assembly (lit., "the Many") which had no reproach
> before witnesses. (*Rule of the Community* 5:24–6:1)

Here we have an understanding of the verse quite similar to those
seen above; the act of reproach is an antidote to hating one's
brother in one's heart. What, however, is one to make of the last
sentence? It is clarified in the so-called *Damascus Document,* another
text connected with the Qumran community:

> Any man from those who have entered the covenant [of the Sect] who
> brings against his fellow a matter which had no reproach before wit-
> nesses, but he brought it in anger or told his elders in order to shame
> him—he is taking vengeance and holding a grudge; and it is written
> [in the Bible about God Himself] that He takes vengeance on his
> enemies and holds a grudge against his foes [see Nah. 1:2]. If he was
> silent towards him from day to day and [then] in his anger against him
> spoke against him for some capital crime, his sin is upon him insofar
> as he did not carry out the commandment of God that said to him,
> "You shall surely reproach your fellow and shall bear no sin because
> of him." (*Damascus Document* 9:2–8)

The point of departure of this second passage is the verse that
follows Lev. 19:17 and to which we have heretofore given little
attention: "You shall not take vengeance or bear any grudge against
the sons of your people." This, our anonymous exegete is telling us,
is not unrelated to the verse that just precedes it, namely, "You shall
not hate your brother in your heart." For in what sense can the
Torah prohibit vengeance and grudges? In a *judicial* sense—as
might seem only apparent in the light of the general injunction
which began our whole passage, "You shall do no injustice *in judgment.*" Everything that follows, according to this interpretation, has
to do with legal proceedings, so that when it comes to "You shall
not hate your brother in your heart," this verse too should be
understood in the same courtroom atmosphere. In a sense it means,
simply, "Stay out of court," reproach your fellow on your own first;
but the Qumran community seems even to have interpreted it as a
legal prerequisite to bringing formal action—one had to "re-

proach" the guilty party "before witnesses" before being able to lodge a formal complaint. One who acted otherwise was not only failing to fulfill the terms of Lev. 19:17 but violating the prohibition of Lev. 19:18 ("You shall not take vengeance . . ."), for while it is proper for God (and hence human beings) to take revenge on actual *enemies* (as the proof text from Nahum seems to argue), to seek vengeance or hold a grudge "against the sons of your people" is clearly forbidden.

It is, finally, to be noted that this "judicial" reading of our Leviticus passage is not known solely to the Qumran sect. The same *Sifra* cited above also understands some of these miscellaneous commandments in a judicial way; thus, "You shall not go as a tale-bearer among your people" is, in one interpretation, taken to refer to a judge who, at the conclusion of a proceeding, reveals how he and his fellow judges voted. Philo of Alexandria (*On the Special Laws* 4.183) likewise sees the same precept as applying not to the people as a whole but specifically to "one who has undertaken to superintend and preside over public affairs," perhaps a vestige of the same judicial interpretation. Similarly, "You shall not stand idly by the blood of your neighbor" is understood in *Sifra* and elsewhere in a judicial sense—that is, do not withhold testimony which might vindicate your neighbor of a capital charge. There may be a hint of the Qumran approach to Lev. 19:17 in the New Testament, Matt. 18:15 (cf. Luke 17:3), where in any case the theme of reproach or reproof is well known and at times suggestive of the tradition we have been tracing (see also Gal. 6:1; Titus 3:10–11).

VI

Our last example concerns a biblical verse that to many an exegete, ancient or modern, must at first (and even second) glance have seemed utterly incomprehensible. It comes in Genesis 49, the moment in which the aged Jacob, close to death, "blesses" each of his sons with a pithy little saying. The Hebrew of these blessings is particularly difficult and in more than one place challenges the interpreter's imagination and skill. The verse we shall look at is Gen. 49:22, the opening of Jacob's blessing of his beloved Joseph. The popular Revised Standard Version translation renders the cryptic words as follows:

> Joseph is a fruitful bough,
> a fruitful bough by a spring;
> his branches run over the wall.

This translation—ultimately based, as we shall see, on ancient exegesis—connects the Hebrew phrase *ben porat* with the root meaning "be fruitful," hence, "fruitful bough." This is fine, though far too certain-sounding for an essentially incomprehensible phrase; if the root has been correctly derived, the phrase means something closer to "son of fruitfulness"! As for "his branches run over the wall"—the branches here are apparently engendered by the nonexistent "bough" that precedes them; the Hebrew word *banot* (if indeed this is how it is to be read) means simply "daughters" or "girls." Sometime ago, the biblical scholar A. B. Ehrlich argued that this word and the apparent verb that follows it are really a single noun construct, *benot sa'adah*, which, on the basis of an Arabic cognate, he translated as "wild asses." Picking up on this suggestion, E. A. Speiser then suggested that *ben porat* ought really to be derived from *pere'*, "wild donkey," and translated the whole in strikingly different language:

> Joseph is a wild colt, a wild colt by a spring, wild asses on a hillside.

This translation has not won unanimous approval, however, and modifications continue to be put forward.

The point here, however, is not what the verse *originally* meant but what various ancient writers *thought* it meant and, moreover, how their writings bear witness to the process of sifting and meditating upon biblical texts that began still earlier. Some of this process can be seen, for example, in the Aramaic targums, which, though late when compared to some of the other exegetical material seen, nevertheless can sometimes elucidate the earlier stages of thinking about a particular problem. The following is the rendering of our verse in Targum Onkelos:

> My son that will grow great, Joseph, my son that will be blessed like a vine upon a spring of water; two tribes will proceed from his sons, [each] receiving an inheritance-share.

This, it will be noted, is somewhat reminiscent of the "fruitful bough" reading seen above, but it has other distinctive features. To begin with, it apparently associates the verb "be fruitful" with its frequent biblical companion "grow great" (see, e.g., Gen. 1:22, 28; 8:17; 9:1, 7; 35:11). It may be that here the translator was anxious to avoid mere "fruitfulness," inasmuch as Joseph is distinguished not by the *number* of his immediate descendants but by the "greatness" that is thrust upon them and, hence, upon him. For as the Genesis narrative relates, Joseph's two sons, Ephraim and Manasseh, end up being elevated to the same status as their uncles, Joseph's brothers, in their inheritance from Jacob ("Ephraim and Manasseh shall be mine," Jacob says in Gen. 48:5, "as Reuben and Simeon are"). Thus Joseph, by way of his sons, inherits a double share—indeed, the "double portion" usually associated with the firstborn. (This, in turn, is connected to the "interpretation" of Joseph as Jacob's firstborn witnessed even in 1 Chron. 5:1 and discussed in chapter 2.) Thus Joseph will indeed "grow great," being ultimately responsible for two among the twelve tribes descended from Jacob.

The translation of Targum Onkelos is further influenced by the fact of a repetition in the Hebrew text of Gen. 49:22. Operating on the assumption, commonly attested in rabbinic exegesis, that there is no such thing as needless repetition in the Bible, our translator is at pains to render the word "fruitful" in two different ways. The first is the more literal "grow great," though even this represents a departure from the words of the text; the second, "be blessed," is a further interpretation, or detailing, of the ultimate significance of Jacob's words. How so? Consider the rest of the verse: The "spring of water" comes from the potentially ambiguous '*ayin,* one of whose meanings in Hebrew is "spring," and no doubt the whole image is influenced by various metaphorical appearances of the well-watered plant within the Hebrew Bible, especially Jer. 17:8 and Ps. 1:3. These in turn provide another dimension to Joseph's "greatness"; he is great in the manner of the righteous man compared, in Jeremiah and Psalm 1, to a tree planted on a spring. He will grow great, true, but this is a reflection of, a result of, his happy condition. For he is "blessed," planted upon water like the righteous and steadfast individuals in these two biblical texts—and, indeed, Joseph himself has already proven to be righteous and steadfast (Gen. 39). Finally, it is to be noted that Targum Onkelos compares him to a *vine* (rather than a tree) precisely because a vine is a proverbial image of fruitfulness (see Ps. 128:3) from which can proceed the two "daughter vines" of Ephraim and Manasseh, whose existence is being alluded to, according to our targum, by the plural "daughters" in the latter part of the verse.

Let us look now at another translation, representative of the so-called "Palestinian" targum tradition. The following is from Targum Pseudo-Jonathan:

My son who has grown great, Joseph, my son who has grown great and strong, and it was further necessary for you to be strong, in that you overcame your evil impulse in the matter of your mistress [Potiphar's wife] and in the matter of your brothers. I compare you to a vine

planted upon a spring of water that sends forth its roots and breaks
the teeth of the peaks and with its branches conquers all the trees of
the field—so, Joseph my son, did you conquer with your wisdom and
your good deeds all the magicians of Egypt. And when they praised
you, the daughters of the rulers would walk on the walls and cast down
before you bracelets and golden jewelry so that you might set your eye
upon them [the daughters], but you did not set your eye upon a single
one of them.

Obviously, this is not "translation" in the commonly accepted
sense, but a discursive translation/retelling/elaboration based on
the bare bones of the text. The reader will nevertheless recognize
here certain elements seen before. The desire to give the phrase
ben porat ("son of fruitfulness"), repeated in the biblical text, added
significance the second time around now leads this translation into
the notion of Joseph's "strength." Where did this come from? The
same word *'ayin,* understood by Onkelos as "spring," is here being
taken in its commoner meaning of "eye," which in the Bible is
frequently symbolic of desire, sometimes especially sexual desire.
Joseph, the "son of fruitfulness," is no longer "upon a spring" but
"above the eye"—that is, above his desires—an allusion to the incident with Potiphar's wife (Gen. 39), which as early as 1 Maccabees
(dated to the first century B.C.E.) had been seen as the central incident of Joseph's life (see 1 Macc. 2:53). This incident showed Joseph's great strength. In similar fashion, the image of the vine—but
here the vine has become rather treelike—leads to another excur-
sion into Joseph's past, his outshining Pharaoh's magicians and wise
men in interpreting Pharaoh's dream. Note that there is no mention
of Ephraim and Manasseh here, or even an allusion to Joseph's
"double portion." For this translation seems bent on associating the
words of the blessing with incidents in Joseph's past life rather than
with his future or offspring. This in turn would suggest that this
particular targum tradition is secondary to the previous one: It has
inherited the "fruitful vine" image but, having no real use for its
fruitfulness, turns it into an aggressive plant that "conquers all the
trees of the field."

But what of the last sentence, wherein the daughters of the rulers
of Egypt walk along the walls and cast their jewelry down before
Joseph? This too, *mirabile dictu,* is based on our biblical text. For it
will be recalled that in the phrase translated in the RSV as "his
branches run over the wall," the word corresponding to "branches"
is really the Hebrew word "daughters" or "girls." To our translator,
this word has summoned up a host of new associations. Recalling
Joseph's extraordinary good looks (Gen. 39:6; this theme figures

prominently in the *Testament of Joseph* and other early retellings) and the fact that Joseph's rise to power must have made of him a most eligible bachelor, our translator understands the "daughters" as real daughters, the daughters of the Egyptian ruling class, who now *climb a wall* in order to be seen by him. In fact, this reading existed even before our present translation, for it has been conflated with a second reading: *'alei šor,* "upon a wall," is now further interpreted by him as *'alei šur,* "in order to look"—that is, in order that he look at them. The same tradition is witnessed in, for example, the *Pirqei di R. Eliezer,* a late Jewish retelling of parts of the Bible:

> Moreover, Joseph rode in a chariot and crossed the whole territory of Egypt, and the Egyptian girls would climb up on the wall and cast down upon him golden rings that he might perchance look upon their beauty.

The motif of the golden jewelry being cast down deserves a word of comment, for this too is generated by the words of Gen. 49:22. The word that corresponds to "climb up" or "walk" in the versions cited is potentially troubling, since it seems to be singular, while its subject is plural. Obviously this bothered exegetes of the girls-climbing-up school, and one solution apparently was to connect it to another word, a rare word that appears only two other times in the Hebrew Bible. *'Eṣ'ada* is some kind of bracelet or ornament, perhaps worn on the arm (see 2 Sam. 1:10). It seems to have intruded itself into the translation tradition we have been tracing, so that the verse now becomes one of almost telegraphic compression: *banot*—the daughters climb up upon the wall; *('e)ṣ'ada*—they throw down their jewelry; *'alei šur*—so that Joseph might look at them.

Both Pseudo-Jonathan and *Pirqei di R. Eliezer* are from a period far removed from the one we have been considering, yet there is ample ground for believing that the interpretations that these works embody are far older than the date of their final compilation. One earlier witness is Jerome's Vulgate, going back to the end of the fourth century, which translates in accordance with the same tradition: "A growing son, Joseph, a growing son and handsome of mien; the girls ran about upon the wall." Elsewhere Jerome elaborates, "O Joseph . . . who are so fair that the whole throng of the young girls of Egypt looked out at you from the walls and towers and windows." And there is a still earlier source that may embody the same tradition. It is the retelling and elaboration of the Joseph story called *Joseph and Aseneth,* written in Greek (probably by an Egyptian Jew) around the turn of the era. Here the motif is garbled somewhat but nonetheless recognizable. Joseph, young ruler of Egypt, goes to the house of his future father-in-law Potiphera (here called Pentephres). As he arrives, he catches sight of Aseneth looking down at him from the upstairs window:

> Joseph said to Pentephres, "Who is that woman who is standing on the upper storey next to the window? Have her removed from this house." For Joseph was afraid, saying, "Let not this woman also trouble me." For all the wives and daughters of the rulers and satraps of the whole land of Egypt had troubled him that he lie in bed with them. And many wives and daughters of the Egyptians had suffered when they saw Joseph because of his beauty. They sent their emissaries to him with gold and silver and gifts of great value. And Joseph sent them back with threats and insults, saying, "I will not sin before the Lord God."

Here we may be correct to see both the themes of young-woman-atop-a-wall (here the "upper storey") and the golden jewelry (here "gold and silver and gifts of great value").

Of course a casual reader of *Joseph and Aseneth* would never recognize in these sentences an *allusion* to an already existing tradition of understanding the words of Joseph's blessing in Genesis 49. Indeed, they are not an allusion, they are more like an internalization, or a reflection, of an exegetical tradition-turned-legend. Early exegesis is full of such instances; for imaginative and creative readings, devised to account for difficult or incomprehensible aspects of the Hebrew text, often take on a life of their own and soon become independent of the exegetical necessity that gave them their birth. But there is another point in our last example as well; the key to a proper understanding of the first-century *Joseph and Aseneth* lay with texts whose final compilation belongs to a much later period. And so it often is with the history of early exegesis as a whole. Again and again, the entire interpretive tradition proves relevant, so that one can only fully grasp the implications of early material by having reference to later sources and, in so doing, trace the evolution of complicated motifs from simpler ones. Our history of early exegesis thus ends as it should, with a gesture outward—to the great exegetical traditions of rabbinic Judaism and Christianity that were to build upon its already elaborate beginnings.

The exegetical movement we have been tracing was many centuries in the making; its roots, as we have seen, lie even in preexilic Israel, and some of its most characteristic features owe their existence to the peculiar history, political and social, of the period that followed the restoration from exile. But if this movement was the product of a long sequence of events, its influence and importance are still more long-lasting. The emergence of the Bible itself—the very idea, that is, of a corpus of sacred texts, whose words would constitute a body of divine instruction given to each generation— is intimately tied to this movement. Moreover, as we have glimpsed, how that Bible was to be read, in myriad little details as well as in general lines of approach, was in large measure already determined by the end of the period we have surveyed. Exegesis hardly stopped. On the contrary, century after century produced more elaborations, syntheses, new insights. But not only was this work in itself a carrying out of an earlier program, it was an expression of the magnitude of our movement's accomplishment, for it had done nothing less than make of the interpretation of Scripture a fundamental religious activity.

Further Reading

General Works

Blenkinsopp, J. *A History of Prophecy in Israel.* Westminster Press, 1983.
———. *Prophecy and Canon: A Contribution to the Study of Jewish Origins.* University of Notre Dame Press, 1977.
The Cambridge History of the Bible. Vols. 1–3. Cambridge University Press, 1963–1970.
Charles, R. H., ed. *The Apocrypha and Pseudepigrapha of the Old Testament in English.* 2 vols. Oxford: Clarendon Press, 1913.
Charlesworth, J. H., ed. *The Old Testament Pseudepigrapha.* Vols. 1–2. Doubleday & Co., 1983–
Coats, G. W., and B. O. Long. *Canon and Authority: Essays in Old Testament Religion and Theology.* Fortress Press, 1977.
Crenshaw, J. L. *Old Testament Wisdom: An Introduction.* John Knox Press, 1981.
Cross, F. M. *The Ancient Library of Qumran and Modern Biblical Studies.* Rev. ed. Baker Book House, 1980.
Davies, W. D., and L. Finkelstein. *The Cambridge History of Judaism.* Vol. 1. Cambridge University Press, 1984.
Dupont-Sommer, A. *The Essene Writings from Qumran.* Translated by G. Vermès. Peter Smith, 1973.
Finkelstein, L. *The Pharisees.* Jewish Publication Society of America, 1963[3].
Fishbane, M. *Biblical Interpretation in Ancient Israel.* Oxford University Press, 1985.
Ginzberg, L. *The Legends of the Jews.* Jewish Publication Society of America, 1913.
Hanson, P. D. *The Dawn of Apocalyptic: The Historical and Sociological Roots of Jewish Apocalyptic Eschatology.* Fortress Press, 1979[2].
———, ed. *Visionaries and Their Apocalypses.* Fortress Press, 1983.
Hengel, M. *Judaism and Hellenism: Studies in Their Encounter in Palestine During the Early Hellenistic Period.* 2 vols. Translated by John Bowden. Fortress Press, 1974.
Kugel, J. "Two Introductions to Midrash." *Prooftexts,* Vol. 3 (1983):131–55.

Lieberman, S. *Hellenism in Jewish Palestine.* Jewish Theological Seminary of America, 1950.

Neusner, J. *From Politics to Piety: The Emergence of Pharisaic Judaism.* Prentice-Hall, 1973.

———. *Rabbinic Traditions About the Pharisees.* 3 vols. Leiden: E. J. Brill, 1971.

Nickelsburg, G. W. E. *Jewish Literature Between the Bible and the Mishnah.* Fortress Press, 1981.

——— and M. E. Stone. *Faith and Piety in Early Judaism.* Fortress Press, 1983.

Patte, D. *Early Jewish Hermeneutic in Palestine.* Society of Biblical Literature Dissertation Series 22. Scholars Press, 1975.

Sanders, J. A. *Torah and Canon.* Fortress Press, 1972.

Schalit, A., ed. *The Hellenistic Age: Political History of Jewish Palestine from 332 B.C.E. to 67 B.C.E.* Vol. 6 of *The World History of the Jewish People.* Rutgers University Press, 1972.

Smith, M. "Palestinian Judaism in the First Century." In *Israel: Its Role in Civilization,* edited by M. Davis, 67–81. Jewish Theological Seminary of America, 1956.

———. *Palestinian Parties and Politics That Shaped the Old Testament.* Columbia University Press, 1971.

Stone, M. E., ed. *Jewish Writings of the Second Temple Period. Compendia Rerum Iudaicarum ad Novum Testamentum* 2:2. Fortress Press, 1984.

———. *Scriptures, Sects, and Visions: A Profile of Judaism from Ezra to the Jewish Revolts.* Fortress Press, 1980.

———. "Why Study the Pseudepigrapha." *Biblical Archaeologist* 46 (1983): 235–43.

Tcherikover, V. *Hellenistic Civilization and the Jews.* Jewish Publication Society of America, 1966.

Urbach, E. E. *The Sages: Their Concepts and Beliefs.* 2 vols. Jerusalem: Magnes Press, 1975.

Vermès, G. *Post-Biblical Jewish Studies.* Leiden: E. J. Brill, 1975.

———. *Scripture and Tradition.* Leiden: E. J. Brill, 1961.

von Rad, G. *Wisdom in Israel.* Translated by J. D. Martin. Abingdon Press, 1972.

Weingreen, J. *From Bible to Mishna: The Continuity of Tradition.* Manchester University Press, 1976.

Special Subjects

Bickerman, E. J. *Four Strange Books of the Bible: Jonah, Daniel, Koheleth, Esther.* Schocken Books, 1967.

Brownlee, H. W. "The Background of Biblical Interpretation at Qumran." In *Qumran: Sa piété, sa théologie et son milieu,* edited by M. Delcor, 183–93. Paris: Editions J. Duculot, 1978.

Collins, J. J., and G. W. E. Nickelsburg. *Ideal Figures in Ancient Judaism: Profiles and Paradigms.* Scholars Press, 1980.

Cross, F. M. "A Reconstruction of the Judean Restoration." *Journal of Biblical Literature* 94 (1975):201–17.

―――. "Aspects of Samaritan and Jewish History in Late Persian and Hellenistic Times." *Harvard Theological Review* 59 (1966):201–11.

Daube, D. "Rabbinic Methods of Interpretation and Hellenistic Rhetoric." *Hebrew Union College Annual* 22 (1949):239–64.

DeVries, S. J. "Observations on Quantitative and Qualitative Time in Wisdom and Apocalyptic." In *Israelite Wisdom: Theological and Literary Essays in Honor of Samuel Terrien,* edited by J. G. Gammie et al., pp. 263–76. Scholars Press, 1978.

Finkel, A. "The Pesher of Dreams and Scriptures." *Revue de Qumran* 4 (1963): 357–70.

Fischel, H. "Story and History . . ." *American Oriental Society Semi-Centennial Volume* (1969):59–88.

Fishbane, M. "Revelation and Tradition: Aspects of Inner-Biblical Exegesis." *Journal of Biblical Literature* 99 (1980):343–61.

Gager, J. G. *Moses in Greco-Roman Paganism.* Abingdon Press, 1972.

Goppelt, L. *Typos: The Typological Interpretation of the Old Testament in the New.* Translated by D. H. Madvig. Wm. B. Eerdmans Publishing Co., 1982.

Gruenwald, I. "Jewish Apocalyptic Literature." In *Aufstieg und Niedergang der römischen Welt,* Vol. 19.1, 89–118. Berlin: Walter de Gruyter & Co., 1979.

Horgan, M. P. *Pesharim: Qumran Interpretations of Biblical Books.* Catholic Biblical Quarterly Monograph Series 8. Catholic Biblical Society of America, 1979.

Japhet, S. "Conquest and Settlement in Chronicles." *Journal of Biblical Literature* 98 (1979):205–18.

―――. "Sheshbazzar and Zerubbabel." *Zeitschrift für die alttestamentliche Wissenschaft* 94 (1982):66–98.

Knibb, M. A. "Prophecy and the Emergence of the Jewish Apocalypses." In *Israel's Prophetic Tradition,* edited by R. J. Coggins et al., pp. 155–80. Cambridge University Press, 1982.

Kugel, J. " 'The Bible as Literature' in Late Antiquity and the Middle Ages." *Hebrew University Studies in Literature and the Arts* 11 (1983):20–70.

―――. "Torah." In *A Handbook of Jewish Theology,* edited by A. Cohen and P. Mendes-Flohr. Charles Scribner's Sons, 1985.

Leiman, S. *The Canonization of Hebrew Scripture.* Shoe String Press, 1976.

Lemaire, A. *Les écoles et la formation de la Bible dans l'ancien Israel.* Fribourg: Éditions Universitaires, 1981.

Levenson, J. D. "From Temple to Synagogue: I Kings 8." In *Traditions in Transformation: Turning Points in Biblical Faith,* edited by B. Halpern and J. D. Levenson, pp. 143–66. Eisenbrauns, 1981.

―――. "Who Inserted the Book of the Torah . . .?" *Harvard Theological Review* 68 (1975) 203–33.

Mantel, H. "The Nature of the Great Synagogue." *Harvard Theological Review* 60 (1967):69–91.

Naveh, J., and J. Greenfield. "Hebrew and Aramaic in the Persian Period." In *The Cambridge History of Judaism,* edited by W. D. Davies and L. Finkelstein, Vol. 1, pp. 115–29. Cambridge University Press, 1984.

Petersen, D. L. *Late Israelite Prophecy: Studies in Deutero-Prophetic Literature and in Chronicles.* Society of Biblical Literature Monograph Series 23. Scholars Press, 1977.

Porton, G. "Midrash: The Jews and the Hebrew Bible in the Greco-Roman Period." In *Aufstieg und Niedergang der römischen Welt,* Vol. 19.2, 103–38. Berlin: Walter de Gruyter & Co., 1979.

Rendtorff, R. "Esra und das Gesetz." *Zeitschrift für die alttestamentliche Wissenschaft* 56 (1984):165–84.

Silberman, L. H. "Unriddling the Riddle." *Revue de Qumran* 4 (1963): 357–70.

Stern, E. "The Province of Yehud: The Vision and the Reality." In *The Jerusalem Cathedra: Studies in the History, Archaeology, Geography, and Ethnography of the Land of Israel,* edited by L. I. Levine, Vol. 1, pp. 9–21. Wayne State University Press, 1982.

Specific Texts Discussed in Chapter 5

On Abraham and Gen. 12:1: G. Vermès, *Scripture and Tradition in Judaism* (Leiden: E. J. Brill 1961), pp. 67–126.

On the Qumran "Law of Reproof" and Lev. 19:17: L. H. Schiffman, *Sectarian Law in the Dead Sea Scrolls* (Scholars Press, 1983), pp. 89–109.

On Joseph in Gen. 49:22: V. Aptowitzer, "Asenath, the Wife of Joseph," *Hebrew Union College Annual* 1 (1924):239–306.

PART TWO

The Christian Bible
and Its Interpretation

by Rowan A. Greer

1

The Rise of a Christian Bible

[handwritten annotation: Governed by ?]

It is not until the time of Irenaeus, about 180 C.E., that we can speak with any confidence of a Christian Bible. Irenaeus, who had grown up as a disciple of Polycarp, the bishop of Smyrna in Asia Minor, became the bishop of Lyons shortly after the persecution in Lyons and Vienne (177 C.E.) during which his predecessor, bishop Pothinus, was martyred. His major literary work, usually called *Against Heresies,* gives us our first clear evidence for the existence of a worldwide Christian church that can be called the Great Church. While the Christian communities that thought themselves members of the Great Church possessed no absolute uniformity in their beliefs and practices, they were united on a broad level in several respects. They were governed by the threefold ministry of bishops, presbyters, and deacons; and their life centered upon the sacraments of Baptism and the Eucharist. Their belief was defined as the apostolic faith, preserved in their sacred writings and in the authoritative summary of those writings known as the Rule of faith.

Like the Hebrew Bible, the Christian Bible of Irenaeus and the Great Church was a collection of books, and this library of sacred writings had become authoritative for Christians. First of all, it included the Greek translation of the Hebrew Bible known as the Septuagint. According to legend, Ptolemy II Philadelphus in the third century B.C.E. commissioned seventy (or seventy-two) learned Jews to make a translation into Greek of the Hebrew Scriptures for his library. This translation included books not finally admitted into the canon of Hebrew Scripture established by the Jewish rabbis in the first two centuries of the common era. These books, known as the Old Testament apocrypha, are Tobit, Judith, Esther, the two books of the Maccabees, 1 Esdras, Wisdom, Ecclesiasticus, Baruch, the Song of the Three Holy Children, Susannah, Bel and the Dragon, and the Prayer of Manasseh. In addition to this "Old Testament," Irenaeus' Bible had a "New Testament" made up of Christian writings. The four Gospels (Matthew, Mark, Luke, and John) and a collection of Paul's letters were the heart of Irenaeus' New Testament canon, but he also cites Acts, Revelation, 1 Peter, and 1 and 2 John. It seems likely that Irenaeus' New Testament was the same as ours, except for the omission of James, Jude, 2 Peter, and Hebrews.[1]

The Christian Bible just described was the product of decisions that were only gradually made and that were forced upon the church during the century and a half following the crucifixion of Christ (30–180 C.E.). During this formative period of early Christianity it was by no means clear that Christians should retain the Hebrew Bible, nor was it easy to decide what Christian writings should be regarded as authoritative. With respect to the Hebrew Scriptures the issue was complicated by the fact that they could be retained only if they were given a specifically Christian interpretation. Consequently, preserving the Hebrew Scriptures meant transforming their meaning according to Christian beliefs. With respect to the New Testament, two controversies were particularly important in the development of a canon. Shortly before the middle of the second century, Marcion taught a Christian faith that rejected the God of the Hebrew Bible and proclaimed that Christ had revealed a God hitherto unknown. Moreover, Marcion regarded only the letters of Paul and an expurgated version of the Gospel of Luke as authoritative. Both Marcion's theological views and his list of authoritative Scripture were rejected by the developing Great Church. Shortly after the time of Marcion, Montanus and his followers began teaching that a new dispensation of the Holy Spirit was at work in them, and the Montanists held their own new writings to be of at least equal authority with the Gospels and the Pauline letters.

In thinking through the vexed question of which Christian writings were to be authorities for Christians, the Great Church concluded that "apostolicity" should be the criterion for the inclusion of books in the New Testament canon. No novel writings were to be admitted, and only those books which could claim to preserve the apostles' witness to Christ could claim authority. This decision avoided the danger of Montanism, that is, the implication that the revelation in Christ was not final and could be superseded. Of course, the problem became that of deciding what constituted the apostolic witness; and it is reasonably clear that theological considerations were crucial. For example, a number of writings that circulated under the name of Peter were rejected because they taught views uncongenial to the Great Church, while the Gospels of Mark and Luke (not written by apostles) were accepted on the grounds that Mark preserved the apostle Peter's preaching and Luke the apostle Paul's. What demonstrated that a given writing did indeed constitute part of the apostolic witness to Christ was not so much historical considerations as the conformity of the writing to what the church came to regard as a true understanding of Christ.

The points just outlined will explain what may seem to be two peculiarities in the discussion that follows. First, Irenaeus will be the focus of attention, since he is the first witness both to the existence of a Christian Bible and to a framework for interpreting it. Even though earlier writers interpret the Hebrew Scriptures and, to some degree, make use of the writings that became part of the New Testament, Irenaeus is the first Christian writer to think clearly about a Christian Bible and how to interpret it. Second, the argument will place emphasis upon the fact that the early Christians read their Bible theologically. Indeed, the decision to retain the Hebrew Scriptures was a theological one. The church came to insist that the God of Israel was the God of Jesus Christ and also that the significance of the Hebrew Scriptures lay in the testimony they bore to Christ. And the decision as to which Christian writings could be considered the apostolic witness to Christ was really a decision that these books interpreted Christ correctly from a theological point of view. For Christians, the dialogue between God and his people found its fullest expression in Christ, and so Christ became the key to the whole of Scripture. The theological and even Christological convictions that determined how a Christian Bible was to be constituted then became central in shaping the interpretation of that Bible.

The points that have just been made are integral to the thesis of the argument that follows, an argument that may be stated in these terms:

1. A Christian Bible is the product of the formative period of early Christianity (30–180 C.E.). Before Irenaeus, we find the church struggling to define its Scriptures and to come to terms with their interpretation, but it is only by the end of the second century that the diversity of earliest Christianity has yielded to an ecumenical unity. The emergence of a Christian Bible is a central feature of that unity.
2. Basic to the task of the formative period is the transformation of the Hebrew Scriptures so that they may become a witness to Christ.
3. With Irenaeus we find the first clear evidence of a Christian Bible and also a framework of interpretation in the church's

Rule of faith. The Rule of faith, as a kind of creed, outlines the theological story that finds its focus in the incarnate Lord.

4. To treat the Rule of faith as the general principle by which Scripture should be interpreted leaves several important questions open. What method should be used in applying the theological principle to the text? How should troublesome details of the Rule of faith be resolved? In particular, how should Christ's relationship to the Father be defined, and how should the lofty Christ "in the form of God" be related to the lowly Christ "in the form of a servant" (Phil. 2:6ff.)? How may Scripture be allowed to function in the Christian life? And, finally, may Scripture be interpreted for its own sake?

The first of these four stages of the argument will be treated in the rest of this chapter; the other three, in chapters 2 through 4.

One last preliminary point needs to be made by warning the reader that in some respects the argument cuts across our modern expectations. We are accustomed to treating Scripture as historical evidence for reconstructing imaginatively the earliest Christian communities or the history of Israel. Or we treat Scripture as a source for the religious teaching we suppose to be central to the Judeo-Christian tradition. If we are to understand the ancient church's use of Scripture, we must learn to suspend our modern expectations. The early Christians asked what the Bible meant theologically rather than historically. And their theological concern centered upon the question of defining the Redeemer who was the object of their piety. In the West, since Augustine the theological agenda has been largely anthropological—what is faith? what is grace? who will be saved? But for the early church the chief question was, who is Christ? At one level, the answer to this question involves the doctrinal development of the early councils and the dogmas of the Trinity and of Christ's person. But at another level, the answer involves what Christ has done. And so the meaning of salvation and its implications for the Christian life were a part of discovering Christ's identity.

Reading Scripture theologically, as the ancient church did, often appears to the modern reader to be a subjective forcing of the biblical text into a preconceived set of theological convictions. Theology appears as much read into Scripture as read out of it. There may be some justice in this reaction; but we need to beware of the claim that our modern historical interpretation of Scripture is somehow objective and, therefore, correct. One cannot interpret Scripture without presuppositions, nor can one altogether avoid a hermeneutical circle that derives from the correlation between question and answer. It is possible to argue that modern critics are just as much in danger of reading their historical presuppositions into the Bible as ancient Christians ran the risk of imposing their theology on the text. For this reason, we need to take seriously the theological approach of the ancient church to its sacred writings. And we need to begin by discussing the formative period of early Christianity in order to see how it was that a Christian Bible came to be.

The Evidence for the Formative Period of Early Christianity (30–180 C.E.)

It is not difficult to list the writings preserved to us from the first century and a half of Christianity's existence. The books of our New Testament, a miscellaneous collection of documents written after the apostolic period but called the Apostolic Fathers, and the works of the Greek apologists who sought to defend Christianity and to recommend it to the surrounding pagan culture are the major survivals from the period before Irenaeus and contemporary with him. It may be possible to add some of the materials found in the collection published in English translation in 1963 and 1965 and called the *New Testament Apocrypha.* [2] And certain of the Gnostic documents discovered at Nag Hammadi in Egypt in 1945 may be dated before the end of the second century. [3] We must also note that certain writings in the Pseudepigrapha were used and revised by Christians in the first two centuries. [4] The difficulty in using this evidence attaches not only to its fragmentary character but also to the fact that we can seldom be certain about the time and place of the writings in question. It would take us beyond the scope of the argument to discuss the evidence in detail, but some indication must be given as to what it shows us about Christian attitudes toward Scripture before Irenaeus' time and what it indicates about the diversity of Christianity during the formative period.

Both the New Testament writings and the apostolic fathers oblige us to conclude that the Bible of the earliest church was what Christians today call the Old Testament. Nevertheless, it is worth noting that many of the early Christian writings we possess fail to cite the Old Testament either explicitly by using an introductory formula (e.g., "it is written") or implicitly by reproducing a recognizable Old Testament verse or verses. In the New Testament, many of the Pauline letters (Philippians, Colossians, 1 and 2 Thessalonians, Titus, Philemon), the Johannine letters, Jude, and Revelation fail to cite the Hebrew Bible in either fashion. Yet, of course, Revelation, to cite but one example, is saturated with allusions to the Hebrew Scriptures and presupposes their authority. Of the apostolic fathers, only *1 Clement* (a letter from the church in Rome to the church in Corinth written in the last decade of the first century), *2 Clement* (probably a sermon written in Rome or Corinth in the first half of the second century), and *Barnabas* (written in Alexandria in the early second century) make any real and direct use of the Hebrew Bible. The Greek apologists such as Justin Martyr, Tatian, Athenagoras, and Theophilus (second half of the second century) appeal to the Hebrew Scriptures but cite them infrequently in their apologies. Only with Justin's *Dialogue with Trypho* do we find any extensive use of the Hebrew Scriptures.

That we do not find so full a use of the Hebrew Scriptures in the early sources as we might expect does not mean that their authority was questioned, at least in what eventually were regarded as "orthodox" circles. The rejection of the Hebrew Scriptures by Marcion and the Gnostics was immediately resisted by the mainstream of Christianity. There remains, however, the issue of how that authority was understood. The problem becomes vivid for us in a brief account that Ignatius gives of a debate he had with "some men" who appear to have been Jewish Christians (*Epistle to the Philadelphians* 8.2). Ignatius, the bishop of Antioch, was under arrest and on his way to Rome and his eventual martyrdom, when he met with representatives of several of the churches in Asia Minor (ca. 107 C.E.). His opponents refused to accept any teaching in the "Gospel" unless they could find it in "the charters." Their view was almost certainly that the authority of the Hebrew Scriptures ("the charters") determines the meaning of the Christian preaching (the "Gospel"). Ignatius, of course, accepted the authority of the Hebrew Scriptures. The Christian must "give heed to the prophets" (*Epistle to the Smyrneans* 7.2). But he insisted that the Christian preaching has prior authority and must determine the meaning of the Hebrew Scriptures. "But to me the charters are Jesus Christ, the inviolable charter is his cross, and death, and resurrection, and the faith which is through him" (*Epistle to the Philadelphians* 8.2). What he must mean is that the Hebrew Scriptures have authority only when read in the light of the Christian faith. The book is less important than the message that gives it its proper meaning. If we may take Ignatius' view as the one that prevails in the early church, we may conclude that while the Hebrew Scriptures were the Bible of the church, their authority was secondary to that of the Christian preaching.

We may not yet, however, think of a "New Testament." To be

sure, the writings of our New Testament were known to Christians before the end of the first century. The very fact that Matthew and Luke used Mark shows that Mark was widely known. And as early as 2 Peter (3:15f.) we find evidence for a collection of Pauline letters. A detailed examination of the apostolic fathers and the Greek apologists reveals that these writings had wide currency and were sometimes even called "Scripture" (e.g. *Barnabas* 4.14; *2 Clement* 2.4; 14.1). Moreover, Justin, writing about 155 c.e., tells us that the written Gospels were used in Christian worship in Rome (*First Apology* 66–67), and he can appeal to their authority (e.g., *Dialogue with Trypho* 100). Yet even Justin characteristically cites not the written Gospels but the early gospel tradition, which seems to have continued to circulate in an oral form.[5] Papias of Hierapolis earlier in the second century in discussing the Gospels had said that he preferred "a living voice" to a book, and this preference seems to have remained dominant into the last part of the second century.[6] In short, while the Gospels and the collection (or collections) of Pauline letters were known and used in the church and while they came to have considerable authority, they were treated as witnesses to the Christian preaching rather than identified with it. One interesting illustration of this point is the *Diatesseron* (a musical term meaning "harmony") of Tatian, a pupil of Justin Martyr. Tatian composed his Gospel harmony about 160 c.e., reducing the four Gospels to one; and this *Diatesseron* became the standard Gospel of Syriac-speaking Christianity until the fifth century. Tatian's enterprise suggests that there was nothing sacrosanct about the four Gospels.

It is Irenaeus who first uses the expression "New Testament" (e.g., *Against Heresies* 4.9.1). The authority of the Christian preaching is now vested in a canon of books. This development should not be regarded as a radical break with earlier attitudes. It is simply a question of taking seriously the authority of the Christian writings that constituted the apostolic witness to Christ and of the inevitable eclipse of the oral tradition, the content of which differed in no way from what could be found in the New Testament writings. Moreover, Irenaeus is not alone in beginning to speak of a "New Testament." At the end of the second century Melito, the bishop of Sardis in Asia Minor, speaks of the "books of the Old Testament" and so implies that he is comfortable with thinking of a "New Testament" (see Eusebius, *Ecclesiastical History* 4.26.14). And the Muratorian Canon, a late-second-century Latin document discovered in the eighteenth century and probably deriving from Rome, gives a canonical list of New Testament books.

It is no exaggeration to say that Christian attitudes toward Scripture remain obscure and confused until the time of Irenaeus. The same point can be made more generally concerning the character of the Christian communities reflected in the evidence from the formative period. Some of these writings are extremely Jewish in nature. For example, the Gospel of Matthew seeks to underline the continuity between old and new; and in a more extreme fashion Paul's opponents in Galatia insist that this continuity means that one cannot be a Christian without being circumcised. While it is fragmentary, there is a good deal of evidence that there were Christians throughout the formative period who thought of themselves also as Jews. The *Preaching of Peter*, included in the New Testament apocrypha and to be dated about 200 C.E., reflects a similar point of view. Another sort of Jewish Christianity sought to employ Jewish categories and traditions to reject Judaism altogether. The *Didache*, written in Syria about 100 C.E., and *Barnabas*, written in Alexandria shortly afterward, both reject Judaism completely, even though they are evidence for a Jewish Christianity. At what seems the opposite extreme we find writings that employ the cosmological and mythological themes of a Gnostic Christianity. These writings include not only the works of the Christian Gnostics that survive but also the letters of Ignatius, the sermon known as *2 Clement*, and in some respects the *Letter of Barnabas*.

Putting the matter this way is to suggest that the mainstream of Christianity found itself obliged to steer between two extremes. Christians could not remain a peculiar kind of Jew, nor could they abandon their Jewish heritage and embrace the full acculturalization represented by the Gnostics. At least this is how Ignatius saw the matter. He fought a battle on two fronts, against Jewish Christians who denied the divinity of Christ and against the Docetists, who were Gnostic Christians that denied the reality of Christ's human experience, death, and resurrection. And it was this sort of path that was taken by the Great Church. By retaining the Hebrew Scriptures, it avoided the danger of Gnosticism and rejected Marcion's view of the absolute novelty of Christianity. By developing a New Testament, it insisted upon a measure of discontinuity with Judaism and upon a Christianization of the Hebrew Scriptures. As we shall see, we cannot confidently reconstruct the diversity of early Christianity. And it seems likely that Judaizing and Gnostic Christians persisted to the time of Irenaeus and beyond. Nevertheless, we can say that the unity of the church, or at least the existence of the ecumenical Great Church, was the achievement of the late second century rather than the condition of the earlier period. Consequently, we must speak of a progress from diversity to unity, a progress that culminates in the Great Church and its Christian Bible.

From Diversity to Unity

We have seen that it is only by the time of Irenaeus toward the end of the second century that we can speak of a Christian Bible. And it is only then that we find any firm sense of a Christian church spread throughout the Mediterranean and identifiable as the Great Church. One important and interesting piece of evidence for this second conclusion is an inscription found in Asia Minor and dating from the end of the second century. Abercius, the bishop of Hieropolis in Phrygia, caused a brief and deliberately cryptic account of his trip to Rome to be placed on his tombstone. In it he said: "And everywhere I had associates. Having Paul as a companion, everywhere faith led the way and set before me for food the fish from the spring."[7] What he means is that wherever he traveled, he found Christian communities that were recognizable to him. We need not suppose he found uniformity of practice and belief. The important point to make is that by his time Christians of the Great Church were able to find the same faith and the same community life in churches throughout the cities of the Mediterranean. Moreover, those loyal to the Great Church anachronistically presumed that their understanding of the church had obtained from the beginning. In their minds there was no fundamental difference between the church of the New Testament and their own.

It is from this perspective that writers such as the second-century church historian Hegesippus, Justin, Irenaeus, and later the fourth-century church historian Eusebius of Caesarea recognize diversity in early Christianity and Judaism. They know of the existence of communities not their own that nonetheless claim to be Christian. Justin Martyr supplies us with a typical perspective in his *Dialogue with Trypho*.[8] He says that there are "many pure and pious Christians" who do not agree with his belief in a millennium. He also refers to people who are "Christians in name" but are really "godless and impious heretics." And he exhorts Trypho not to consider as "real Christians" those who deny the millennium and the resurrection of the dead. Similarly, "one, after careful examination would not acknowledge as Jews the Sadducees or the similar sects of the Genistae, Meristae, Galileans, Hellenians, and the Baptist Pharisees." In a similar way, Hegesippus recognizes "heretical" sects in both Christianity and Judaism.[9]

It is almost certainly a hopeless task to identify the heretical groups listed by Justin, Hegesippus, and others. It is, of course, possible to add to the evidence. Justin, Hippolytus, Irenaeus, Tertullian, and the fourth-century heresy hunter Epiphanius give elaborate lists of Christian heretics. Moreover, the discovery of a collection of Gnostic documents at Nag Hammadi adds new evidence that must somehow be fitted into the picture. The rabbinic writings supply us with many references to the *minim* (heretics) and to those who speak of "two powers," thus compromising monotheism. And we can assume that there were actually existing religious communities that corresponded in one way or another to the designations we find in the writers of the Great Church. But pressing beyond this broad generalization is impossible for two reasons. First, what the church fathers tell us hinges upon their assumption that the Great Church which they experienced in their time was identical with the church of the New Testament. And, second, they attribute to the heretical sects the same sort of definition and organization that characterized their own; heresy is treated as a perverse mirror image of the Great Church. These perspectives generate a fog that obscures for us the true character of the diversity of early Christianity. It is not just that our evidence is fragmentary, though that is certainly true and cannot be stated too strongly. It is also that the character of much of our evidence is colored by an interpretive point of view in the sources, which blocks the way for us.

The first of the points made above is probably the more important. To identify the Great Church with the original church is to suppose that heresy is novelty. We need to remember the ancient mentality that regarded what was "new" as strange, suspicious, and erroneous. Truth precedes error just as goodness precedes evil. Thus, as Hegesippus puts it, "they called the church virgin, for it had not yet been corrupted by vain messages."[10] Eusebius, writing in the early fourth century, follows his predecessor and elaborates his point of view. In the *Ecclesiastical History* he takes a triumphalist point of view about the progress of the church. Despite the devil's attempts to rape the virgin church through persecution and heresy, the church triumphs over its foes. That triumph is made evident by God's punishment of the Jews for their rejection of Christ and by the spread of the gospel among the Gentiles.[11] These themes, which inform Eusebius' account of the church up to Constantine's time, have their roots in earlier writings and even in the New Testament itself. And they conspire to exclude diversity from the church and to relegate it to novel and heretical sects.

The second aspect of the point of view prevailing from the late second century onward has to do with the way in which the heretical sects are understood by their "orthodox" foes.[12] The Gnostics are thought of as a perverse mirror image of the Great Church with their own succession of teachers and their own Rule of faith. Justin attributes the formation and origin of Gnosticism to Simon Magus, who is mentioned in Acts 8. Irenaeus and Hippolytus follow him, and Irenaeus goes a step farther by beginning his refutation of the Gnostics through "detecting" their erroneous Rule. These approaches to polemic succeed in conveying the impression that the heretical communities are easily definable, clear in their beliefs, and organized on the model of the Great Church. There may be some basis for thinking of Gnostic communities such as the Valentinians in this way. But it is easy enough to read between the lines of what the heresiologists are saying and to discover that they are setting up their opponents for refutation. Irenaeus, for example, notes the Hydra-like character of the Gnostics and suggests that it is rather like stepping out of one's front door in the morning to discover that mushrooms have sprouted everywhere.[13] He recognizes that Gnosticism is far more difficult to pin down and to define than he would wish. And so, we must suppose that the religious communities opposed by the fathers were far less organized and far more diverse than the evidence at first suggests.

The conclusion seems inescapable that we cannot be very sure how to describe the diversity of early Christianity. Our evidence not only is partial but derives for the most part from sources toward the end of the second century and afterward. Even Eusebius admits that in telling the story of the church's progress he is like a "traveller on some desolate and untrodden way."[14] It is not so much that these sources are inaccurate as that they adopt a point of view so highly interpretive that a veil is placed between us and the communities described as "heretical." Moreover, we have no statistical evidence at all and cannot even be certain that the majority of "Christians" in Irenaeus' day were members of the Great Church. The best a considered imagination can do is to suggest that the Christian who belonged to the Great Church found a worldwide community in a way impossible for the Gnostic or the Jewish Christian. Presumably, it was the ecumenical nature of the Great Church that ensured its future, while it was the more local and fissiparous aspect of the heretical communities that doomed them. We cannot accept the view of the Great Church that its position was the original one and that those who differed from it in the past were heretics who had departed from the truth. Instead, we must understand what happened as the gradual emergence of unity out of diversity. At another level, however, the point of view of the Great Church does explain what characterizes the movement from diversity to unity. The key to the development is defining the relationship of the church to Israel.

The Church and Israel

Paul's anguished question as to why the Jews rejected their own Messiah (Rom. 9–11) is really the fundamental preoccupation of all the writers of the New Testament. They take differing approaches to the problem, but in one way or another insist upon a qualified continuity between the church and Israel. The church is identified as Israel—a new, a true, an eschatological, or a purified Israel, but nonetheless Israel. Paul himself gives us the fullest and clearest solution in Romans 9–11. It looks as though God, an arbitrary and tyrannical sovereign, has rejected his ancient chosen people, just as in the past he had rejected Ishmael and Esau. And it looks as though the Jews of their own volition have rejected God and his Messiah. But if one presses beyond the appearances, one can see that a righteous remnant of Israel has been preserved so that the Gentiles may be incorporated into the people of God. Finally, the incorporation of the Gentiles into Israel will provoke the Jews to return to the newly defined Israel. Matthew in a similar fashion sees Christians as those who remain truly loyal to the law by accepting the messianic Torah which deepens and clarifies its meaning (Matt. 5:17). For Luke, it is the Jews who are the apostates from Israel. When Paul addresses the Sanhedrin after his arrest in Jerusalem, he insists that Christians by their belief in the resurrection have preserved the true heritage of Israel (Acts 23:6), and John may be encouraging the sympathetic Jews of his time to remain, like Nicodemus, secret Christians even within the synagogue (John 3:1–2; 7:50; 19:39). Without sacrificing claims made about Christ, the New Testament writers are reluctant to posit a total breach between Christianity and Israel.

It is easy to see why the distinction between the church and the synagogue did not take place quickly and easily. The diverse character of both Christianity and Judaism in the first century meant that it was not always easy to decide who was a Jew and who a Christian. And there must have been many reluctant to make that decision. But Christians began increasingly to renounce the strict observance of the law and to insist on calling Christ "God." And once Rabbi Johanan ben Zakkai had established the school at Jabneh, rabbinic Judaism began increasingly to clarify what observing the law meant and to define their religious platform as obedience to the one God and his Torah. These two developments, reacting against each other, led to a gradual but inevitable parting of the ways.[15] It may well be that this is what lies behind Claudius' expulsion of the Jews from Rome in the 40s. Suetonius refers to riots in the Jewish quarters "at the instigation of Christus" *(impulsore Chresto)*, and "Christ" may have been the bone of contention rather than the ringleader of the mob.[16]

In any case, once the school at Jabneh had been founded after the destruction of Jerusalem in 70 C.E., rabbinic Judaism began to take measures against those who confessed Christ. John's Gospel alludes to the danger of expulsion from the synagogue (John 9:22). And Justin Martyr in the middle of the second century puts the matter rather strongly.[17] The sufferings of the Jews in Palestine after the repression of Bar-Cochba's rebellion in 132 C.E. are thought to be the retributive consequence of their rejection of Christ and his followers:

> Now you spurn those who hope in Him and in Him who sent Him, namely, Almighty God, the Creator of all things; to the utmost of your power you dishonor and curse in your synagogues all those who believe in Christ.

The cursing to which Justin refers is probably the anathema of the heretics that had been added to the Jewish prayer known as the Eighteen Benedictions. In this way rabbinic Judaism sought to exclude those who confessed Christ. And in a similar way the church sought to exclude those who observed circumcision, the Sabbath, and the food laws.

One factor that contributed to the disengagement of Christianity from Judaism was Jewish rebellion against Rome. The first revolt, which ended in 70 C.E. with the destruction of Jerusalem, the revolts in the diaspora under Trajan, and the Hadrianic revolt under Bar-Cochba, which ended in the exclusion of all Jews from Jerusalem in 135, all failed to command the support of Christians. The concern of Christians, widespread though not universal, to recommend the church to the Roman government involved, as well, the dissociation of Christians from the rebellious Jews. The book of Acts in the New Testament and works of Christian apologists such as Justin Martyr show us that Christians felt obliged to argue that they were not subversive of Roman society. The assumption of Romans that the Christians hated the human race, were immoral people, and rejected the religious and social conventions of the empire needed to be countered. And it was possible to argue that the popular prejudice was based upon a misunderstanding of Christian principles. In

Justin's view, this misunderstanding was the product of demonic instigation. In one sense Christians inherited prejudices that had already been directed toward the Jews, as well as a Jewish party platform that was designed to claim a place for Israel in Roman society. But the Jewish revolts tended to force Judaism out of that society, while the Christians were free to exploit the universalist aims of the religion from which they had sprung. And it was easier for Gentiles who had been attracted to Judaism to become Christian, since they were not obliged to be circumcised and to observe the law and since they were placed on an equal level with Jewish Christians.

Nevertheless, another factor is at work. Rabbinic Judaism remained a proselytizing religion much later than has usually been supposed, and the withdrawal of Judaism from the surrounding society was not complete until, during the Christian empire, that withdrawal was forced upon the Jews. The legislation of the fourth and fifth centuries protected the Jews but prohibited them from any real participation in the life of the empire. At the same time, it was the "concurrence" of Christianity and Judaism that forced rabbinic Judaism to abandon many earlier Jewish notions and to take its stand on the one God of Israel and his Torah. For example, Jewish speculation about Wisdom could go so far as to treat Wisdom as a symbolic figure representing aspects of God or to identify Wisdom with the Torah. But when Christians identified Christ with Wisdom, monotheism seemed compromised; and the Jews were obliged to abandon ideas that might well imply a sort of polytheism.

As Christians and Jews moved apart from one another, there arose the possibility that Christianity would renounce its Jewish heritage altogether. The seeds of such a rejection may be found as early as the Pauline letters. A one-sided emphasis upon Paul's contrast between the law and faith could easily lead to the notion that the Christians were a new people. The *Letter to Diognetus* (ca. 170? c.e.), distinguishes Christians so sharply from Jews that the inference of total discontinuity can be drawn. The *Preaching of Peter*, cited by Clement of Alexandria (ca. 200 c.e.), speaks of Christians as a "third race," neither Jewish nor Gentile. All ambiguity is removed by Marcion, who repudiates Judaism, the Hebrew Scriptures, and the God of Israel altogether. Moreover, the Valentinians and the other Christian Gnostics treat the God of Israel as inferior to the God who sent Christ. The role of the Hebrew Scriptures becomes problematic, since they are treated as a witness to the inferiority of the old dispensation and to the novelty of the new one. Redemption for the Gnostics represents an overcoming of the created order and, consequently, of Israel, the Hebrew Scriptures, and the creator God.

The mainline development of Christianity rejected these extreme statements of the disjunction between Jews and Christians, Israel and the church. The writings recognized as apostolic and ultimately placed in the canon of the New Testament agreed in insisting that the one creator God of the Hebrew Scriptures was the God of Jesus Christ. By the time of Irenaeus, the Great Church drew the conclusion that redemption must somehow be described as the completion of God's creative purpose, the church the completion of Israel, and the New Testament the completion of the Hebrew Scriptures. At its most basic level, these convictions resolved the fundamental problem we are addressing. Nevertheless, how could the early Christian polemic against the Jews be reconciled with a rejection of views like Marcion's? How could the discontinuity of the church with Israel be balanced by an insistence on continuity? The answer lay in the idea of a sacred history presided over by God's providence. Irenaeus, basing his view partially on Justin's thought, treats the Hebrew Scriptures as a providential dispensation of God, pointing beyond themselves to their consummation in the Christian revelation. The Hebrew Scriptures become a witness to Christ.

The argument thus far has been that the separation of Christianity from Judaism and the dialectic that attended it forced the developing Great Church to insist simultaneously on the continuity and the discontinuity of old and new. Irenaeus supplies us with evidence of a theological framework in which this double insistence makes sense. But he also shows us what the Great Church took to be the warrant and authority for this theological framework. Discussion of Irenaeus' theology in its relation to scriptural interpretation will be reserved for chapter 3. Here the question has to do with the authority for his theology and, specifically, with the creation of a Christian Bible. Irenaeus' authority is what he calls the apostolic faith, and this faith is in part embodied in Scripture. We must describe how Irenaeus understands the apostolic faith and may then argue that this understanding is directly related to theological decisions that establish the church as both continuous and discontinuous with Israel and to a Christian Bible that is equally constituted on the basis of these decisions.

The apostolic faith, for Irenaeus, is the norm for Christian belief and the point of departure for its theological articulation. By committing themselves to the apostolic faith, Christians remain loyal to their heritage and faithful to their witness to Christ. Thus, the faith is both the product of a theological tradition and the basis for its further development. This faith, Irenaeus says, "we do preserve, and it always, by the Spirit of God, renews its youth."[18] In other words, the apostolic faith, though preserved from the past, is constantly made alive in the present. Putting the matter in terms of Scripture, the church preserves the Bible from the past, but constantly allows it to "renew its youth" by interpreting it for contemporaries. Interpretation, then, is involved at two levels. Constituting the apostolic faith is interpretive, and expounding it simply continues the interpretation.

By the apostolic faith Irenaeus really means two things, Scripture and the Rule of faith. His metaphors clarify his point of view. The apostles, like rich men putting money in the bank, deposited in the church the Scriptures and the Rule of faith.[19] By Scriptures he means the Greek translation of the Hebrew Bible (the Septuagint) and a New Testament virtually identical with ours.[20] By the Rule of faith he means a summary of the faith that is not totally fixed verbally but that is recognizable as an ancestor of later Christian creeds. In principle, Irenaeus insists upon the identity of Scripture and the Rule. Scripture, like a mosaic, is made up of many distinct passages; and the Rule of faith is the "hypothesis" or plan that enables one to arrange the passages in the right order.[21] What becomes an either-or question at the Reformation in the sixteenth century is for Irenaeus a both-and question. The Rule derives from Scripture and is applied to it. The bishops of the church, then, are the guardians of this double apostolic deposit. Thus, by the time of Irenaeus we find not only a clear definition of the Christian Bible but also the idea of a hermeneutical principle that derives from it but can be applied to it, together with an authority structure capable of making judgments about valid interpretations of Scripture. Irenaeus' point of view is not merely his own but reflects the community theology of the Great Church; and we can see in it the term of a development that is not merely reactive to Judaism and Gnosticism but that also involves the generation of positive norms for Christian belief and life.

Nevertheless, the content of the apostolic faith insists upon the paradox already mentioned that the church stands in continuity and discontinuity with Israel. Continuity centers upon the claim that the creator God of the Hebrew Scriptures is the same as the God of Jesus Christ. Discontinuity derives from belief that both creation and the Hebrew Scriptures point beyond themselves to Christ. From this point of view, then, the apostolic faith is really the result of a decision to define the church's unity by avoiding the two extreme positions represented by Judaizing Christians, on the one hand, and Marcion and the Gnostics, on the other. And this decision was also one about the content of a Christian Bible. Consequently, creating a Christian Bible was not only an interpretive but also a theological task. Chapter 2 will examine one aspect of this task by treating ways in which Christians transformed the Hebrew Scriptures during the formative period. Chapter 3 will examine Irenaeus' completion of this task and his use of a New Testament in expounding the faith of the Great Church.

2
Christian Transformations of the Hebrew Scriptures

To the modern reader, early Christian interpretations of the Hebrew Scriptures appear to be transformations of the biblical text that alter its meaning. We tend to think of an original sense, understood historically, and to regard theological interpretation as a departure from the true meaning of the text. Nothing could be farther from the point of view of religious writers in late antiquity. Pagan, Jew, and Christian were united in assuming the general correlation of sacred texts with the beliefs and practices of religious communities. Scripture represented the authority for those beliefs and practices, but at the same time the religious convictions of the community unveiled the true meaning of Scripture. Far from supplying a new meaning, the transformations of sacred books disclosed their true significance. It is from this point of view that all Christians during the formative period before Irenaeus were obliged to come to terms with the Hebrew Scriptures by interpreting them in a "Christian" sense. The writers of the New Testament assume the authority of the Hebrew Bible and make use of it not only by citing it but also by using its categories to explain Christ and his significance. Most other Christians take the same approach, and even the Gnostic Christians were obliged to interpret the Hebrew Bible in order to show why it should be rejected or at least placed firmly on a level inferior to new Christian writings. And, paradoxically, many Gnostic ideas appear rooted in theosophical understandings of the Hebrew Bible although those very ideas demand the rejection of it and its God. In what follows, most of the evidence to be considered will be from the New Testament, the apostolic fathers, especially *1 Clement* and *Barnabas*, and from Justin Martyr. The reason for this is quite simply the fact that only there do we find any full and explicit use of the Hebrew Scriptures. Nevertheless, whenever possible, evidence from the

Gnostic writings and from the New Testament apocrypha will be considered.

In describing the earliest Christian interpretations of the Hebrew Scriptures several assumptions suggest themselves and will orient the reader to the argument of this chapter. First, there is no need to speak in a complicated way about "methods." Indeed, the only method used is that of claiming that the interpretation given is the clear meaning of the text, that is, proof texting. Scripture becomes a warrant for a wide range of Christian convictions. Nonetheless, the proof texting does fall into two general categories. On the one hand, the Hebrew Scriptures are used to demonstrate the validity of Christian moral injunctions. It is, of course, not the detailed law of the Jews that is at issue; but Christian exegesis from this point of view bears a family relationship to rabbinic halakha. On the other hand, the Hebrew Scriptures are used to demonstrate that Christ is the fulfillment of Israel's hope. Here three somewhat differing approaches are taken. The Hebrew Scriptures prophesy Christ and the events surrounding his life and fate. Or the Hebrew Scriptures foreshadow Christ. It is the type, the mark of the seal ring in the wax of the past, that points to the reality of Christ. Or, finally, the relationship of old and new is transformed into the relationship of earthly to heavenly; and the Hebrew Scriptures become a mysterious allegory of Christian truths. And from these three points of view, Christian interpretation bears a striking resemblance to the pesher method employed by the Qumran community and, with respect to allegorism, to the exegesis of Philo. In all these cases, however, the Christian message is assumed to be the key to the Hebrew Scriptures.

In addition to regarding these "methods" as differing ways of proof texting Christian beliefs, two other assumptions are being made. Second, the moral proof, the proof from prophecy, typology, and allegorism do not always appear in a pure form, nor do we find writers adopting one of these approaches in isolation from the others. The use of examples from the Hebrew Scriptures is found in combination with specific proof texts. The proof from prophecy sometimes appears in lists of testimonia. Midrashic weaving together of a variety of texts occurs, as does a kind of targumic or haggadic elaboration of biblical stories. Third, the decisive feature of Christian interpretation is found not in methods or forms but in the function of the exegesis. The biblical text is used to explain what Christian virtues are, to deny the validity of Jewish practices such as circumcision, sacrifices, the observance of the Sabbath, and the food laws, and to prove the truth of Christ, of his saving work, and of the rejection of the Jews and the inclusion of the Gentiles. We shall begin by discussing the uses that the New Testament writers made of the Hebrew Scriptures; both form and function will be considered. Then, after examining a number of examples of the forms in which Christian approaches to the Hebrew Scriptures appear, the argument will turn to their functions in order to suggest that we find a quest for a unifying framework by which the Hebrew Scriptures may be understood in a Christian sense.

The New Testament Writers and the Hebrew Scriptures

The writers of the New Testament all make use of the Hebrew Scriptures both to justify Christian moral teaching and practices and to proclaim Christ. It is important to note that in speaking of "the writers of the New Testament" we are not yet speaking of a New Testament. Instead, we are treating the documents as the earliest evidence for Christian responses to Christ's life and fate. And we need to remember that these writers were almost certainly converted Jews who accepted the God of Israel and the authority of Scripture. Their common concern was to find in Scripture a warrant for their practices and beliefs, and their common assumption was that approaches they had taken to Scripture as Jews could be adapted to Christian purposes. Rabbinic (or better, Pharisaic) proof texting, the pesher method, and the sort of allegorical approach we find in Philo are all used, often all three by the same author. We shall begin by showing how Scripture is used as a warrant for Christian morality and practice and then turn to the earliest apologetic for the preaching of Christ's death and resurrection. Particular versions of this apologetic will then be discussed.[1]

The letters of the New Testament provide us with the best examples we have of Christian moral teaching in the earliest period. Often the teaching is adapted and addressed to specific problems in the different churches. But sometimes we find passages that presumably draw upon "the standard of teaching" given those who were prepared for baptism (Rom. 6:17; cf. Titus 1:9; 1 Cor. 11:2; 2 Thess. 2:15; 3:6). One example is Romans 12–13, where Paul prefaces his advice about the specific problem of the "weak" and the "strong" in the Roman church with a reminder of familiar norms for the Christian life. One such norm is the nonretaliation required by Christian love. The Christian must not return evil for evil (Rom. 12:17) either to a fellow Christian or to a hostile pagan and must be obedient to the state (Rom. 13:1–7). The rule in its various aspects hinges upon words that Paul does not cite as sayings of Jesus but that are preserved in that form in the Gospels. "Bless those who persecute you" (Rom. 12:14) is found on Jesus' lips in Matt. 5:44 and Luke 6:28 (cf. Acts 7:60; 1 Cor. 4:12). The possible implication is that Jesus' words are authoritative for Christian moral teaching. But Paul also appeals to the Hebrew Scriptures. Allusions to texts from Proverbs and the explicit citation ("for it is written") of Deut. 32:35, together with the words of Prov. 25:21–22, confirm the rule that Paul is explaining. Since vengeance is the Lord's according to the law in Deuteronomy, Christians must never avenge themselves. In principle, Paul's reasoning differs in no way from rabbinic justifications of the oral law. In practice, the development we find in rabbinic Judaism never takes place in Christianity, since it is the preaching of the dead and risen Lord rather than Christian moral teaching that comes to be developed and systematized. Finally, Paul's approach to the law of nonretaliation is not peculiar to him. The same law ("Do not return evil for evil or reviling for reviling") is stated in 1 Peter 3:8–12 with a possible allusion to Jesus' words in Matt. 5:44, and he grounds the law in Ps. 34:12–16 ("Let him keep his tongue from evil. . . . Let him turn away from evil").

The same sort of development is indicated by Rom. 13:8–10. There the fulfillment of the law is equated with loving one another. The text bears a striking resemblance to Jesus' summary of the law as love of God and love of neighbor (Mark 12:28–34 and parallels) and to his words in the story of the rich young ruler (Mark 10:17–22 and parallels, where Matt. 19:19 adds Lev. 19:18). And, while Paul does not formally cite the texts, he makes clear reference to Ex. 20:13ff.; Deut. 5:17ff.; and Lev. 19:18. Galatians 5:14 and James 2:8 also cite the verse from Leviticus ("You shall love your neighbor as yourself"). It is difficult to escape the conclusion that the summary of the law, drawing upon crucial passages in Scripture, represents a chief point of departure for the Christian teaching.[2] Very little more can be said with certainty about the development of early Christian moral teaching. Passages such as Eph. 5:22–6:9 demonstrate that Christians drew up "rules for households" (*Haustafeln*) that have roots in both Jewish and pagan ethical teaching. And occasionally texts from the Hebrew Scriptures are used (Eph. 5:31/Gen. 2:24; Eph. 6:2/Ex. 20:12/Deut. 5:16; 1 Peter 5:5/Prov. 3:34). But to risk a conclusion, it appears that we are in the presence of an abortive development. What might have become a Christian mishnah fails to grow, and the halakhic approach to Scripture is placed in the shadow by a preoccupation with the message of salvation.

One final example concerns Christian practice rather than moral teaching. In 1 Corinthians 9, Paul refers to the right of apostles "to our food and drink" and "to be accompanied by a wife." What this amounts to is a rule that Christian teachers and their families are to be paid, or at least to be relieved of the necessity of employment. The rule is quite the opposite of the custom that came to prevail among the Jews, where rabbis were forbidden payment for their teaching. The Christian practice is justified for Paul by the law, since Deut. 25:4 forbids the muzzling of a threshing ox (1 Cor. 9:9). Presumably, Paul treats the verse in an allegorical fashion. The ox that deserves food in return for its work stands for the apostle who must be cared for by the community. A parallel passage in 1 Tim. 5:17–18 refers to the same rule and the same scriptural proof text. And it also bases the rule on Jesus' saying that "the laborer deserves his wages" (Matt. 10:10; Luke 10:7). At a later period we encounter church orders that set forth rules for the Christian community; the *Didache* is the earliest example. But as is the case with Christian moral teaching, a halakhic concern to ground Christian practice in Scripture seems largely to have disappeared. The *Didache* makes surprisingly little use of the Hebrew Scriptures.

The exegetical energy of early Christians was primarily directed toward finding in Scripture a warrant for the Christian preaching, the message of salvation. First Corinthians 15:1–11 will orient us to this enterprise. Beginning with v. 3, Paul cites the tradition of the preaching he had received himself. The creedal affirmation that follows consists of two points: "Christ died for our sins" and "he was raised on the third day." Both points are supported by empirical proof; he was buried and appeared to various disciples. But both points are described as "in accordance with the scriptures." In other words, Christ's death and resurrection are somehow thought to be proved by Scripture, and the earliest Christian apologetic sought to demonstrate this. The New Testament writers appear to presuppose such an apologetic, but they do not expound it apart from elaboration and adaptation. In the speeches of the book of Acts, for example, we find the main lines of the apologetic, but it has been integrated with Luke's more developed theological view. And in writings such as Romans and Galatians the apologetic has been adapted to Paul's arguments about faith and the inclusion of the Gentiles, that is, to his preoccupation with the dilemma of the Christian's relationship to Israel.

Nevertheless, by examining key texts of the Hebrew Scriptures as they are used throughout the New Testament writings, we can deduce something of the character of the earliest Christian apologetic for Christ's death and resurrection. In Acts 8, Philip finds the

Ethiopian eunuch reading Isaiah's description of the suffering servant. Isaiah 53:7–8 is explicitly cited and Philip takes the opportunity to preach Jesus to the eunuch, "beginning with this scripture" (Acts 8:35). If we discard the specifics of the narrative context, there can be little doubt that Luke is giving us a fair account of the earliest passion apologetic.[3] The suffering righteous one of Ps. 22 and 69 corresponds to the suffering servant of Isaiah, and these psalms also belong in the earliest passion apologetic.[4] Detailed examination of the use of these passages from the Hebrew Scriptures by the New Testament writers shows us how the early apologetic begins to attract other texts to itself in order to elaborate the proof and how the apologetic adapts itself to details of Jesus' story and its significance.

The same patterns may be found in scriptural proof of the resurrection. A few central texts constitute the proof and begin to draw other scriptural texts into the argument. The texts sometimes shift their application to related themes, and even begin to be worked into theological constructs. It is by no means clear what constitutes the scriptural proof for the resurrection in 1 Cor. 15:4. The "third day" might find support in Hos. 6:2 ("On the third day he will raise us up") and Jonah 1:17 ("Jonah was in the belly of the fish three days and three nights"). Matthew 12:40 uses the verse from Jonah this way. But it seems likely that Ps. 110:1 is at the heart of the resurrection apologetic: "The Lord says to my lord: 'Sit at my right hand, till I make your enemies your footstool.' " Both the exaltation to heaven implied by Jesus' resurrection and the final triumph of God over all his enemies may be found in the verse. Its original function as a resurrection apologetic is best preserved in Peter's speech at Pentecost, where it is included as one among other proof texts (Acts 2:34–35). Jesus' resurrection has exalted him to God's right hand and has demonstrated him to be Lord and Christ. And it is the risen Lord who has poured forth the Spirit on the apostles. The first part of this interpretation is implied in the passion narrative of the Synoptic Gospels by Jesus' answer to the high priest's question whether he is the Christ (Mark 14:62 and parallels):

> I am; and you will see the Son of man seated at the right hand of Power, and going [RSV: coming] with the clouds of heaven.

Jesus' answer conflates Ps. 110:1 ("seated") with Dan. 7:13 ("going"), and the two verses are used to predict the glorious exaltation of Jesus' resurrection. Hebrews uses Ps. 110:1 this way repeatedly (1:3; 1:13; 8:1; 10:12; 10:13; 12:2), and the interpretation informs such passages as Rom. 8:34; 1 Cor. 15:25; Eph. 1:20; and

Col. 3:1. Other texts besides Dan. 7:13 are drawn into the pattern. For example, Peter's Pentecost speech uses Ps. 16:8–11. And Hebrews uses the parallel of Ps. 8:4–6 ("the son of man . . . crowned . . . with glory and honor, putting everything in subjection under his feet") to define Christ's exaltation in the resurrection (Heb. 2:6–9).

Not only do we find other biblical texts drawn into association with Ps. 110:1 to constitute scriptural proof of Christ's resurrection, we also discover new applications of the psalm to other aspects of the Christian claim. In the Synoptic Gospels (Mark 12:36 and parallels), Jesus cites the first verse to confound the scribes' understanding of the Messiah as David's son rather than his Lord. Here we find a question of Jesus' identity as Lord rather than of his resurrection which demonstrates that identity. This shift in application lies behind later uses of the psalm verse to prove the preexistence and divine status of Christ. Another shift in the application of Ps. 110 may be found in the use of the fourth verse by the author of Hebrews. The king of v. 1 is also the "priest after the order of Melchisedek" of v. 4 (Heb. 5:6, 10; 6:20; 7:3, 17, 21). What had proved the resurrection now also proves Christ's identity as the true priest-king. And it is not going too far to say that this interpretation of Ps. 110 is constitutive of the Christology we find in Hebrews, a Christology that integrates the themes just mentioned with the myth of the Redeemer who descends and is exalted to accomplish God's saving purpose.

One other example of the early Christian apologetic may be given. The rejected stone that has become "the head of the corner" (Ps. 118:22) refers to Christ's death and resurrection. In the Synoptic Gospels (Mark 12:10–11 and parallels), Jesus cites the psalm verse immediately after the parable of the wicked husbandmen who kill the son of the vineyard's lord. The scriptural proof text is applied both to Christ's death and to his resurrection. The same use is made of the verse in Acts 4:11. Psalm 118:26 ("Blessed is he who comes in the name of the Lord") is used in the Palm Sunday narratives (Mark 11:9 and parallels; John 12:13) and in Jesus' lament over Jerusalem (Matt. 23:39‖Luke 13:35), where the coming is eschatological. Attention has shifted from one verse of the psalm to another. But the most interesting development is the integration of the rejected stone (Ps. 118:22) into a midrashic treatment of Scripture in 1 Peter 2:1–10. The rejected stone is a firm foundation for believers (Isa. 28:16), who as "living stones" are built into a spiritual house. But it is a "stone of stumbling" (Isa. 8:14) for the disobedient. Exodus 19:5–6; Hos. 2:23, and other texts are fashioned into a description of the new people of God. Several of these texts are cited by Paul (Isa. 8:14/Rom. 9:33; Isa. 28:16/Rom. 9:33; 10:11; Hos. 2:23/Rom. 9:25), who is also concerned with the respective fate of believers and Jews. The apologetic has moved from Christ's death and resurrection to the broader implications of his fate.

In attempting to reconstruct the earliest Christian use of Scripture to prove the claims made about Christ we have found a very complex and dynamic enterprise. One proof text draws others into its wake, and passages from Scripture are combined in various ways. The texts are applied to different aspects of Christ's fate and identity and of the Christian story. They are integrated into developing theological structures. Two conclusions force themselves upon us. First, the earliest Christian attempts to explain Christ are in great measure exegetical in character. What is said of Christ is rooted in the details of Scripture. But, second, what gives form to the exegetical work is the Christian story. Christ's life, his death and resurrection, his session at God's right hand, the rejection of the Jews and the preaching to the Gentiles, and Christ's return at the end of the age—all of this is a story that gives some order to the scriptural texts that are used. It is in this sense that Christ is regarded as the key to the meaning of Scripture.

If we turn from the earliest Christian apologetic that can be deduced from the New Testament to the New Testament writers themselves, we can find a number of different developments and elaborations of it. In general terms, the New Testament writers do more than cite the text of Scripture. They are saturated in it, and the biblical idiom comes naturally to their lips. Constant allusions may be found to the Hebrew Scriptures. We cannot read Luke's infancy narratives without being reminded of the story of Samuel's birth. Matthew's Sermon on the Mount is clearly meant to take us to a new Sinai. The miraculous feeding of the multitude in the wilderness harks back to the manna miracle in the wilderness, as John 6 makes explicit. Behind Christ hover the figures of Adam, Abraham, Moses, and David. This constant reference to Scripture can, from one point of view, be regarded as a rebirth of images. Revelation, for example, nowhere cites the Hebrew Scriptures; but the book can scarcely be understood without reference to the biblical themes and categories that are used for Christian purposes. From another point of view, the Hebrew Scriptures become a type of Christ, foreshadowing him and his work, or an allegory in which the letter of Scripture points toward the timeless truths to which Christians are committed. There are only a few types explicitly defined in the New Testament writings. John 3:14 treats Moses' lifting up of the serpent in the wilderness (Num. 21:9) as a type of Christ's exaltation on the cross. Matthew 12:39ff. (cf. Matt. 16:4) treats Jonah's three days in the belly of the whale as a type of Christ's three days in death, but Luke 11:29ff. interprets Jonah as a sign of repentance. 1 Peter 3:21 understands the deliverance of Noah as a type of Christian baptism. And in Galatians 4, Paul interprets the story of Abraham's two children in a partly typological, partly allegorical fashion to argue for the incorporation of the Gentiles into God's people. In this way, Christian interpretation of Scripture presses beyond the proof texting that is characteristic of the early apologetic.

Let us conclude discussion of the New Testament writers by making some observations about the approach several of them take toward interpreting Scripture. And we may begin with Paul. The most striking feature of Paul's letters from this point of view is that they seldom speak of the fulfillment of prophecy. Indeed, Rom. 1:2 is the only clear example of the idea; and here Paul may be employing an earlier creedal tradition. His own approach to Scripture is best indicated in 2 Cor. 3:12–18. The meaning of the Hebrew Scriptures is obscured for the Jews. It is as though a veil has been placed over them, and Moses' veiled face (Ex. 34:33ff.) is an allegorical warrant for the metaphor. But Christ has removed the veil, and those who are in Christ can now read Scripture and understand its true meaning for the first time. The mystery is unveiled for the Christian. It is this approach which explains why the story of Abraham establishes the law (Rom. 3:31–4:25). Within his discussion in Romans 4, Paul cites scriptural proof texts (Gen. 15:6; Ps. 32:1–2; Gen. 17:5; 15:5) and draws the first two texts together, since "reckoning" occurs in both. But these methods, which are standard rabbinic ones, are used in the interest of a broader purpose. It is almost as though Paul were saying that as a Jew he had misread the story of Abraham to mean that steadfast obedience is in the long run rewarded by friendship with God. Now, however, as a Christian he can see that the friendship comes first and the obedience follows from it. The story of Abraham, then, becomes an allegory of justification by faith; and the true meaning of Scripture is related to the unveiling of that timeless truth.

At the same time, Paul does not altogether remove the element of time and, with it, the implication that there is a predictive dimension of the Hebrew Scriptures. In Galatians 3 the story of Abraham is treated as the story of a promise made in the past and fulfilled in Christ. Deuteronomy 27:26 and 21:23 ("cursed") are brought together to describe the curse of the law as the curse taken by Christ on the cross. And a second comparison of texts contrasts the life that comes from faith (Hab. 2:4) with the life that, in principle, comes from keeping the law (Lev. 18:5). The detailed argumentation drives to the conclusion that the law brings a curse instead of life, while Christ's abolition of the curse enables the promise made to Abraham (Gen. 12:3, 7) to come to fulfillment. The law of Moses comes between the promise and its fulfillment, but far from interfering with that fulfillment, it functions to hasten its coming. Moreover, just as Abraham appropriated the promise in faith (Gen. 15:6), so Christians must embrace its fulfillment in faith. In this way, Paul's interpretation is correlated with his understanding of the salvation history, and the unveiled mystery of Scripture is related to the unfolding of events in time. The same observation may be made concerning Paul's discussion of God's mysterious plan for saving Jews and Gentiles in Romans 9–11. Very many scriptural passages are cited, and what they reveal is God's eternal and saving purpose which unfolds itself in time. To the remnant of Israel (e.g., Rom. 9:29/Isa. 1:9; Rom. 11:4/1 Kings 19:18) are added the Gentiles (e.g., Rom. 9:25/Hos. 2:23; Rom. 10:20/Isa. 65:1). Finally, the conversion of the Gentiles will provoke the Jews to jealousy and to a return to Israel (e.g., Rom. 10:19/Deut. 32:21).

In contrast to Paul, Matthew strongly emphasizes the predictive aspect of Scripture. The Hebrew Scriptures are no longer so much a mystery revealed in Christ as a detailed prophecy of him. The five infancy stories that Matthew tells (Matt. 1:18–2:23) are all constructed around prophetic texts and are said to "fulfill what was spoken by the prophet." Isaiah 7:14 and Micah 5:2 predict the virgin birth of the Messiah in Bethlehem. Hosea 11:1 predicts the flight to Egypt; Jer. 31:15, the slaughter of the innocents; and the words "he shall be called a Nazarene" (Judg. 13:5?), the return to Nazareth. Nine other times in the Gospel, Matthew uses his formula of prophecy fulfillment (Matt. 4:14; 8:17; 12:17; 13:14; 13:35; 21:4; 26:54, 56; 27:9). Yet even without the formula, the Hebrew Scriptures are used as a prophecy fulfilled by Christ. While the emphasis on the predictive character of Scripture does seem to be Matthew's, the idea may be found in other New Testament writers. Luke 4:21 tells of Jesus' claim in the synagogue at Nazareth that the passage from Isaiah he has just read (Isa. 61:1–2) "has been fulfilled in your hearing." John uses a formula very much like Matthew's to speak of the fulfillment of Scripture (John 12:38; 13:18; 15:25; 17:12; 19:24, 36). The proof from prophecy seizes upon one aspect of Paul's approach to Scripture and gives it pride of place.

We may turn finally to Luke, where we find what can be described as promise fulfillment rather than prophecy fulfillment. In his resurrection narratives Luke reveals to us his basic approach to Scripture. It is the risen Lord who explains to the disciples on the road to Emmaus "in all the scriptures the things concerning himself" (Luke 24:27). And in his last encounter with the disciples Jesus says that "everything written about me in the law of Moses and the prophets and the psalms must be fulfilled" (Luke 24:44). The content of this fulfillment is "that the Christ should suffer and on the third day rise from the dead, and that repentance and forgiveness of sins should be preached in his name to all nations, beginning from Jerusalem" (Luke 24:46–47). According to Luke, the risen Lord reveals the true meaning of Scripture as fulfilled in him. And, of course, this fulfillment can be regarded as prophecies come true. But Luke's tendency is to think more generally of promises that are fulfilled. Stephen's speech in Acts 7 is a narrative of the history of Israel from Abraham to Moses to David and the Temple. The promise (Acts 7:5, 17) gradually unfolds itself but is completed only in Christ. Luke's theology revolves around the salvation history, and he divides that history into succeeding epochs. Each epoch becomes a promise fulfilled in the succeeding one. The decisive fulfillment is, of course, found in Christ, but that fulfillment in turn becomes a promise of the final consummation at the end of the age.

If nothing else, our discussion has demonstrated the complexity of the use made of Scripture by the New Testament writers. The Hebrew Scriptures become a warrant for Christian practice, but, more important, for the preaching of the gospel. Not only are proof texts used, but as well Scripture echoes in almost every verse of the New Testament. The focus, however, may be found in citing texts to demonstrate the truth of the gospel. The proof texts may be regarded as prophetic, typological, or allegorical; but it is not always easy to be sure which label to use in a given case. Luke's schema of promise and fulfillment looks like a version of prophecy fulfillment, but it also has affinities with typology. Paul's proof texting can sometimes look more like allegorism than proof from prophecy. And it is difficult to say whether Galatians 4 is a type or an allegory. The same fluidity attaches to early Christian interpretation of the Hebrew Scriptures after the apostolic period. Here, too, the one thing that is clear is that Christ and his story reveal the true meaning of Scripture and so unveil its authority. In what follows we shall turn, first, to different approaches taken by Christians to the Hebrew Scriptures and, then, to functions of those approaches in telling the Christian story. We shall keep the New Testament in mind but shall focus on the apostolic fathers and Justin Martyr.

Christian Approaches to the Hebrew Scriptures

Exempla

It is no surprise to find Christian writers using biblical examples in their exhortations. Both Jews and pagans adopted this obvious approach.[5] We should probably think of the Christian sermon and its roots in Jewish synagogue practice where the homiletical use of biblical figures can treat them as models to be followed or cautionary tales to be avoided. The most obvious instance of the use of examples in the New Testament occurs in Hebrews 11 which uses examples to illustrate the kind of faith the readers are to have as they press forward toward perfection. "By faith," repeated sixteen times, introduces the examples that include Abel, Enoch, Noah, the patriarchs and Sarah, Moses, and Rahab. The list at the end of the chapter goes on to add judges, prophets, and the righteous. It is not necessary to analyze the passage in detail to realize that these figures and their stories do not obviously illustrate faith. Other virtues come as easily to mind—obedience in the case of Abraham, righteousness in the case of Noah. There need be no problem, since as any preacher knows, the same story can be used to illustrate a number of different points. But what is surprising when one examines Hebrews with rabbinic passages in mind is that exegetical proof texts are missing and the biblical verses that are cited do not supply the proof that a given figure exemplifies faith. Hebrews 11 does make use of the Hebrew Scriptures, but we find no precision of interpretation by which details of the text are used to prove the homiletical point.

In *1 Clement* we find one list of examples that does make use of specific biblical proof texts. After describing Christ's humility (*1 Clement* 16), *1 Clement* goes on to list biblical examples of humility (*1 Clement* 17–18). Elijah, Elisha, and Ezekiel are simply mentioned. But Abraham, Job, Moses, and David each are given a double proof, the divine testimony to their excellence and a text proving their humility.[6] This particular list in *1 Clement* puts us in touch with a use of examples that is precise and carefully exegetical. Elsewhere in *1 Clement*, as in Hebrews, such rabbinic care is conspicuous by its absence. It looks as though Christians remain concerned with the results of midrashic exegesis, but no longer understand or worry about the detailed proof texting that enables those results. There are other listings of examples in *1 Clement*—jealousy in 4–6, repentance in 7–8, obedience in 9–12, and self-sacrifice in 55. Nowhere do we find the precise proof texting that occurs with the examples of humility. Moreover, Abraham exemplifies obedience, faith, and hospitality, as well as humility. And the examples given in 11 and 12 fail to continue the theme of obedience and instead speak of Lot's hospitality and piety and Rahab's faith and hospitality. Taken as a whole, *1 Clement* adopts the same loose way of using examples that we find in Hebrews. Unlike Hebrews, *1 Clement* adds not only Christ but Christian and pagan examples to instances from the Hebrew Scriptures. Peter, Paul, and other Christian martyrs illustrate the effect of jealousy (*1 Clement* 5–6). "Kings and rulers" embody the virtue of self-sacrifice (*1 Clement* 55). In sum, *1 Clement* is not so much interested in a careful interpretation of the Hebrew Scriptures as a basis for Christian ethical norms as he is in using Scripture to make a homiletical point directly related to the Corinthian situation. Only by abandoning jealousy and embracing repentance, obedience, humility, and self-sacrifice can the Corinthians restore order to their church.

Testimonia

Another approach to the Hebrew Scriptures that we find in our literature is that of testimony lists, that is, short collections of biblical verses. Here the aim is not to find in Scripture a warrant for moral norms but rather to demonstrate the truth of Christian claims.[7] The testimony lists that we possess are stereotyped in character as a comparison of *Barnabas* with Justin's *Dialogue with Trypho,* Irenaeus' *Demonstration of the Apostolic Preaching,* Tertullian's *Against the Jews,* Cyprian's *Testimonies,* and other sources shows. As well, a form critical study of certain of the lists suggests that their anti-Jewish function is secondary and that we may be dealing with collections of proof texts used in the Hellenistic Jewish synagogue to show "what the Lord requires" and adapted to Christian purposes.[8] Furthermore, the testimony lists discovered at Qumran supply another Jewish precedent for what we see in early Christian writings. Finally, the sort of assembling of proof texts found in Romans 9–11, Hebrews 1–2, and the opening verses of Mark suggests that lists of crucial proofs began to be made very early. It is unlikely that we can uncover the details of the process by which testimonia developed, and it is reasonably clear that at one level we are dealing with stock Christian proof texts rather than with documentary sources. In any case, the testimonia are used to legitimate the Christian rejection of Jewish practices and Christian claims about Christ. Particularly in this second area we are dealing with an elaborated form of the proof from prophecy.

Barnabas uses Scripture testimonies to reject Jewish sacrifices (*Barnabas* 2), fasting (3), circumcision (9), and Sabbath observance (15); but these negative uses of texts are balanced by testimonies designed to prove that Christian baptism and Christ's cross fulfill the ancient promises (11–12).[9] We find more than a straightforward listing of proof texts. *Barnabas* 11, which argues that "the water and the cross" were revealed beforehand, begins by citing Jer. 2:12f. and Isa. 16:1f. to show that the Jews reject baptism and build "cisterns of death" for themselves.[10] The text continues by citing Isa. 45:2–3, which has no apparent connection either with baptism or with the rejection of the Jews. Perhaps the last part of v. 3 ("who call you by your name") supplies a connection with baptism, while v. 6 in speaking of the universal knowledge of God supports the Christian claim about the choice of the Gentiles and the rejection of the Jews. The chapter concludes by using Ps. 1 and Ezekiel 47 to show that the water and the cross are mentioned together. Here we may be in the · presence of an early Christian interpretation of Ezekiel's Temple vision that identified the rivers of paradise flowing from the Temple Rock with the water of baptism, and the trees planted beside the rivers with Christ's and Christians' crosses.[11]

Barnabas 12 adds further complexities. The statement of "another prophet" that "all these things" shall be accomplished "when the tree shall fall and rise, and when blood shall flow from the tree" cannot be found in the Hebrew Scriptures, though it is cited by Pseudo-Gregory of Nyssa in *Testimonies* 7. *Barnabas* 12 continues by adding typological demonstrations of the cross (Moses' uplifted arms at the battle with Amalek and his lifting up of the brazen serpent in the wilderness) and concludes by identifying Jesus as the true Joshua and the "Lord" of Ps. 110:1 and Isa. 45:1. The Isaiah passage has been altered to read, "The Lord said to the *Lord (Kyrio)* my Christ" instead of, "The Lord said to *Cyrus (Kyro)* my Christ." This altered verse occurs elsewhere in our sources.[12] Could it be that the consonants are immutable jots and tittles, while the vowels can be changed, just as the rabbis felt able to alter the vocalization of the Hebrew text for purposes of interpretation, provided the consonants were preserved?

We cannot pretend to be able to explain the details that have been described. Suffice it to say that *Barnabas'* testimony lists are not merely a simple listing of proofs from prophecy. They are the end product of an interpretive task that includes altering texts as well as assembling them. They reflect the use of books outside the Hebrew Scriptures. And they betray fuller interpretations of some of the texts involved, notably Ezekiel 40ff. In general terms, however, it is easy enough to see how the testimony lists function for Barnabas. They belong in the context of his interpretation of Christian *gnōsis*. This knowledge is designed to instruct Christians in the deeper meaning of their baptismal faith, a deeper meaning that revolves around the rejection of the Jews and their practices and the mystery of the Christian's incorporation into Christ through baptism. And there is more than a hint that the "knowledge" is to be equated with a Christian and esoteric interpretation of Scripture.

Types and Allegories

We have already seen that Barnabas integrates two types with his list of testimonies to the cross in ch. 12. Moses' lifting up of the brazen serpent in the wilderness (Num. 21:6ff.), a type mentioned in John 3:14f., is understood by Barnabas not only to show that the death of Christ brings life to Christians but also "to convince them [the Jews] that they will be delivered over to the affliction of death because of their transgression." The serpent is, as well, related to the serpent in Genesis 3. The other type of the cross is Moses' lifting up of his hands in the battle with Amalek (Ex. 17:8ff.). In *Barnabas* 7–8 the scapegoat of Leviticus 16 and the red heifer of Numbers 19 are examined typologically. They foreshadow Christ, as does the sacrifice of Isaac (Gen. 22/*Barnabas* 7.3), but they are also interpreted in reference to the necessity for Christians to attain Christ's kingdom "through pain and suffering," to the Christian's destiny, and to the Jews' rejection of Christ. Moreover, the details of the two rituals are interpreted. For example, the three boys who sprinkle the people with the water mixed with the ashes of the red heifer are "a testimony to Abraham, Isaac, and Jacob." Barnabas depends upon an elaboration of Numbers 19 that specifies details of the ritual, and he gives what should probably be called an allegorical interpretation of those details. If Barnabas can sometimes draw typologies that relate old to new into allegories that claim to open the hidden and spiritual meaning of the text, he can also make a straightforward use of allegorism. In *Barnabas* 10 the food laws of the Hebrew Scriptures are thought to signify different forms of moral behavior. A precedent for this sort of interpretation of the food laws is found in Judaism as early as the *Letter of Aristeas* (second century B.C.E.). The confusion between typology (understood as relating old to new) and allegorism (understood as relating earthly to heavenly) should not surprise us. Paul's treatment of Abraham, Hagar and Ishmael, Sarah and Isaac, and the two Jerusalems in Galatians 4, as we have suggested, poses the same ambiguity. The story in the

Hebrew Scriptures foreshadows Christ and the Christians typologically, but the letter of Scripture points beyond itself to a heavenly meaning. The juxtaposition of a cosmological perspective with a salvation history one creates the perplexity.

Midrashic and Haggadic Developments

Another approach taken to Scripture that we find in *Barnabas* involves the elaboration of a text's meaning either by relating it to other texts or by expanding it in what almost seems a haggadic fashion. The first sort of elaboration may be found implicitly and explicitly in *Barnabas* 6. Passages from the Hebrew Scriptures concerning stones (Isa. 28:16; 50:7; Ps. 118:22ff.) are related to one another and referred to Christ as the stone that saves believers and crushes unbelievers. The pattern is one that may well depend on Jesus' citation of Ps. 118 in Mark 12:10f. and parallels and, as we have seen, is found in the New Testament as early as 1 Peter 2:4–10. Hermas' vision of the tower (*Visions* 3; *Similitudes* 9) depends upon this midrashic development.[13] The brief passage in *Barnabas* implies the whole story of Christ rejected by the Jews and believed in by the Gentiles. A more explicit midrash in *Barnabas* 6 can best be understood as part of a baptismal homily expounding the Christian's death and resurrection with Christ in baptism by the use of creation and exodus themes. Entering the promised land really means union with Christ and can also be understood as a new creation. In a similar fashion, Hebrews equates the "rest" of the promised land in Ps. 95 with God's Sabbath rest after creation (Heb. 3:7–4:11). Specific verses from the Hebrew Scriptures are used in both *Barnabas* and Hebrews, but the passages in question drive toward a moving and powerful description of baptism and the Christian passover. To die and rise with Christ is to die to the old creation and to bondage in Egypt and to rise to the true promised land of heaven itself, the new creation.

A different sort of elaboration of the text of the Hebrew Scriptures is Barnabas' haggadic development of the story of the golden calf in Exodus. Barnabas tells the story twice, more or less in the same way (*Barnabas* 14; 4:6–8). Moses, fasting on Mt. Sinai for forty days and forty nights, receives the two tables of the law written by the finger of God. He is told to go down quickly because of the idolatry of the people in making the golden calf to worship, and he breaks the stone tables of the law. The story is, of course, based upon Exodus 31–32; but details are borrowed from Ex. 24:18; 34:28; and Deut. 9:12–17. The point of the story for Barnabas is that

the covenant which God intended to make with Israel was with-
drawn because of Israel's apostasy and given to the Christians. The
last point is demonstrated by Isa. 42:6f.; 49:6f.; and 61:1f. Barnabas
does not make explicit the strict exegetical proof of his interpretation. Presumably that would hinge upon the fact that the first set of
tables was written by the finger of the Lord (Ex. 31:18), while the
second set was written by Moses (Ex. 34:28). For Barnabas, however, the elaborated story is what suffices to prove that the covenant
is not "both theirs and ours"; "it is ours" (*Barnabas* 4:6–7). We shall
encounter this use of the golden calf story again.

The Functions of Christian Approaches
to the Hebrew Scriptures

The brief descriptions that have been given of Christian exegesis
point toward the conclusions suggested earlier. First, the fundamental method employed is the use of proof texts to demonstrate
Christian convictions. At the level of the Christian message of salvation the proofs from prophecy, typology, and allegorism do not
always appear in a pure form. Barnabas, for example, uses all three
methods, tends to mix them together, and integrates them with
testimony lists and midrashic elaborations of the Hebrew Scriptures. Second, it begins to appear that the exegetical conclusions
are more important than careful and precise exegesis. The authority
of the Hebrew Scriptures is unlocked only when the Christian message is used as the key to its interpretation. For this reason, the
functions of Christian interpretation dominate. It is to those functions we must now turn, and we shall focus discussion upon the
evidence found in Justin's *Dialogue with Trypho*.

Proof of the Rejection of Jewish Practices

Justin's *Dialogue with Trypho* almost certainly reflects the way the
developing Great Church in the middle of the second century understood the debate between Christians and Jews. The issue, as
Trypho tells us in *Dialogue* 10, revolves around Christian rejection
of circumcision and the keeping of the law and "resting your hopes
on a man that was crucified." The first of these points means that
Justin must show why it is legitimate for Christians to reject circumcision, the Sabbath observance, the food laws, and the Temple
sacrifices. And, since he accepts the authority of the Hebrew Scriptures, he must argue his case from it. Justin's basic perspective is
that the law of Moses was instituted "on account of your transgres-

sions and the hardness of your hearts" (*Dialogue* 18). God uses the prophets to repeat Moses' commands, but it is "on account of the hardness of your hearts, and your ingratitude towards Him, that He continually proclaims them" (*Dialogue* 27). Like Barnabas, Justin uses the golden calf story to argue that "God, accommodating Himself to that nation, enjoined them also to offer sacrifices, as if to His name, in order that you might not serve idols" (*Dialogue* 19). Unlike Barnabas, however, Justin does not go so far as to claim that Israel never possessed the covenant. Instead, he argues that the covenant given for Israel's sin points beyond itself to "an eternal and final law" promised by Isa. 51:4f.; Jer. 31:31f.; and Isa. 55:3ff. (*Dialogue* 1–12). It is with this fundamental perspective in mind that Justin uses the Hebrew Scriptures to demonstrate the abolition of Jewish practices.

Christian rejection of circumcision was a crucial issue for the Jews, since it carried with it the rejection of an obligation to observe the law. Paul, particularly in Galatians, insists that the Jews are misled. To reject circumcision is to reject the law of Moses; but far from rejecting the moral demand of God, it enables a deeper obedience that springs from full and mature fellowship with God. Abraham supplies Paul with his chief example, since Abraham receives the promise and his friendship with God *before* his circumcision (Gal. 3). Justin cites Gen. 15:6, one of Paul's chief proof texts, to make precisely the same point (*Dialogue* 92). In a similar way, Justin argues that God did not teach "those who are called righteous and pleasing to Him who lived before Moses and Abraham" to be circumcised and to observe the Sabbath (*Dialogue* 27). Enoch and Noah, for example, were uncircumcised (*Dialogue* 92). God would not have made Adam uncircumcised had circumcision been required to make him pleasing to God (*Dialogue* 19). Justin does not employ proof texts to make his point but simply employs the biblical stories. It is arguable that the burden of proof is on the Jews to counter Justin's interpretation. And indeed we do find in Aboth de Rabbi Nathan careful proof that Adam was made circumcised and that others of the righteous before and including Moses were born uncircumcised.[14] Another aspect of Justin's argument is that nations besides Israel practice circumcision (*Dialogue* 28). Circumcision, then, is of no avail.

Justin presses beyond the idea that circumcision is unnecessary to argue that it is a sign given the Jews by God to signify their hardheartedness. Deuteronomy 10:16f. and Lev. 26:40f. speak of the uncircumcision of Israel's heart (*Dialogue* 16). Justin interprets this uncircumcision as though it indicated fleshly circumcision. The outward sign points to an inward wickedness and functions "that you may be separated from other nations and from us, and that you alone may suffer that which you now justly suffer; and that your land may be desolate, and your cities burned with fire; and that strangers may eat your fruit in your presence, and not one of you may go up to Jerusalem" (*Dialogue* 16). Hosea 1:9 is also referred to circumcision as a sign that the Jews are rejected as God's people (*Dialogue* 19). The texts of the Hebrew Scriptures are brought into relation with the aftermath of the Hadrianic revolt, especially the prohibition of all Jews from Jerusalem; and circumcision becomes a sign of God's rejection of Israel.

Justin exploits the contrast between circumcision of the flesh and circumcision of the heart by identifying Christian baptism with the latter. In this way Jer. 4:4 and 9:25f. are interpreted as stating the contrast, and Mal. 1:10f. and Ps. 18:43 are drawn into the argument as proof that the Gentiles are the true people of God (*Dialogue* 28). Circumcision, according to Justin's interpretation of Jer. 2:13, is "the useless baptism of cisterns" (*Dialogue* 19, 114) in contrast to the Christian baptism of life. The type of Joshua's circumcision of the Children of Israel with "knives of stone" (Josh. 5:2) is fulfilled in Christian baptism, which constitutes the new people of God prophesied by Isa. 65:1–3 (*Dialogue* 24). The "knives of stone" are the words of Christ, who is the Stone; and their effect is to cut off idolatry (the worship of stones) and every kind of wickedness (*Dialogue* 113–114). Baptism with knives of stone is contrasted with circumcision by iron instruments. The iron, of course, symbolizes the hard-heartedness of the Jews. Justin employs the proof from prophecy, typology, and what looks like an allegorical treatment of the type to make his point. In all these ways the rejection of circumcision is grounded in the text of the Hebrew Scriptures.[15]

Justin treats the other Jewish practices in precisely the same way. The observance of the Sabbath, the food laws, and the Temple service were all given to the rebellious people who worshiped the golden calf and have no abiding value (*Dialogue* 19–27; 40–42). Yet in some respects they can be understood spiritually to foreshadow Christ. The Temple service, in particular, supports Justin's view. The destruction of Jerusalem and the Temple means that the laws for the Temple service are a dead letter and demonstrates that the sacrifice of the paschal lamb was a temporary injunction (*Dialogue* 40). Indeed, the whole of the Temple service enjoined in the Hebrew Scriptures, having come to an end, remains significant only as a type or symbol of Christian truths. Justin follows the approach already found in Hebrews and *Barnabas*. The paschal lamb, as in John 19:36 and 1 Cor. 5:7–8, is a type or symbol of Christ on the cross. The two goats of the Day of Atonement ritual stand for the two appearances of Christ. As the scapegoat, Christ was humiliated and crucified. As the other goat, he will return in glory at the end of the age (*Dialogue* 40). The offering of fine flour (Lev. 14:10) is a type of the Eucharist, the pure offering prophesied by Mal. 1:10–12 (*Dialogue* 41). The twelve bells on the high priest's robe (cf. Ex. 28:33) symbolize the twelve apostles whose "sound has gone forth into all the world and their words to the ends of the world" (Ps. 19:4),[16] converting the wicked to childlike obedience (Isa. 53:1–2) (*Dialogue* 42). The literal meaning of the Temple service is abolished, but the spiritual meaning is fulfilled in Christ and the church.

Gnostic Use of the Hebrew Scriptures

Barnabas and Justin give us a rather full idea of the character of early Christian arguments against the Jews, but their point of view seems moderate when compared to that of the Christian Gnostics. Scripture is used to show that Jewish practices are to be rejected and that the destruction of their Temple and nation is retribution for their sins, which began with making an idol in the wilderness and culminated in their rejection of Christ. But the Gnostics take this attitude a step farther by denying that the creator God of the Hebrew Scriptures is the God revealed by Christ. And, paradoxically, they use the Scriptures, particularly Genesis, as a point of departure for complicated myths that equate creation with the Fall and the material universe with evil.[17] It will suffice to take one chief example and to show how the Hebrew Scriptures are used to prove the inferiority of their God. In the *Second Treatise of the Great Seth*, for example, the Cosmocrator or Archon is a laughingstock "because he said, 'I am God, and there is none greater than I. I alone am the Father, the Lord, and there is no other beside me. I am a jealous God, who brings the sins of the fathers upon the children for three and four generations.' "[18] Clear reference is made to Ex. 20:1–6; Deut. 5:9; Isa. 43:11; and Isa. 45:5. These biblical verses are thought to demonstrate the folly and vainglory of the creator God in believing himself sole Lord. This Gnostic exegesis, taken together with Marcion's, reveals the fundamental danger in the anti-Jewish polemic of the early church. It is a simple step from rejecting the Jews and their practices to rejecting their God and their Bible, a step neither Barnabas nor Justin wishes to take. Some framework is required in order to block this step. When Irenaeus begins to argue that the law was given to Israel in its childhood to educate the people for Christ, it becomes possible to treat the temporary character of the Jewish law in a new way that begins to make more sense of it in both its continuity and its discontinuity with Christ.

Proof of Christ and the Church

To return to the *Dialogue with Trypho,* we must continue by showing how Justin uses the Hebrew Scriptures positively and argues that Christ supplies the key to interpreting them. Elements of this more positive use have already been described. Circumcision points to the true circumcision of the heart, which is Christian baptism. The Temple service has a spiritual meaning that is embodied in Christ and the church. But the focus of Justin's interpretation of the Hebrew Scriptures is found in his reference of them to Christ. There is nothing surprising in this, since the New Testament and the early church are agreed in seeing Christ as the fulfillment of the hope of Israel. The details of Justin's interpretation are, as well, coherent with the New Testament and the developing Great Church. In *Dialogue* 126 we read:

> "But if you knew, Trypho," continued I, "who He is that is called at one time the Angel of Great Counsel (Isa. 9:6), and a Man by Ezekiel (40:3), and like the Son of Man by Daniel (7:13) and a child by Isaiah (9:6), and Christ and God to be worshipped by David (Ps. 2), and Christ and a Stone by many (Ps. 118:22f., Isa. 8:14, 28:16, 50:7, Dan. 2:34, 44f.), and wisdom by Solomon (Prov. 8:22ff.), and Joseph and Judah and a Star by Moses (Gen. 49, Num. 24:17), and the East by Zechariah (6:12), and the Suffering One and Jacob and Israel by Isaiah again (42, 43, 52–53), and a Rod, and Flower, and Cornerstone, and Son of God (Isa. 8:14, 28:16, 11:1), you would not have blasphemed Him who has now come, and been born, and suffered and ascended to heaven, who shall also come again, and then your twelve tribes shall mourn (Zech. 12:10). For if you had understood what has been written by the prophets, you would not have denied that He was God, Son of the only, unbegotten, unutterable God."

The probable scriptural allusions have been indicated in the citation, and the passage looks not at all unlike a testimony list. Many of the passages will be considered later in the argument. But the preliminary point to make is that Justin's interpretation of these and other passages from the Hebrew Scriptures proceeds by relating the details of the text to details of the story of Christ's preexistence, birth, death, resurrection, and second coming. Although doing so anticipates our conclusions, we shall use these points of reference to organize the discussion that follows.

Justin insists that the Hebrew Scriptures prove the existence of the Word of God before his incarnation. The puzzles found in the narrative of God's destruction of Sodom and Gomorrah (Gen. 18–19) may be resolved by equating the Lord who speaks to Abraham with the preexistent Word of God (*Dialogue* 56). This explains why the "three men" of Genesis 18 become "two angels" in Genesis 19, and the interpretation is confirmed by Gen. 19:24 ("the *Lord* [the Word] rained on Sodom sulphur and fire from the *Lord* [God the Father] out of heaven"). Whenever the Hebrew Scriptures speak of God's descents and appearances, they refer to the Word rather than to the Father (*Dialogue* 126–27). It is the Word who wrestles with Jacob (Gen. 32), comes down to see the tower of Babel (Gen. 11:5), shuts Noah in the ark (Gen. 7:16), and speaks to Moses from the burning bush (Ex. 3). Specific proof texts for Justin's view include, as well as Gen. 19:24, Ps. 110:1, where two "Lords" appear, Ps. 45:6–7, where two "Gods" appear,[19] the use of the plural by God (Gen. 1:26, 28; 3:22), and Prov. 8:22ff., where "Wisdom" is the "beginning" of God's ways and his agent in creation (*Dialogue* 61–62).[20]

This preexistent Word of God becomes incarnate by being born of a virgin. Isaiah 7:10–17 supplies Justin with his chief proof text (*Dialogue* 43, 66–67, 77–78, 84; *First Apology* 33), but he uses other passages the same way. When Isaiah asks "who shall declare his generation" (Isa. 53:8), he refers to the miracle of Christ's birth (*Dialogue* 43). Isaiah 11:1ff. shows that the Christ-child receives all the differing spirits of prophecy, that thereafter prophecy ceases in Israel, and that the sevenfold Spirit is given by Christ to the church in accordance with Ps. 68:18 and Joel 2:28 (*Dialogue* 87; cf. *First Apology* 32). Isaiah 9:6 refers not only to Christ's birth but also to his cross, the "government" on his shoulders (*First Apology* 35). Justin also employs types or examples to make his case. The virgin birth is like the miraculous births of Eve, Samuel, Isaac, John the Baptist, and others (*Dialogue* 84). Occasionally Justin presses beyond using Scripture as a prophetic or typological proof of the virgin birth. For example, he inserts Isa. 8:4 ("For before the child knows how to cry father or mother, he shall receive the power of Damascus and the spoil of Samaria in the presence of the king of Assyria") into his citation of Isaiah 7, employing the parallel between Isa. 8:4 and Isa. 7:16. This enables him to give an allegorical interpretation of Isaiah 7 (and Isa. 8:4) that sees in it Matthew's story of the visit of the Magi to the Christ-child (*Dialogue* 77–78).

The king of Assyria is Herod, and Damascus and Samaria refer to the power of magic. By worshiping Christ, the Magi prove magic to be subservient to him.

Justin is preoccupied with the cross and finds it predicted and foreshadowed by the Hebrew Scriptures in many ways. Noah, for example, shows that the "mystery of saved men appeared in the deluge" (*Dialogue* 138). The wood of the ark symbolizes the cross; the water symbolizes Christian baptism; and the eight people saved "were a symbol of the eighth day, whereon Christ appeared when He rose from the dead." It is important to note that Justin does not distinguish the cross from Christ's resurrection. Indeed, the cross stands for both Christ's death and his resurrection, regarded as a single event. And the cross is a sign of victory, not an instrument of torture. In this respect, Justin's view is characteristic of the attitude of the early church toward the cross. It is a sign of deliverance. And so stories of deliverance in the Hebrew Scriptures are a way of speaking of Christ's death and resurrection. Noah and Jonah (*Dialogue* 107) are used by Justin in this typological fashion. It is remarkable that these are precisely the stories we find portrayed in the early catacomb frescoes. The literary and the iconographic sources agree in presenting early Christianity as a deliverance foreshadowed in the Hebrew Scriptures and consummated in Christ. Here we are at the heart of the early church's reading of the Hebrew Scriptures.

Justin finds many other types of the cross in Scripture. In *Dialogue* 86 he lists the tree of life in paradise, Moses' rod, the tree that sweetened the bitter waters of Marah, Jacob's rod and his ladder, Aaron's rod, the oak of Mamre, the seventy willows of Ex. 15:27, Elisha's stick, and Judah's rod. To these types he adds the prophetic verses of Isa. 11:1; Ps. 1:3; Ps. 92:12; and Ps. 23:4. Wherever wood is found in the Hebrew Scriptures, there we find the cross. The paschal lamb and the scapegoat, as we have seen, are types of Christ's death (*Dialogue* 40, 111), as is Rahab's scarlet rope (Josh. 2:18/*Dialogue* 111). Two central types are found in Moses' lifting up his hands in the battle with Amalek (Ex. 17:8ff./*Dialogue* 90, 111) and in his lifting up the serpent to heal the people (Num. 21:4ff./*Dialogue* 91; *First Apology* 60). The second of these types is related to the blessing of Joseph in Deut. 33:13–17 (*Dialogue* 91) and to Plato's description of the world soul in the *Timaeus* (*First Apology* 60). The cross is not only revealed in the Hebrew Scriptures but is equated with a cosmic principle that orders and preserves human life and that expresses itself in the keels of ships, plows, an army's standards, and the human form (*First Apology* 55).

In discussing the types of the cross that Justin identifies, we have also seen that he uses the proof from prophecy. The long discussion of *Dialogue* 94–106 focuses upon the predictions of the cross found in the Hebrew Scriptures. The first three of these chapters deal with the curse of the cross in very much the same way that Paul does in Gal. 3:7ff. Deuteronomy 27:26 and 21:23 are correlated with each other to show that Christ on the cross takes upon himself the curse laid upon us for failing to do the law. Beginning with *Dialogue* 97, Justin discusses Ps. 3:4–5; Isa. 65:2 (also cited in Rom. 10:21); Isa. 53:9; and Ps. 22. Isaiah 53 and Ps. 22 as proofs from prophecy may also be found in *1 Clement* 16 and *Barnabas* 5. Justin frequently employs verses from Isaiah 53 in his passion apologetic (*First Apology* 50–51; *Dialogue* 13, 42–43). He relates the passage not only to the cross but also to Christ's preexistence (*Dialogue* 63) and to his second, glorious advent (*Dialogue* 118). Psalm 22 is given lengthy treatment in *Dialogue* 98–106 and is cited in *First Apology* 35 and 38. *Dialogue* 72–73 gives us three proofs from prophecy that Justin claims the Jews have expurgated from their copies of Scripture. The first is Jer. 11:19, where Justin is simply following the Septuagint. The second, attributed to Jeremiah by Justin and by Irenaeus (*Against Heresies* 4.22) and to Isaiah by Irenaeus (in *Against Heresies* 3.20), cannot be identified. The third adds "from the tree" to Ps. 96:10: "Say among the nations, the Lord reigns." One possible explanation is that a midrashic interpretation of the verse has been confused by Justin with the text itself.

Justin's demonstration of the cross by typology and the proof from prophecy already can be seen as, equally, a demonstration of the resurrection. But we need to add his treatment of Ps. 110. The psalm is used in a central way by the New Testament to demonstrate Christ's resurrection and, in Hebrews, his eternal priesthood. It is used as a resurrection proof in *1 Clement* 36 and *Barnabas* 12. Justin uses the psalm in a number of different ways. David is prophesying the resurrection and exaltation of Christ, but also his session at God's right hand, which precedes his second, glorious advent. The "mighty sceptre" of v. 2 is the mighty word of Christ "preached everywhere" (*First Apology* 45; cf. *Dialogue* 83). In *Dialogue* 32–39, Ps. 110 is part of an argument that proves to Trypho "that it is declared in the Scriptures that Christ must suffer, and come again with glory, and receive the eternal kingdom over all the nations, every kingdom being made subject to Him" (*Dialogue* 39). Thus, the psalm, while related to the resurrection, is interpreted to refer more specifically to Christ's heavenly session and, consequently, to his second advent. The psalm does not refer to King Hezekiah (*Dialogue* 33, 83) any more than Ps. 72 refers to Solomon (*Dialogue* 34). Rather, it refers to the universal reign of the risen Lord which will be consummated by his return at the end of the age. The same reference is given to Ps. 72 (*Dialogue* 34); Ps. 24 (*Dialogue* 36); Ps. 46 and 99 (*Dialogue* 37); and Ps. 45 (*Dialogue* 38). Justin preserves the resurrection apologetic but sets it in the broader context of the two advents. As we have seen, the first verse of Ps. 110 is used to prove the existence of two Lords (*Dialogue* 56, 127). And Justin also uses the third verse as a prophecy of Christ's birth (*Dialogue* 63, 76).

What we begin to see in Justin's proof from prophecy is a tendency to relate the text of the Hebrew Scriptures to as many of the details of Christ's story as possible. His interpretations are quite coherent with the earliest Christian apologetic use of Scripture, but he expands and elaborates that apologetic. Justin's use of the blessing of Judah in Gen. 49:8f. supplies a clear example of his comprehensive approach. The passage is understood to predict Christ's suffering at his first advent, the cessation of kings and prophets among the Jews, and the Gentiles' expectation of Christ's future appearance (*Dialogue* 52). "Binding his foal to the vine" (Gen. 49: 11) predicts the Gentiles' embrace of the yoke of Christ as well as the events of Palm Sunday. The predictions of Zech. 9:9 and 13:7 fill in details (*Dialogue* 53). "He shall wash His garments with wine, and his vesture with the blood of the grape" refers to the washing of Christians in Christ's own blood, which is derived from the power of God (*Dialogue* 54), as well as to his passion (*First Apology* 32). Genesis 49:10 predicts that prophets and kings shall cease for the Jews after Christ's passion. And the phrase "desire of nations" in the same verse is fulfilled in the Gentiles who look for Christ's future appearance (*Dialogue* 52).[21] The entire Christian story is predicted. Christ comes in humility, is crucified, and will return in glory. The Jews are rejected for their disbelief, and the Gentiles are given the hope of the second advent.[22]

Two points must be made by way of concluding this discussion of Justin's *Dialogue with Trypho*. First, the patterns of interpretation that we find are not confined to Justin's writings but are current throughout the early church. The earliest apologetic that may be deduced from the New Testament writers is enshrined in the *Dialogue with Trypho*, and the expanded and elaborated version we find there is a constant in early Christianity. The argument for this cannot be made convincingly by using the sources earlier than or contemporary with Justin. There are points of contact, particularly with Barnabas. But the other evidence we possess is extremely fragmentary and makes surprisingly little direct use of the Hebrew Scriptures. That Justin's interpretation does represent the church's view of the Hebrew Scriptures and is a view that in large measure he inherits and transmits may be shown by its coherence with what we find in Tertullian's *Against the Jews* and Cyprian's *Testimonies*. The way the Old Testament functions for Justin is, generally speaking, the way it continues to function for the Great Church of Irenaeus and the third century, and indeed for the whole of the patristic period. The second point is that the pattern we find in Justin's interpretation is a functional one. Justin uses all the different methods we have mentioned—the proof from prophecy, typology, and allegorism. These methods are mixed with one another not only by being placed side by side but also by being used simultaneously on the same texts. Types, for example, tend to be allegorized; and proofs from prophecy also seem at times allegorical. The quest for a framework of interpretation is a quest not as much for method as for a way of finding coherence between the Hebrew Scriptures and the Christian story. Interpretation has as its purpose showing how the Hebrew Scriptures bear witness to Christ. Of course, this involves the reapplication of the text to changed circumstances. Nevertheless, since the only changed circumstance that really matters is the coming of Christ, it makes more sense to think of Christian interpretation as a gradual bringing into focus of the biblical testimony to Christ than as a series of adaptations of the text to the fate of the church. The first step in acquiring this focus is to find a basic framework for interpreting the Hebrew Scriptures. The final section of this chapter will argue that before Irenaeus we can find only a quest for such a framework.

Toward a Framework for Interpreting the Hebrew Scriptures

In the Christian writings before the time of Irenaeus that have been preserved for us there remains only a single extended discussion of how the Hebrew Scriptures should be interpreted, and that discussion is from a Gnostic. Epiphanius, the late-fourth-century heresiologist, preserves a letter to Flora, written by Ptolemey, one of Valentine's followers. The letter was written in Rome in the third quarter of the second century, and "Flora" may even symbolize the Roman church. In any case, it is a writing designed to invite its readers to the Valentinian community, where they may receive the fuller and esoteric teaching. It may be supposed that Ptolemey is aware of the debate over Marcion; and even if he has not read Justin Martyr, he is certainly capable of using the same arguments to a somewhat different purpose. Ptolemey proposes the first framework for interpreting the Hebrew Scriptures we know of. At the heart of his proposal is the insistence that the God who legislated the divine part of the Hebrew Scriptures is neither the perfect God and Father nor Satan, the opposing power. Rather, he is a secondary God, imperfect, one in need of completion by another (3). He is, in fact, the Demiurge, the intermediate creator God, who is neither good nor evil nor unjust, but merely just (7).

The Demiurge, however, is not the author of the entire Hebrew Scriptures. By using Christ's words, Ptolemey argues for a threefold division. The first part of the law was given by the creator God himself. A second part was given by Moses, since Christ distinguishes Moses' permission of divorce from God's command of life-long marriage in Genesis (cf. Matt. 19:6–8). Finally, a third part is contributed by the elders of the people, since Christ contrasts their tradition with the command in the Decalogue to honor father and mother (cf. Mark 7:5–13 and Matt. 15:4–9/4). The first, divine part of the law, is in turn divided into three. First, there is pure legislation, unmingled with evil. This is identified as the Decalogue, which the Savior fulfills. Second, there is the legislation mixed with evil and injustice. This was just and was given because of the weakness of those receiving it to enable them to follow the pure legislation. This second kind of legislation is the law of strict justice, "an eye for an eye and a tooth for a tooth"; and it is abolished by the Savior. The third form of legislation is typological and symbolic and consists of laws for circumcision, the Sabbath, fasting, the paschal lamb, the unleavened bread, and similar institutions. This law is transposed by the Savior from the perceptible to the spiritual and invisible realm.

If we compare Ptolemey's framework with what we find in a writer like Justin, there emerge both similarities and differences. The persistence of the moral law and the abrogation of the ceremonial law in favor of its spiritual meaning are both themes that appear in the mainstream of early Christianity. And Ptolemey's explanation of the spiritual meaning of Jewish practices does not differ significantly from what we have already seen. Moreover, his notion that the law was accommodated to the condition of the people is one we find in Justin and Irenaeus. On the other hand, to attribute the divine law to a God other than the God of Jesus Christ marks the Gnostic character of Ptolemey's view. He has not taken the anti-Jewish polemic of the early church as far as Marcion did, but he has exploited its logic more fully than the Great Church would allow. His conclusion in the long run implies the Gnostic denials of the goodness of creation, the continuity of redemption with creation, and the identity of the God of Jesus Christ with the God of the Hebrew

Scriptures. Not only are the authors of the two testaments different, but there are two authors of the Hebrew Scriptures in addition to the creator God.

Although we find in the mainstream of Christianity no explicit framework for interpreting the Hebrew Scriptures until Irenaeus, it is arguable that Justin is moving toward such a framework. In *Dialogue* 93 we read:

> Unless, therefore, a man by God's great grace receives the power to understand what has been said and done by the prophets, the appearance of being able to repeat the words or the deeds will not profit him, if he cannot explain the argument of them.

The word translated "argument" is actually *logos,* and Justin identifies the *logos* of Scripture with the Christian story. Elsewhere he says that "those events which have happened, and those which are happening, compel you to assent to the utterances made by them [the prophets]" (*Dialogue* 7). What Justin appears to be saying is that experience of the Christian story alone provides the perspective from which the true meaning of the Hebrew Scriptures can be seen. It is only in retrospect and from the point of view of the Logos (word) made flesh that the Hebrew Scriptures make sense. Like Paul, Justin believes that Christ unveils them and makes their meaning clear for the first time. This understanding of the matter may be related to Justin's apologetic use of the Logos theology. The Word of God is to be identified with the whole of Truth and of the Good. This Word was known partially by the philosophers and the righteous before Christ and was revealed in the Hebrew Scriptures. But just as the demons counterfeited the parts of the Truth they read in Scripture by concocting mythologies and theologies, so the Jews' understanding of Scripture was partial because they lacked the fulfillment that could alone make sense of their own book. The "logos" of Scripture can be known only when the Logos (Word) of God is revealed completely and to all in the incarnation.

Although the true meaning of the Hebrew Scriptures can be seen only retrospectively from their fulfillment in Christ, there remains an ambiguity. To look back on the past can mean to reject it. And this was the approach of Marcion and, in the long run, of the Gnostics. But to look back on the past can equally mean to see its continuity with the present, and this was the solution of Irenaeus and the Great Church. Justin's thought drives in both directions. On the one hand, to regard the law as given because of Israel's hard-heartedness is to imply a gap between old and new. Justin is by no means a Gnostic, but he has not altogether blocked a Gnostic interpretation. The basic issue is Justin's treatment of those aspects of the law which do not obviously point forward to Christ. On the other hand, Justin does insist that the same God is revealed in the Hebrew Scriptures and in Christ. And he treats much of the Scriptures as "types, symbols, and proclamations of what would happen with respect to Christ and of those foreknown to believe in him and likewise of what would be done by Christ himself" (*Dialogue* 42). In other words, the Hebrew Scriptures can be regarded as a type, an allegory, and a prophecy of Christ and the church.

One simple step forward is necessary to turn Justin's view into a framework for interpretation. His own notion of a God who providentially dispenses the course of human history must be used to resolve the ambiguity of the retrospect from Christ. That aspect of the Hebrew Scriptures which has to do with Israel's history must be regarded as temporary not because Israel deserves punishment but because Israel needs to be educated. The law, then, would be dispensed so as to prepare Israel for Christ. Though accommodated to Israel's hard-heartedness, that very hard-heartedness can be regarded as the product of immaturity. Thus, the function of the law in every aspect is to point toward Christ. Instead of speaking of the dispensations of different Gods and human beings as Ptolemey does, the church learns to speak of different economies of the same God. The step described as the one taken by Irenaeus, and by taking it he finds a way of including the aspects of the Hebrew Scriptures abolished by Christ within God's providential purpose. In this way, Irenaeus offers a Christian transformation of the Hebrew Scriptures that makes them wholly integral to a Christian Bible. In one further respect Irenaeus takes us beyond Justin by clarifying the identity of Christ. These two steps succeed in articulating a framework for interpreting the whole of Scripture, and Irenaeus identifies this framework with the Rule of faith.

3
A Framework for Interpreting a Christian Bible

In the early church all roads lead not to Rome but to Irenaeus and the last quarter of the second century. His writings represent the term of Christianity's formative period. For the first time we find reflected in his understanding of the church the practical and theoretical structures that had come to give Christianity the ecumenicity enabling it to develop into the Catholic church destined to receive imperial patronage from Constantine not much more than a century after Irenaeus' death. The two sacraments of Baptism and the Eucharist, together with the threefold ministry of bishops, priests, and deacons, gave the church an outward structure that was identifiable throughout the Roman empire and even, to some degree, beyond its borders. At the level of theory, the significance of this ecumenical institution found its exposition in a Christian Bible and a Rule of faith thought to be derived from Scripture and supplying the proper key to the meaning of Scripture. We have already seen something of the beginnings of this development by regarding the formative period of early Christianity as what created a Christian Bible, consisting of the Septuagint and the apostolic writings that came to be called the New Testament. And we have seen how the Christian writers before Irenaeus transformed the Hebrew Scriptures so that they could act as an authority for Christian practice and teaching.

Before Irenaeus, however, we find no fully articulated definition of a New Testament canon and no clear framework for interpreting a Christian Bible. There were disputes over which of the apostolic writings should be regarded as authoritative as well as over the status of the Hebrew Scriptures. And, as we have seen, transforming the meaning of the Hebrew Scriptures meant a number of different things. At one level, the enterprise involved an ambiguity, and even from our modern perspective a fundamental theoretical contradiction. The majority view saw in the Hebrew Scriptures a set of warrants for Christian practice and belief, and yet the authority of Israel's Bible for the church depended entirely upon reading it in particular ways. The central development of Christianity insisted equally that the Hebrew Scriptures promised Christ and that Christ was the key to their meaning. But at another level, granted the paradox of using the Scriptures this way, the transformed meanings they were given did not completely cohere with one another. On the one hand, the text proved that the Jews were wrong, and it was used to authorize the abolition of the practices central to Judaism. On the other hand, Christians used it positively to show how it pointed beyond itself to its fulfillment in Christ. Finally, at an even deeper level, if Christ and the Christian preaching supplied the key to interpreting the Hebrew Scriptures, the question remained which Christ was being assumed by the interpreter. Anyone who has studied the New Testament has been obliged to face the fact that it includes a number of different Christologies which do not seem to be altogether coherent with one another.

Irenaeus addresses all these issues and does so by employing the notion of a salvation history that focuses on the story of the incarnate Word of God but relates that story to the Word's activity in creation and in the history of Israel. By defining the incarnate Lord, Irenaeus clarifies the identity of the hero of the Christian story, a story that includes all of human history. This, in turn, enables him to give a coherent account of the story as a whole, that is, of what he calls the apostolic faith. And the clarified view of the Christian preaching embodied in the Rule of faith supplies him with a framework of interpretation that orders Christian transformations of the Hebrew Scriptures into a coherent pattern. We cannot be sure how much of Irenaeus' thought can be regarded as his own contribution. Some would deny him any originality at all and would regard him as the spokesman for earlier traditions that contradict one another at crucial points. Others would regard him as innovative, the first writer to create a catholic synthesis of Christian belief. The truth probably lies somewhere between these two extreme views. In any case, Irenaeus does not claim to be expounding his own faith but that of the Great Church; and this is how he was understood by his immediate posterity.

We can argue, then, that Irenaeus brought the church's faith to bear upon two issues—the meaning of the Hebrew Scriptures and the identity of Christ. Both these issues were crucial to the debate with Gnosticism, which denied or devalued the Hebrew Scriptures and which separated the Savior in one way or another from the creator God of the Hebrew Scriptures. We have already seen something of the way the meaning of the Hebrew Scriptures was an issue before Irenaeus. Now, before turning to Irenaeus himself, we must say something about the issue of Christ's identity. We can do so largely by posing the question in terms of the New Testament itself and by arguing that the various writers of the New Testament create a problem for the church by defining Christ in a number of different ways. In other words, an exegetical puzzle is posed for a writer like Irenaeus by the New Testament canon. Only by solving that puzzle can he come to conclusions about the apostolic faith, and only by clarifying the apostolic faith can he find the key that unlocks the ordering of Christian interpretations of the Hebrew Scriptures. We could say that the quest which Irenaeus accomplishes is basically the discovery of a principle of interpretation in the apostolic Rule of faith. At the same time, as we shall see, it is in another sense Scripture itself that supplies the categories in which the principle of interpretation is expressed. Text and interpretation are like twin brothers; one can scarcely tell the one from the other. What emerges is an unbroken dialogue or discourse between a book and a people, between Scripture and tradition, between the letter and the spirit, and between the word and the experience of those hearing it.

New Testament Understandings of Jesus

No matter how complicated Christianity became or even was from the very beginning, there can be little doubt that in all its forms it was and remains in one way or another a response to Jesus of Nazareth. For this reason, if the central problem for the New Testament writers was the relationship of the church to Israel, their central preoccupation was to explain Jesus and his significance. To say this presumes the "historical Jesus," but it does not explain the point of departure of the earliest Christians. Modern preoccupation with the historical questions about Jesus and Christian origins have made it seem as though we have no certain historical knowledge. Actually, more is known of Jesus' life and work than of most ancient figures; and certainly the details of the evidence have been subjected to a scrutiny that would be astonishing in any other historical field. There can be little doubt that Jesus was a Galilean prophet, who had been a disciple of John the Baptist but who broke with him and established his own mission with a preaching centered upon "the kingdom of God." There is widespread agreement that this message was double in character, that it proclaimed the near but future reign of God, but also the present inbreaking of that triumph. Moreover, Jesus was executed by the Roman government on the, presumably, false charge of teaching rebellion against Rome; he was crucified under Pontius Pilate about 30 C.E. Finally, a number of those who had been his disciples claimed that they had encountered him alive after his death and explained their experience by saying that God had raised him from the dead in anticipation of the general resurrection at the end of the world. Only the last of these conclusions is problematic, but even here the difficulty lies not with whether the claim that God had raised Jesus from the dead was made, but only with the truth and the meaning of that claim.

It is tempting to suppose that these facts are the basis for interpreting the meaning of Jesus' teaching, life, and fate. And much of modern critical New Testament study has proceeded on the assumption that if only we could recover the facts, we should then be in a position to give a decisive interpretation of them. That no one has succeeded in doing this presupposes a set of problems. It is not merely a question of failure to find agreement about the facts. More than that, it is that we cannot suppose that even if the facts were known in detail, they would automatically imply a correct interpretation. We can, in principle, know all the essential facts about Napoleon, but such knowledge gives us no certain interpretation of his significance in European history. At still deeper a level, we may question whether there is such a thing as a brute fact. Certainly in the New Testament, fact and interpretation are inextricably woven together. And, more important from our present interest, the New Testament writers do not make the historical Jesus their point of departure in responding to Jesus' person. There seem to have been those in the first century who oriented their response to his teachings, his miracles, or to his supposed identity with an apocalyptic figure of some kind.[1] But the canonical writers of the New Testament are agreed in taking Jesus' death and resurrection as the basis for their accounts of his significance.[2] In this way, their theology is based partly on an event that took place in the full light of history, but partly on an event—or another dimension of the cross—that by definition transcends what historians can say one way or another. To be sure, the focus upon the dead and risen Lord by no means yields any single interpretation of his significance, nor does it mean that his teaching and miracles must of necessity be neglected. But it is important to understand that there is agreement in the New Testament about where to begin.

Once this has been said, what strikes the reader of the New Testament is the very different directions taken by its writers in explaining Jesus. For Paul and the tradition on which he depends, as 1 Corinthians 15 shows, all that matters is that Christ died and was raised the third day. Negatively, Paul appears to insist on this preaching against those who based their apostleship and message on the earthly Jesus. Second Corinthians 5:16 presumably excludes the "fleshly" Jesus from serious consideration. And this is why Paul seldom, if ever, appeals either to Jesus' message or to his deeds, his example, and his miracles. Positively, he places the death and resurrection of Christ in a cosmological and mythological framework. Thus, the evil angels who rule this world are ultimately responsible for Christ's death (1 Cor. 2:8). Christ's death and resurrection, then, are integrated with the story of a heavenly redeemer, equal to God, who empties himself, is obedient to death on the cross, and is now highly exalted by God (Phil. 2:6ff.). That Paul's view is not totally idiosyncratic is demonstrated by its basic coherence with what we find in deutero-Pauline writings such as Hebrews and in the Fourth Gospel. At the same time, we cannot simply identify Paul's views with those of Hebrews and John, nor can we argue that the assessment he gives of the dead and risen Lord is the only one we find in the New Testament.

The Synoptic Gospels both agree and disagree with Paul. For example, Mark portrays Jesus as the hidden Messiah, whose identity is evident to the pagan centurion at the moment of Jesus' death on the cross, even though no one in the story has quite guessed the secret previously (Mark 15:39). This and other features of Mark betray his commitment to the "gospel" of the dead and risen Lord, but, unlike Paul, he sees no contradiction between this claim and Jesus' words and deeds.[3] What for Paul was either-or is for Mark both-and. Matthew represents a variation on the theme. The gospel of Jesus' death and resurrection is central to his faith, as the final commissioning of the disciples by the risen Lord shows (Matt. 28:16ff.). But even the Jesus of Easter is portrayed as the Teacher, and for Matthew, Jesus is not only the giver of the messianic Torah but also, as Wisdom, is himself that Torah.[4] Luke's emphasis is upon the miracles of Jesus, and these he regards as prophetic in character, so that Jesus is a prophet "mighty in deed and word" (Luke 24:19). The Synoptic Gospels do not desert the Pauline focus on the cross and the resurrection, but they do include Jesus' earthly ministry. And for Matthew, the risen Lord is first of all the teacher and the teaching, while for Luke he is the prophetic healer. Moreover, none of the Synoptic Gospels employ the redeemer myth found, for example, in Philippians 2. At first this seems surprising, since the redeemer myth is clearly far older than the Synoptic Gospels. Two considerations, however, help explain the anomaly. First, the Gospels are concerned with the traditions about Jesus, which drive away from myth and cosmological speculation. Second, and probably more important, they may well be reacting to a Gnostic misuse of the redeemer myth, which divorced the Savior from his actual history and rendered the cosmological myth problematic for the church.

In the Fourth Gospel, however, the redeemer myth reappears. John is not so much concerned to set the earthly events of Jesus' life and fate in a cosmological framework as he is to use that very framework as a starting point for explaining Christ. It is the Word of God, the one who descended from heaven, that reveals his glory in the cross. And it is the cross that represents the "hour" in which "glory" is revealed. Jesus' "lifting up" on the cross is his "exaltation," and it coincides, as well, with his return to the disciples in the gift of the Spirit. In contrast to Luke, who supplies a narrative framework for what we call Good Friday, Easter, Ascension, and Pentecost, John identifies all these events with aspects of the cross. John's point of view differs from Paul's chiefly in moving from the cosmological myth to the historical Jesus rather than the other way around. It should be added that he, like the other writers of the New Testament, preserves earlier identifications of Jesus within his broader theology. All the New Testament writers consider different aspects of Jesus' messianic character, and all four Gospels reproduce his own mysterious self-identification as Son of Man.

If the diversity of New Testament Christology is demonstrated by isolating the leading perspectives of the various writers, the picture becomes still more complex when we try to press behind the redactional level of the writings themselves to the earlier traditions they employ or at least reflect. Of course, it is Jesus' identity as the Messiah that supplies the most obvious example of this. But in trying to understand the texts, we find that two sorts of problems emerge. Who was the Messiah supposed to be? When was Jesus designated Messiah? The obvious answer to the first question is to identify the Messiah with the descendant of David commissioned by God to restore the kingdom to Israel (Acts 1:6). And certainly much of the New Testament reflects this view. At the same time, it is clear that Jesus is thought to be the Messiah because he is the prophet like Moses predicted by Deut. 18:15, 18 (John 6:14–15; Acts 3:22; 7:37). And, for Hebrews, Ps. 110:4 demonstrates Christ to be the priestly Messiah (Heb. 5:5ff.). That Jesus' messianic status can define him now as king, now as prophet, and now as priest almost certainly reflects the diversity of messianic expectations in first-century Judaism. And the only rule that works for the New Testament is that Jesus fulfills whatever is expected. The second problem with Jesus as Messiah is best indicated by a careful reading of Acts 2:36 and Rom. 1:4. These texts appear to reflect a very ancient Christology that saw the resurrection as the point at which Jesus became the Messiah, a role he would presumably fulfill when he returned at the end of the age. Needless to say, the logic that began to operate is the one we find in Paul's use of the tradition in which the messianic designation at the resurrection "with power" simply makes manifest a previous designation less obvious. The stories of Jesus' baptism and transfiguration include messianic appointments; and with the birth narratives of Matthew and Luke, we find Jesus born the Messiah. Of course, we cannot discuss either of the two problems that have been indicated. The point has been simply to show that claiming Jesus as the Messiah is far more complicated than might at first appear.

The same point is more obvious with respect to the title "Son of Man." The title occurs only in words of Jesus and always in the third person. Moreover, three sorts of sayings are involved: references to a future, heavenly figure, who will appear as judge to vindicate Jesus; references to a present, lowly but authoritative figure, who seems to be Jesus himself; and the Marcan passion predictions, where the Son of Man dies and is raised. The usual view would regard the first set of sayings as authentic and argue that Jesus is really predicting the advent of another figure. Then, since Jesus had identified his own authority with that of the future Son of Man, it was not illogical for the church to identify Jesus' person as well as his authority with the Son of Man. The result is the reading of the title into the other sorts of sayings and the identification of Jesus as Son of Man.[5] Recent work, however, by G. Vermès and Norman Perrin has challenged this view.[6] "Son of Man" is a common Aramaic way of referring to oneself obliquely, and so there is no reason to suppose that Jesus' use of the third person must refer to someone else. Moreover, there is no clear evidence of the use of Son of Man as a technical title before the New Testament. The usual evidence in Daniel 7, *Ethiopian Enoch*, and 4 Esdras need not involve a titular use of the term. Finally, the first group of sayings about the future, heavenly Son of Man seem to have grown from exegetical reflection on Ps. 110, Daniel 7, and Zechariah 12. All this begins to point toward the likelihood that Son of Man is a category elaborated by Christians through reflecting upon Jesus' words and upon crucial passages in the Hebrew Scriptures. The Gospel of Mark, in which we find the title used fully for the first time, really uses it to tell a simple story about Jesus. As the Son of Man he is the lowly but authoritative figure who dies and rises and who will come in glory at the end of the age to vindicate his work. Looking at the problem this way suggests two important points. First, Mark's use of the title correlates with Jesus' message of the kingdom of God. Just as the kingdom is both present and future, both lowly now and glorious hereafter, so it is with the Son of Man. And the passion predictions function to tie together present lowliness and future glory. Second, the pattern bears a striking resemblance to the story of the redeemer myth.

The redeemer myth is another Christological construct found in the New Testament that has never been satisfactorily explained. The older view, best known through Rudolf Bultmann's writings, argued that a pre-Christian Gnostic redeemer myth had been used by Paul, John, and others as a way of explaining Christ. The difficulty with this view is that there is no clear evidence that such a pre-Christian myth existed. The issue is, of course, complicated by the debate about Gnosticism; and it would be foolish to claim to solve the problem. At the same time, elements of the redeemer myth can be simply explained in terms of what we do know about first-century Judaism and Christianity. First, we must recognize that when the redeemer is identified with "the first-born of all creation" (Col. 1:15), the biblical text involved is certainly Prov. 8:22, where "Wisdom" is created by God to be his agent in creating the world. For the Jew, "Wisdom" was to be identified with the Torah (Sirach 24:23). Thus it is easy to see why, for the Christian, Wisdom is Jesus. We are not dealing so much with a redeemer myth as with the transformation of a Jewish exegetical theme. A second point concerns the obedience of the redeemer. Here it is not impossible that notions of Christ as the new Adam, bringing life by obedience instead of death by disobedience, are involved. Finally, the exaltation of the redeemer bears a striking relationship to the interpretation of Christ's resurrection by the use of Ps. 110:1 in the speeches of Acts. In other words, the elements of the redeemer myth correlate with Christological themes that may be found in the New Testament. And, whatever its origin, the myth as we actually find it tells a story. A divine figure descends to earth, where he lives a human life of obedience, culminating in the death of the cross. The crucified one then is exalted and returns to his place of heavenly origin.

To anticipate, this is how Irenaeus attempts to resolve the dilemma of the diversity of New Testament judgments about Christ.

Irenaeus and His Savior

Irenaeus' positive teaching in *Against Heresies* must be disengaged from his polemic against Gnosticism. To refute the Gnostics he is obliged to deny their tendency to fragment the Godhead, their opposition of the creator God and the God of Jesus Christ, their denial of the unity of the Hebrew Scriptures and the New Testament, and their refusal to see any continuity between creation and redemption. Consequently, his argument tends to reduce itself to the claim that there is but one God, the creator, who is the God of Jesus Christ and of both the Hebrew Scriptures and the New Testament. If, however, we press beyond his argument with the Gnostics, we begin to see that his understanding of Christianity focuses upon Jesus Christ as Savior. As God delivered Jonah from the whale, so the Word of God in the incarnation rescued humanity from its ancient enemy (*Against Heresies* 3.20.1). Moreover, Irenaeus presides over a martyr church; and he insists that the whole point of his faith would be lost if the Word of God made Son of Man had not truly suffered, died, and been raised (*Against Heresies* 3.18.6). The object of Irenaeus' piety, then, is the dead and risen Lord; and he must integrate this Christ with his conviction that this Lord is God incarnate and that there is, nonetheless, but a single God. Thus, at a very early stage in the history of Christian theology we see the issues already raised that were to preoccupy the church in the fourth and fifth centuries. If Christ is God, how is he related to the Father? If Christ is God, how can he suffer and die? The Trinitarian and Christological issues need not preoccupy us, but we can see how Irenaeus' depiction of his Savior raised them.

We may gain a preliminary understanding of Irenaeus' definition of Christ by examining a passage in which he appeals to the apostolic Rule of faith (*Against Heresies* 1.10.1). The church, he says, believes

> in one God, the Father Almighty, Maker of heaven, and earth, and the sea, and all things that are in them; and in one Christ Jesus, the Son of God, who became incarnate for our salvation; and in the Holy Spirit.

The third clause of this creedal statement goes on to define the Spirit as proclaiming through the prophets "the dispensations of God, and the advents, and the birth from a virgin, and the passion, and the resurrection from the dead, and the ascension into heaven in the flesh of the beloved Christ Jesus, our Lord, and His [future] manifestation from heaven in the glory of the Father." We shall return to "the dispensations," but for the moment the point to make is that the list of events that Irenaeus gives is his way of speaking of the incarnation. His word for it is "economy" (*the* dispensation), and what he means by it is the decisive act of God in ordering the household of creation. And this act is really a story that begins with the first advent of Christ when he was born of the Virgin, continues with his death, resurrection, and ascension, and concludes with his second advent at the end of the age. Irenaeus' commitment to his Savior is at the same time a commitment to this story. And the story is one of the divine Word of God who was made Son of Man.

The resemblance of this story to the redeemer myth is no accident. Indeed, in the passage we have been examining, Irenaeus defines the purpose of the second advent by citing Eph. 1:10 ("to gather all things in one") and Phil. 2:10–11 ("every knee should bow . . . and that every tongue should confess"). Throughout his writings Irenaeus appeals to passages from the New Testament that we should associate with the redeemer myth to define his understanding of the story of the Word of God incarnate. Philippians 2 demonstrates both the descent of the divine Word to a human life of obedience, culminating in suffering and death, and the ascent of the crucified Lord to his rightful place with God the Father (*Against Heresies* 4.24.2; 3.12.9). Moreover, the "obedience to death" of the Philippians hymn is the obedience of the new Adam (*Against Heresies* 5.16.3). In Book 3.16, Irenaeus seeks to prove from the apostolic writings "that Jesus Christ was one and the same, the only begotten Son of God, perfect God and perfect Man." Among the texts cited is Col. 1:15, where the phrase "the first-born of all creation" defines the redeemer in the hymn used in Colossians and proves for Irenaeus that it is the Son of God made Son of Man who was raised from the dead. As well, Gal. 4:4–5 ("God sent forth his Son, born of a woman") suggests to Irenaeus the incarnation. Similar uses of Rom. 8:3 ("God . . . sending his own Son in the likeness of sinful flesh") and Gal. 3:13 ("having becomes a curse for us") may be found (*Against Heresies* 3.20.2; 3.18.3). And, of course, the prologue to John's Gospel proves for Irenaeus Christ's divinity, his agency in creation and revelation, his virgin birth, and the saving effect of the incarnation (cf. *Against Heresies* 3.11.1; 3.16.2; 4.20.6, 11; 5.18.2–3). Both details from the New Testament texts and the basic pattern of the redeemer myth contribute to Irenaeus' understanding. But, as we shall see, he adopts a particular understanding of the redeemer myth, and in doing so employs patterns found in Pauline theology to develop his doctrine of Christ's "headship" (recapitulation). Before turning our attention to this doctrine, the heart of Irenaeus' theology, we must, however, ask the question why he is insistent that the redeemer be God. The question draws its force from the fact that seldom in the New Testament do we find Christ called "God." Indeed, the prologue to the Fourth Gospel and doubting Thomas' confession, "My Lord and my God!" in John 20 are the only places where the identification occurs unequivocally. This explains why the Revised Standard Version translates Rom. 9:5: "of their race . . . is the Christ. God who is over all be blessed for ever. Amen." The alternative translation, given in a footnote, is "Christ, who is God over all, blessed for ever"; and, of course, this is the way Irenaeus understands the verse (*Against Heresies* 3.16.3). Designating Christ as "God" becomes a commonplace in the literature after the New Testament, and the most obvious reason is that the church could not worship a Savior who was less than God, nor could it believe that anyone not divine would have been capable of bringing salvation. Irenaeus recognizes that Christ's victory must have been a human one, since only in this way would Satan have been "legitimately vanquished." But "unless it had been God who had freely given salvation, we could never have possessed it securely. And unless man had been joined to God, he could never have become a partaker of incorruptibility" (*Against Heresies* 3.18.7). Thus, the Savior must be God perfectly united with humanity, the Son of God made Son of Man. The passages in the New Testament that appear to give the redeemer divine status, then, give Irenaeus a warrant for the view that lies at the heart of his religion of salvation.

The Economies of God

There is, however, a deeper reason for Irenaeus' insistence that the Savior is God, and that has to do with the Word's function before the incarnation. To say that Christ is God is to suppose that he was begotten by the Father in the beginning and that he preexisted the created order. Irenaeus cites with approval a tradition that interprets Gen. 1:1 as though it referred to God's creation of the Word as his agent in creating the world (*Demonstration of the Apostolic Preaching* 43). Proverbs 8:22ff. had already interpreted the verse to mean "by his first fruits God created the heavens and the earth" and had identified God's "first fruits" with Wisdom, "the first of his acts of old." It was a simple step for Christians to identify Christ with God's Wisdom and to define him as God's agent in creation and revelation. Irenaeus' use of this tradition is complicated by the fact that he identifies the Holy Spirit with God's Wisdom, and so speaks of two hands of God, his Word and Wisdom, who were "always present" with him and "by whom and in whom, freely and spontaneously, He made all things" (*Against Heresies* 4.20.1). Nonetheless, Irenaeus' tendency is to focus upon the Word of God. In the passage to which reference has just been made Irenaeus goes on to argue that, while God is unknown on account of his greatness, "as regards His love, He is always known through Him by whose means He ordained all things" (*Against Heresies* 4.20.4). This is, of course, the Word of God, who is not only God's agent in creation but who also gave the prophets their gift of announcing his "advent according to the flesh." Christ is not confined, then, to the incarnation, but, as the Word of God, is active throughout the whole history of creation. In his polemic with the Gnostics this understanding of the Savior identifies the agent of salvation with the agent of creation and of the dispensations of the Hebrew Scriptures. And quite apart from the polemic, it demands that we set the story of the incarnate Word within the larger story of all God's dispensations beginning with creation itself. Defining the Savior as God integrates redemption with creation and with the sacred history of Israel.

The Son of God, then, "administering all things for the Father," reveals the Father in the created order, in the Hebrew Scriptures, and in the incarnation (*Against Heresies* 4.6.6–7). In revealing the Father, he gives human beings that vision of God which is their life (*Against Heresies* 4.20.7). What Irenaeus means is that the perfect vision of God renders the body incorruptible; the mind is so empowered by its vision of God that it exercises the kind of control over the body that not only equates with the life of virtue but also effects the incorruption of the resurrection from the dead. The end of the process, of course, is reserved for the age to come; but the vision of God begins in the present. Indeed, the incarnation, far from introducing the revelation of God for the first time, brings to focus God's self-disclosure in creation and in the Hebrew Scriptures. Thus, the history of the human race is one of the progressive revelation of God, a revelation that drives toward the final redemption of incorruption in the new age. Irenaeus finds the revelation of God in the Hebrew Scriptures and argues that "the writings of Moses are the words of Christ" (*Against Heresies* 4.2.3). His proof texts are John 5:46–47 and Luke 16:31, where Christ is made to equate believing Moses with believing himself. Christ's revelation of the Father in the Hebrew Scriptures takes place by stages. There are four covenants, under Adam, under Noah, under Moses, and the fourth "which renovates man, and sums up all things in itself by means of the Gospel, raising and bearing men upon its wings into the heavenly country" (*Against Heresies* 3.11.8). These dispensations, or economies, together with other economies of God in, say, the life of Abraham and the prophets, are "fitted for the times" at which they were given (*Against Heresies* 3.12.11). All the economies of God are administered by his Word, and they find their focus and summation in *the* economy of the incarnation.

Irenaeus' understanding of the economies of God is best explained by his use of the metaphor of education. The Word's revelation of the Father is really a teaching and a moral training that is designed to assist humanity's growth and persuade human beings to the perfection that is their destiny in God's purpose. For this reason, Irenaeus insists upon human freedom and upon human obedience to God's teaching as a free response to God's moral persuasion. "For there is no coercion with God, but a good will [toward us] is present with Him continually" (*Against Heresies* 4.37). We find no technical exposition of the relationship between providence and human freedom, but Irenaeus belongs with the other church fathers before Augustine in regarding the two activities as simultaneously operative. And the metaphor of education supplies a commonsense way of insisting upon both, since teaching and learning go together. Regarding human history as an education correlates with another metaphor central to Irenaeus' thought. He understands the history of humanity on the analogy of the development of an individual human being as a growth from the innocence of childhood to adult maturity. God did not create Adam perfect, because created things inevitably fall short of perfection and must grow from infancy to maturity. The creation of humanity is followed by growth, strengthening, abounding, recovering, and finally the glorification of the perfect vision of God that renders humanity incorruptible (*Against Heresies* 4.38).

If the history of humanity is a growth that is an education for the moral, spiritual, and physical perfection of human destiny, then even the fall of Adam and Eve needs to be seen as part of the process that leads from infancy and innocence to mature perfection. From the point of view of Adam and Eve, the Fall is a childish mistake. To be sure, it carried with it the disastrous result that humanity was bound over to Satan and the power of death. And it was a sin that God was obliged to punish. But Adam and Eve scarcely knew what they were doing, and the moment they had sinned they repented and sought to punish themselves by covering themselves with harsh fig leaves. God, however, compassionately removed the fig leaves and clothed them with soft coats of skin (*Against Heresies* 3.23.5, using Gen. 3:7 and 3:21). The implication of Irenaeus' interpretation of Genesis 3 is that the Fall was a necessary stage in human education and growth. Learning is a trial and error affair, and it often comes through suffering. Indeed, the Greek word for education also means punishment, and God's punishment of Adam and Eve is his way of educating them. Only by passing through the stage of knowing good and evil could humanity grow toward the perfect doing of the good. Irenaeus' view of the broader Christian story is not one of a paradise lost in Adam and regained in Christ. Instead, it is a story of the growth from innocence to experience. Moreover, the education begun in Adam continues in the age to come and is related to the understanding of Scripture. If there are some things even in creation that are known only to God, why should we complain that, though we are able by God's grace to explain some things in Scripture, "we must leave others in the hands of God, and that not only in the present world, but also in that which is to come, so that God should for ever teach, and man should for ever learn the things taught him by God?" (*Against Heresies* 2.28.3). And the teacher that God uses throughout human history is the Word, the preexistent Son of God, who dispenses God's economies and, finally, sums them all up by the economy of the incarnation.

Christ's Headship

To speak of Christ as the Word of God integrates redemption with creation and with the Hebrew Scriptures, but it leaves open the question of how the incarnation is to be related to the other economies of God through the Word. Irenaeus' solution to this problem depends upon developing what we should call the redeemer myth into his doctrine of the headship of Christ by which he sums up the previous economies, or dispensations, of God. Irenaeus expresses his view by attacking those who are ignorant that God's

> only-begotten Word, who is always present with the human race, united to and mingled with His own creation, according to the Father's pleasure, and who became flesh, is Himself Jesus Christ our Lord, who did also suffer for us, and rose again on our behalf, and who will come again. . . . There is therefore, as I have pointed out, one God the Father, and one Christ Jesus, who came by means of the whole dispensational arrangements [connected with Him], and gathered together all things in Himself. But in every respect, too, He is man, the formation of God; and thus He took up man into Himself, the invisible becoming visible, the incomprehensible being made comprehensible, the impassible becoming capable of suffering, and the Word being

made man, thus summing up all things in Himself: so that as in super-celestial, spiritual, and invisible things, the Word of God is supreme, so also in things visible and corporeal He might possess the suprem-acy, and, taking to Himself the pre-eminence, as well as constituting Himself Head of the Church, He might draw all things to Himself at the proper time. (*Against Heresies* 3.16.6)

The constant presence of the Word to the human race is contrasted with his union with humanity in the Word made flesh, and the previous dispensations are contrasted with *the* economy that "gath-ers together" and "sums up" all things in himself. In this way all the economies of God find their union and their consummation in the incarnation.

The term that Irenaeus employs, as well as some of his ideas, is borrowed from Eph. 1:9–10: "For he has made known to us in all wisdom and insight the mystery of his will, according to his purpose which he set forth in Christ as a plan for the fulness of time, to unite (*anakephalaiōsasthai*) all things in him, things in heaven and things on earth." The word translated "unite" can as easily be translated "head up," and Ephesians clearly refers to Christ's universal head-ship by which all things are bound together. In the passage from Irenaeus just cited, the Latin uses the term *recapitulare,* the equiva-lent of the Greek *anakephalaiōsasthai,* three times; and the Latin word is rendered by the English phrases "gathered together," "took up," and "summing up." "Head up" or "sum up" translates the word in Irenaeus' understanding of it better than "recapitulate" for the simple reason that Irenaeus is not thinking of Christ's unifying work as a restoration of some original unity. The basic framework of his theology depends upon arguing that the previous dispensations of God are for the first time consummated by being summed and headed up by the incarnate Lord. To use an anachronistic analogy, we may think of the keystone of a medieval cathedral. When placed in its position in the vaulting, the keystone bears the architectural stresses of the cathedral, unifying them and holding the building together. So the creative activity of God finds its consummation in the incarnation, which for the first time binds the created order together in harmony. This heading up, accomplished in principle by the incarnate Lord, will be accomplished in fact in the new age (*Against Heresies* 1.10.1, where Eph. 1:10 is cited).

Irenaeus' understanding of Christ's headship takes its point of departure from Ephesians but goes beyond the Pauline theology of that letter. For Ephesians, the headship of Christ is described largely in cosmological terms, as the spatial metaphors of the tem-ple and the body demonstrate. Christ heads up the whole created order, because he binds together heaven and earth. Irenaeus retains this cosmological interpretation and also employs another theme found in Ephesians, the union of Jews and Gentiles in a new people of God under Christ's headship. As the chief cornerstone, Christ "has gathered into one, and united those who were far off and those who were near; that is, the circumcision and the uncircumcision, enlarging Japhet, and placing him in the dwelling of Shem" (*Against Heresies* 3.5.3, citing Eph. 2:17 and Gen. 9:27). But Irenaeus presses beyond the timeless idea of Ephesians and thinks of Christ's headship in what may be called historical terms. That is, Christ heads up the earlier dispensation of God. That is why, as "Head of the Church" he is constituted as the one who will draw all things to himself "at the proper time" (*Against Heresies* 3.16.6). In one sense, Irenaeus' dominant metaphors of growth and education have transformed the theme from Ephesians. But, in another sense, a second Pauline theme has enabled him to rework the idea. The Adam typology of Romans 5 and 1 Corinthians 15 suggests to Irenaeus that Christ heads and sums up the development of the human race begun in Adam.

At first it looks as though Irenaeus' use of the Adam typology undermines the point of view we have been describing because it presents Christ in contrast to Adam, undoing what was done in Adam. And because "heading up" is more often than not connected with the Adam typology, Irenaeus' doctrine has often been understood as "recapitulation" in the sense of a restoration of paradise lost. It is easy enough to see how this interpretation gained currency. For Irenaeus, following Rom. 5:12ff., Christ's obedience answers to and undoes Adam's disobedience and its effect; life replaces death (*Against Heresies* 3.18.2, 7; 3.21.10; 5.16.3). Similarly, Eve's disobedience is countered by Mary's obedience (3.22.4; *Demonstration of the Apostolic Preaching* 33). The tree of the cross undoes what happened by the tree with the forbidden fruit (*Against Heresies* 5.17.3; *Demonstration of the Apostolic Preaching* 34). And Christ's conquest of Satan in his temptation undoes Adam's defeat by Satan (*Against Heresies* 5.21). All these themes present the typology as one of reversal. Sometimes, however, Adam and Christ correspond with each other. As Adam was born of virgin soil, so Christ was born of the Virgin (*Against Heresies* 3.18.7; 3.21.10; *Demonstration of the Apostolic Preaching* 32). Irenaeus insists that this was to preserve "the analogy." In other words, the typological relationship of Adam and Christ is a relationship meant to be understood in the larger framework of Irenaeus' thought. To be sure, Christ does reverse the Fall, bringing life through obedience to death instead of death through disobedience. But this reversal is only part of the picture, since it is what enables the new Adam to complete God's intent in creating Adam.

That this is how we should interpret Irenaeus is indicated in several ways. First, we must remember that the new Adam is not merely a human being but is the Son of God made Son of Man. And so the new humanity marks an advance over the old because it is fully united with God. Moreover, the seventy-two generations that Luke records between Christ and Adam show that Christ is "He who has summed up in Himself all nations dispersed from Adam downwards, and all languages and generations of men, together with Adam himself." Alluding to 1 Cor. 15:45ff., Irenaeus goes on to say that Adam was "of an animal nature . . . that he might be saved by the spiritual One" (*Against Heresies* 3.22.3). Finally, Irenaeus argues that while it was "said that man was created after the image of God," the image was not actually "shown," with the result that Adam easily lost "the similitude." Christ, then, "both showed forth the image truly, since He became Himself what was His image; and He re-established the similitude after a sure manner, by assimilating man to the invisible Father through means of the visible Word" (*Against Heresies* 5.16.2). The movement from Adam to Christ is one from an intended image and an easily lost likeness to the true and stable image and likeness of God.

The Framework and the Hebrew Scriptures

By his doctrine of Christ's headship, Irenaeus has succeeded not only in defining his Savior but also in clarifying the church's Rule of faith. The story of Christ's incarnation is that of his virgin birth, his life of obedience, his death, resurrection, and ascension, and his coming at the end of the age. And this story is understood as the final and focal economy of God through his Word and so is set within the framework of all the divine economies in creation and the Hebrew Scriptures before the incarnation. This Rule of faith is in one sense built out of specific passages in Scripture and out of the broader patterns of the redeemer myth, the doctrine of Christ's headship found in Ephesians, and the Pauline Adam typology. It purports to make explicit what is implicit in Scripture, and it enables Irenaeus to make sense of the earlier Christian transformation of the Hebrew Scriptures. From a general point of view, it will be seen, the Hebrew Scriptures include the economies of God that are designed to prepare humanity for the incarnation. Thus, the Hebrew Scriptures point beyond themselves to their fulfillment in Christ but at the same time represent a necessary stage of growth and an education that must take place before the final economy of the incarnation. Thus, Irenaeus not only shows how the Hebrew Scriptures are transcended when fulfilled by the New Testament, he also supplies a way of insisting upon the meaning of the Hebrew Scriptures in God's providence. We need to see in somewhat more detail how this is so.

Book 4 of *Against Heresies* focuses upon the relationship of the Hebrew Scriptures and the New Testament and a refutation of their opposition to each other by the Gnostics and Marcion. Irenaeus must show how the Hebrew Scriptures point beyond themselves and yet have value in their own right, and he does this by relating them to God's providence. He thinks of the Hebrew Scriptures under three aspects. "They [the Jews] had therefore a law, a course of discipline, and a prophecy of future things" (*Against Heresies* 4.15.1). By "law" he means the "natural" law embodied primarily in the Decalogue and remaining in force for the Christian. By "course of discipline" he means the Mosaic law and the Jewish practices required by it. And by "prophecy" he includes the typological dimension of the Hebrew Scriptures. We should remember that Christians before Irenaeus had tried to see the Hebrew Scriptures in their different aspects. Irenaeus certainly depends upon views like those of Justin and, in a modified way, of Ptolemey. And his definition of the different aspects of the Hebrew Scriptures is not at first sight very remarkable. What is striking, however, is that he insists upon regarding all three dimensions as dispensed by God for the sake of Israel, as well as in the interest of the Christian dispensation.

As a "prophecy of future things" the Hebrew Scriptures predict and foreshadow Christ. Irenaeus follows the path described in the last chapter. Chapters 42–85 of the *Demonstration of the Apostolic Preaching*, for example, include most of the prophecies and types that may be found in Justin's *Dialogue with Trypho*. There is no need to repeat what we have already seen there. But Irenaeus is not content to stop with this reference of the Hebrew Scriptures beyond themselves to Christ. The prophets also functioned within the ancient people of God by "accustoming man to bear His Spirit [within him], and to hold communion with God" (*Against Heresies* 4.14.2). In other words, the prophets were not only those who predicted Christ and God's plan of salvation, they were also teachers who, like the patriarchs, "prepared a people beforehand." Similarly, the typological aspect of the Hebrew Scriptures was designed for instruction as well as prediction. When Moses constructed the tabernacle "after the pattern . . . shown . . . on the mountain" (Ex. 25:40), he was not only foreshadowing Christ but also instructing the people, "calling them to the things of primary importance by means of those which were secondary; that is, to things that are real, by means of those that are typical; and by things temporal, to eternal; and by the carnal to the spiritual; and by the earthly to the heavenly" (*Against Heresies* 4.14.3). The themes of education and growth inform Irenaeus' understanding of the Hebrew Scriptures as a "prophecy of future things" and give prophecy and type a use and purpose within the people of God before Christ. They are being educated for the decisive economy of the incarnation.

A similar pattern informs Irenaeus' assessment of the natural law included in the Hebrew Scriptures, specifically the Decalogue. One might suppose him to be content with simply underlining the persistence of the natural law. Instead, he treats the natural law as the law of liberty which Christ's teaching fulfills and extends. The prohibition of adultery now includes that of lust, of murder, that of anger. Swearing is totally forbidden, and the new righteousness exceeds that of the scribes and the Pharisees by deepening it (*Against Heresies* 4.13.1, citing Matt. 5). The Sermon on the Mount, then, not only repeats the teaching of the natural law but also uncovers its deeper meaning and so intensifies the righteous demand of God. In this way Christ shows how the law is appropriate for sons rather than slaves (*Against Heresies* 4.16.5).

The last aspect of the Hebrew Scriptures is the one most difficult to fit into Irenaeus' pattern. The "course of discipline" represented by the Jewish practices taught by the Mosaic law was, of course, abolished by Christ. Circumcision, Sabbaths, food laws, and sacrifices have all come to an end. True, their typological meaning enables them to be treated as a spiritual foreshadowing of Christ. But Irenaeus must agree that, taken literally, they have no value; and he even agrees with the earlier tradition by saying that they were given to the people by Moses "on account of their hardness [of heart], and because of their unwillingness to be obedient" (*Against Heresies* 4.15.2, where Matt. 19:7–8 is used as a proof text). Moreover, Irenaeus understands the Mosaic legislation as a penalty for the sin of the golden calf:

> But when they turned themselves to make a calf, and had gone back in their minds to Egypt, desiring to be slaves instead of free men, they were placed for the future in a state of servitude suited to their wish, —[a slavery] which did not indeed cut them off from God, but subjected them to the yoke of bondage. (*Against Heresies* 4.15.1)

Had Irenaeus gone no farther than this, we should be left with the puzzle of how the Hebrew Scriptures can be affirmed in speaking of Christ and denied in giving the Jews their law. Moreover, we should be unable to see beyond the utter rejection of the Jews. Irenaeus, however, uses the notion of the "course of discipline" as a punishment to go beyond his predecessors. The laws of bondage given by Moses were "suited for their instruction or for their punishment" (*Against Heresies* 4.16.5). Whether or not the Latin text simply gives two translations of the one Greek word *paideia*, it is clear that Irenaeus thinks of God's punishment as educative. As he says elsewhere in more general terms, God through the Mosaic law was "teaching the headstrong" to follow him (*Against Heresies* 4.14.2). The principle to which Irenaeus appeals is that the law of bondage "used to instruct the soul by means of those corporeal objects which were of an external nature, drawing it, as by a bond, to obey its commandments, that man might learn to serve God" (*Against Heresies* 4.13.2).

In these ways, then, Irenaeus integrates the three aspects of the Hebrew Scriptures with the larger framework of his thought. By prophecy and type, by the natural law, and by the Mosaic law which was designed to train servants for the free obedience that awaited them, God was instructing Israel. The Hebrew Scriptures turn out to be a necessary preparation for the New Testament. And we should not misrepresent Irenaeus if we were to argue that his view of the Fall correlates with his view of Israel's hardness of heart. Just as the Fall was an inevitable, if not necessary, stage through which humanity had to pass on its way to perfection, so the sin of the golden calf and its punishment in the land of bondage was a stage along the way for the people of God. Irenaeus has managed to circumvent the Marcionite tendency of the early anti-Jewish Christian polemic by treating the history of Israel as part of the total story of humanity's growth toward perfection. And this enables him to place the different Christian transformations of the Hebrew Scriptures in relation to one another within a view of God's providential dispensations which drive toward the economy establishing Christ's headship.

The Framework of Interpretation and Scripture

Implicit in the argument has been the contention that Irenaeus at every step of the way draws upon Scripture in articulating the framework by which he believes it must be interpreted. The Gnostics are "evil interpreters of the good word of revelation" (*Against Heresies*

1., preface), because they fail to observe the "order" of Scripture. They use the obscure passages to explain the clear ones and so compound confusion (*Against Heresies* 2.10.1). It is as though they had composed a false Homeric narrative by piecing together Homeric verses out of their proper place in the poems. The student of Homer will recognize the verses and by restoring them to their proper position will destroy the false narrative. Similarly, the Christian will recognize "the names, the expressions, and the parables taken from the Scriptures" in the Gnostic teaching. And the Rule of faith will enable him to restore these elements to their rightful place and fit them to the body of truth (*Against Heresies* 1.9.4). Thus, the order implicit in Scripture is to be identified with the Rule of faith. From one point of view, it is a kind of canon within the canon that can be deduced by the careful reader who uses the plain passages to interpret the obscure ones (*Against Heresies* 2.28.3). On the other hand, Christ is the treasure hidden in the Scriptures. He is their true order, but is "pointed out by means of types and parables." Only when the predicted Christ appeared did the prophecies of the Hebrew Scriptures have "a clear and certain exposition." Belief in Christ alone reveals the hidden treasure "brought to light by the cross of Christ" (*Against Heresies* 4.26.1). And what is true of one part of Scripture may be presumed true of all. The proper order of the Rule of faith, though implicit in Scripture, is made explicit only by revelation.

Enough has been said to explain how the Rule of faith functions at a general level as a framework for interpreting the Christian Bible. At the particular level much could be said about detailed conclusions that Irenaeus draws in interpreting Scripture. But there is no mystery involved, no recondite method, not even any close attention to lexical problems. It is true that Irenaeus is attentive to details of the text. For example, he exploits Paul's tendency to use dangling phrases to read 2 Cor. 4:4 as though it said "God has blinded the minds of the unbelievers of this world" rather than "the God of this world has blinded the minds of the unbelievers" (*Against Heresies* 3.7). And he uses the present tense in Matt. 11:27 ("No one *knows* the Father except the Son and any one to whom the Son *chooses* to reveal him") to argue that the Son always reveals the Father, against the Gnostics, who claim that the Son's revelation of the Father was the novel revelation of an unknown God (*Against Heresies* 4.6). More important than his lexical observation, however, is the conviction that comes to him from the Rule of faith that the Word always reveals God.

We may conclude that, though Irenaeus has solved the problem of how to interpret the Christian Bible by providing the Rule of faith as a principle generally applicable to Scripture, a great many difficulties remain at a particular level. The church after Irenaeus accepts his basic platform and remains committed to what we should call theological exegesis by regarding the church's faith as the key to unlock the meaning of Scripture. But debates persist at several levels. First, there is the ambiguity of Irenaeus' method. His larger framework would seem to imply that we should understand Scripture in a temporal way, moving from anticipation to fulfillment to consummation. But Irenaeus tends to use "type" to refer to an earthly representation of a heavenly reality, and much of his exegesis seems to be what ought to be called allegory. It is this ambiguity that helps explain the rivalry (to be discussed in the next chapter) between Alexandrian allegorists and Antiochene typologists. Second, Irenaeus' framework leaves two problems more or less unresolved. The Trinitarian and the Christological issues that occupy the next two centuries of the church's life are struggles to make more precise Irenaeus' definition of the Savior, and they have a decided impact upon the interpretation of Scripture. Third, Irenaeus says little about the meaning of scriptural interpretation for the Christian life. Moral and ascetical uses of Scripture, however, are to be found in the early church. Finally, we may raise the question whether Christians ever engaged in the study of Scripture for its own sake and with an eye to using the difficulties in the text as a point of departure for interpretation. These questions will occupy our attention in the final chapter.

4

Applying the Framework

When we conclude that for the early church the Rule of faith supplied the basic hermeneutical principle and framework for interpreting Scripture, we are really saying that for the church fathers the true meaning of Scripture was a theological one. At first this looks like a point of view standing in absolute contrast with a modern historical-critical one that would understand interpretation as describing the original meaning of the text in its historical context. And it is tempting to contrast late antique with modern exegesis by regarding the first as subjective and eisegetical and the second as objective and exegetical in the proper sense. There is, of course, some truth in putting the issue this way, but doing so blocks a correct understanding of patristic exegesis by assuming that a perspective largely the product of the nineteenth-century Enlightenment is alone defensible. Must we grant that the historical meaning of the text is the true one? Must we suppose that there are scientific methods capable of unearthing the historical meaning of the texts? Even in a modern setting these assumptions are problematic, since they imply that the church's use of Scripture in preaching and teaching and in the formulation of doctrine is not interpretation at all but at best a kind of allegorization of the Bible. If, however, we take seriously the use made of Scripture in the contemporary church, we can begin to see that our use of the text is not so radically different from that of the fathers as might at first appear. However much the ancient church supposed the true meaning of Scripture to be theological, it by no means wished to deny the historical setting of the texts; nor did it fail to see most of the problems that have become the stock-in-trade of modern critical study of Scripture.

The point of saying this is to argue that we cannot impose our modern sensibilities upon the difficulties found by the ancient church in applying the general theological framework of interpretation to the details of Scripture. If there was a debate over the proper method of interpreting the Bible, it was not because the fathers presumed that a correct and scientific method could be found. And if it was unclear what Scripture taught theologically, morally, and spiritually, it was not because moving from what the text *meant* historically to what it *means* theologically was a difficulty but because there was disagreement about detailed points of theology, ethics, and spirituality. Finally, our modern assumption that interpretation for the sake of interpretation is objective, while interpretation for the sake of the church's message is subjective, could not be farther from the point of view of the ancient church. To say that interpretation must always in principle conform to the faith of the church by no means prevents Christians in late antiquity from being concerned with interpreting Scripture quite apart from proving Christian beliefs and practices. The difficulties in applying the framework of interpretation that we shall consider in this chapter are not difficulties because the patristic perspective is uncritical and wrongheaded, but are issues that inevitably must be faced in the detailed application of principles. To use a simple analogy, the difficulties encountered by the Supreme Court in applying the Constitution of the United States have to do with the question of what principles mean in practice and not with moving from a historical reading of the Constitution to an allegorical one.

The Question of Method

Sooner or later most discussions of patristic exegesis focus upon the debate between allegorism and typology and upon the views of Origen (d. 254) and Theodore of Mopsuestia (d. 428).[1] Up to a point, this approach is convincing. We have already seen that Irenaeus is highly ambiguous with respect to his method of interpretation. His theology requires that Scripture be understood in reference to the story of human progress from creation to redemption, and we should suppose that his method would be typological, understanding typology as the relationship of events to one another in time. But Irenaeus tends to define typology as the relationship between earthly and heavenly realities, a point of view characteristic of what would normally be called allegory. And he can give allegorical interpretations of, for example, the parables of Jesus. It is possible to argue, then, that Origen (in Alexandria) and Theodore (in Antioch) resolve the sort of confusion found in Irenaeus' work by consciously elaborating two methods opposed to each other. As we shall see, this assessment is correct, but it does not go far enough.

Whatever else we say, it is certainly true that Origen is the first, if not the only one, of the fathers to argue in detail for a method by which to interpret Scripture. His genius was to integrate the wide variety of approaches to sacred texts with which he was acquainted into a coherent methodological theory. As a Christian, Origen was familiar with Christian typology and the proof from prophecy, as well as the allegorical interpretations of early Christian writers. He knew the exegetical work of Gnostic Christians and treated it with respect; his *Commentary on John* is in part a running debate and discussion with that of Heracleon, a Valentinian who wrote the earliest commentary on the New Testament we know of. Origen's education gave him a thorough knowledge of pagan rhetoric and of the Stoic allegorization of Homer and Hesiod. He was acquainted with Philo and the Hellenistic Judaism of Alexandria. And, finally, he went to school under the Jewish rabbis, always citing their opinions with respect and often with approval. He employed the critical tools of his day in establishing the text of the Septuagint. His work, the *Hexapla*, arranged the Hebrew text of the Scriptures, its transliteration, and available Greek translations in parallel columns so that variant readings could be noted and assessed with diacritical marks. A scholar, Origen was also a philosopher and can claim to be a founder of Christian Neoplatonism.

It was as a churchman, however, that Origen used his great gifts and wide knowledge to interpret Scripture for the church. His method draws together the various approaches noted above by making a fundamental distinction between the letter and the spirit, that is, the obvious narrative meaning of the text and its more mysterious spiritual meaning. Employing the conventions of Greek literary criticism, Origen argues that the difficulties and impossibilities that represent stumbling blocks in the biblical narrative demonstrate that a spiritual meaning is woven into Scripture by the Holy Spirit who inspired its authors (*On First Principles* 4.2–3).[2] For the most part, the narrative and the spiritual meanings go hand in hand, and most passages in Scripture admit of both understandings. Certain passages, however, have no narrative meaning—for example, anthropomorphic expressions referring to God. We can immediately see that Origen's fundamental distinction correlates with the Platonic distinction between the perceptible order of sense appearances and the intelligible order of immutable reality and that the biblical distinction between flesh and spirit, the earthly and the heavenly, supplies a warrant for it.[3] The interpretation of Scripture, then, moves from the letter of the narrative meaning to the spirit of the allegorical meaning mysteriously embodied in the text, just as the Christian life moves from the "milk" of the elementary teaching of Christ crucified to the "solid food" of the deeper meaning of that teaching.[4] Indeed, Origen virtually identifies the spiritual life with the interpretation of Scripture, since to begin to penetrate the deeper meaning of the sacred text is to participate so far as possible in the ultimate realities that mark the Christian's destiny. Origen can sometimes distinguish aspects of the spiritual or allegorical meaning from one another. If the "body" of Scripture is the narrative meaning, its "soul" and "spirit" are the moral and spiritual dimensions of the allegorical meaning (*On First Principles* 4.2.4). Alternatively, in his *Commentary on Song of Songs*, Origen distinguishes the allegorical meaning that attaches to the soul's progress from that which refers to Christ and the church. He sets the stage for more complicated theories about the senses of Scripture, but the only distinction that really matters for him is the one between the letter and the spirit.[5]

We might suppose that Origen's method eliminates all possibility of understanding Scripture in terms of past, present, and future and so rejects the traditional Christian use of the proof from prophecy and typology. He does not, however, draw this logic for the simple reason that his theological perspective repudiates a strict pattern of emanation and return and distinguishes the End from the Beginning that it resembles. In the Beginning the rational beings (preexistent souls that become angels, humans, and demons when they fall) are incorporeal and equal. But at the End, when the perfection of a full contemplation of God through his Word is restored and made stable, the rational beings have bodies and are unequal. Thus, Origen's theology retains the teleological character of the Christian story and leaves room for the typological relationship of old to new. For example, the pattern of the heavenly tabernacle revealed to Moses on the mount (Ex. 25:40) corresponds to earthly tabernacles —the one in the wilderness, the Temple in Jerusalem, and the church. But we must also see that the "shadow" of the Temple points forward typologically to the "image" of the church; and that "image" in turn is a type of the true tabernacle that signifies the ultimate destiny of the rational beings.[6] The law is a shadow of future things as well as of heavenly ones (Heb. 10:1; 8:5). The temporal order and, consequently, typology and the fulfillment of prophecy find their place in the larger Platonizing framework of Origen's thought and so in his allegorism. We may draw the conclusion that not only is Origen's allegorical method qualified in this way but also that his method, however much it draws upon the science of his day, is finally nothing but a corollary of his theological vision.

Origen's approach to Scripture provoked opposition even in his own lifetime, and roughly three quarters of a century after his death we find the first surviving repudiation of Origen's interpretation of Scripture in Antioch with Eustace's treatise *On the Witch of Endor* (ca. 320).[7] Somewhat later the Antiochenes Diodore of Tarsus (d. ca. 390) and Theodore of Mopsuestia (d. 428) wrote treatises, now lost, against the allegorical method, with Origen as their chief opponent. To some degree the Antiochene opposition to Origen and his followers was the rejection of a method. We can understand their hostility by Theodore's comments on Gal. 4:24, which he refuses to acknowledge as a warrant for allegorism.[8] His argument is that Paul does not abolish the narrative meaning (*historia*) but insists upon the facts of Abraham's story. The Antiochenes are worried that Origen's allegorism abolishes the significance of the events in time recorded in Scripture, and they present their typological method as an alternative to allegorism. We need to take seriously this opposition of one method to the other, but it does not tell the whole story. For example, Eustace attacks Origen's interpretation of the Witch of Endor story (1 Sam. 28) not because it is allegorical but because Origen takes the narrative too literally. To be sure, he complains that Origen allegorizes everywhere else; but we get the decided impression that Eustace is more concerned with Origen's conclusions than with his method. The same impression comes across in what evidence may be found in the writings of the other Antiochenes. And, as we shall see, Theodore's typological method is just as much a corollary of his theology as Origen's allegorical method is of his.

The fundamental axiom of Theodore's theology is that God has divided the whole creation and human history into two successive ages (*Commentary on Genesis, Patrologia Graeca [PG]* 66.633–34; *Commentary on John*, ed. Vosté, p. 55). For this reason, Scripture always takes seriously what we should call the historical context of its statements and narratives. The Holy Spirit inspired the writers of Scripture but did so in accordance with "contemporary need" (*Commentary on Nahum, PG* 66.401–404). Several implications follow from this basic perception. First, the Hebrew Scriptures know nothing of the Trinity, and so Theodore rejects the traditional use of texts from the Hebrew Scriptures as warrants for the three persons of the Godhead. Second, even those passages which have to do with the Christian dispensation typologically have a meaning quite apart from this reference. For example, when Moses lifts up his arms at the battle with Amalek, the obvious significance of the text has to do with Israel's victory. Finally, Theodore severely limits the proof from prophecy. In his view, David as a prophet predicts in the psalms the whole of Israel's future, but only four of the psalms (Ps. 2; 8; 45; and 110) predict Christ. Thus, psalms traditionally thought to be prophetic of Christ (e.g., Ps. 22; 69) merely used words appropriate to Christ's story. In turn, the prophets (Isaiah, Jeremiah, Ezekiel, Daniel, and the twelve minor prophets) never predict Christ, save that in Malachi, the last of the prophets, we find the revival of David's prediction of Christ. However congenial these views of the Hebrew Scriptures may be to a modern historical-critical perspective, we cannot too strongly emphasize the fact that they cut across opinions almost universally held in the ancient church. In some ways the conclusions of Theodore's method were as radical as those of Origen. Origen's view runs the risk of dissolving the Hebrew Scriptures; indeed, he says that when rightly understood, the whole of Scripture is transformed into the gospel (*Commentary on John* 1.1–15). Theodore, on the other hand, loosens the connections between the Hebrew Scriptures and the New Testament.

At the same time, Theodore's understanding of "type" preserves the possibility of a Christian reading of the Hebrew Scriptures and gives him a way of interpreting the New Testament. The old dispensation not only fulfilled a "contemporary need" but also established a type of the new one, "since it has a certain resemblance (*mimesis*) to it" and supplies "indications" (*menysis*) of it (*Commentary on Jonah*, PG 66.317ff.). For this reason, passages in the Hebrew Scriptures that are denied a prophetic meaning can nonetheless be given a typological one. For example, Zech. 9:9 predicts Zerubbabel ("Lo, your king comes to you"), but it can also be understood to indicate typologically the Palm Sunday story of the Gospels. It is in this sense that the law "possesses a shadow of all the things pertaining to the Lord Christ" (*Commentary on Zechariah*, PG 66.557; cf. Heb. 10:1). Typology enables an interpretation of the Hebrew Scriptures, but it also supplies a perspective for understanding the New Testament. Of course, much of the New Testament can be understood strictly in terms of the narrative meaning (*historia*), since that narrative in general fulfills the types of the Hebrew Scriptures. But many passages in the New Testament point toward the consummation of that fulfillment in the age to come. Theodore's understanding of the church and its sacraments is typological, because in it and them we "perform in this world the symbols and signs of the future things"

(Woodbrooke Studies, Vol. 6, p. 82). The pattern that Theodore establishes argues for the progression from promise to fulfillment to consummation, or, to put it metaphorically, from shadow to image to reality. It is fair to say that this double typology is a method of exegesis, but it is equally obvious that the method is no more than a middle term between Theodore's basic theological assumptions and the interpretation of the biblical text.

One example of the contrast between Origen's and Theodore's exegesis may be given to support the assessment being given. Both wrote commentaries on John's Gospel and were therefore obliged to deal with the obvious discrepancies between John and the Synoptic Gospels.[9] For Origen, the contradictions cannot always be resolved at the level of the narrative meaning. While he appears to argue that the interpreter must begin by seeking such a resolution and so establishing the *historia,* he is willing to suggest that there are passages without a proper narrative meaning. In any case, what matters is the spiritual or allegorical meaning of the text; and this is why John's Gospel is the "spiritual" Gospel. In contrast, Theodore argues that John is more concerned that the other Evangelists to preserve the chronological framework of Jesus' ministry, as the precision of his time references suggests (e.g., John 1:29, 35, 43; 2:1). Consequently, the beginnings of Jesus' ministry according to the Synoptics must be placed after the first two chapters of John. John's description of the cleansing of the Temple at the beginning of Jesus' ministry (John 2:13ff.) is to be explained either by the fact that another such incident took place at the end of Jesus' ministry, as the Synoptic Gospels record, or by the fact that the Synoptic writers were unconcerned with the true chronology. For Theodore, it is crucial to establish the narrative meaning, and symbolic interpretations may be given only when the text itself is metaphorical or when a typological interpretation is required.

The sharp contrast of methods (or, perhaps better, of the results of the methods) that we find in Origen and Theodore cannot so easily be found in other writers. To be sure, Theodoret, Chrysostom, and Nestorius deserve the label Antiochene, while Cyril is obviously an Alexandrian. But none of these figures seem primarily concerned with the issue of method. The debate between Cyril and the Antiochenes can scarcely be explained by a difference of exegetical method. And to cite another example, Jerome's repudiation of allegorism is not total and represents more a rejection of Origenist opinions than a change of exegetical method.[10] In general, the fathers continue to use both typology and allegorism without embracing the extreme positions we find in Origen and Theodore.

It is tempting to make an exception of Augustine, since it was the allegorical interpretation of the Hebrew Scriptures that enabled him to accept them in all their, to him, crudeness and since he delights in the etymologies and numerologies that were a part of the allegorical method. Without denying that exegetical method was an issue for the fathers, we may conclude that the more important question for them was the theological function of interpretation.

The Theological Meaning of Scripture

To argue that the deeper issue that divides Origen and Theodore, Alexandria and Antioch, is theological rather than methodological is by no means tantamount to saying that the fathers simply read their theology into the text. Indeed, if anything, their respect for the text exceeded ours. For them every detail of the inspired Scriptures was important, and theology remained an exegetical enterprise in the ancient church. One example will make the point. The first general council at Nicaea in 325 placed the word *homoousios* ("one in being") in its creed as a way of specifying the relationship of the Son to the Father so as to exclude the Arian belief that the Son was of a created essence different from that of the Father. The term did not find wide acceptance in the church, partly because of its theological implications and the history of its use by Monarchian heretics (unitarians, as it were). But the major objection to the term was that it was unscriptural. The faith of the church, at least in official formularies, ought to be expressed so far as possible in the biblical idiom. To say this does not mean that theologians were limited to that idiom. On the contrary, in their attempt to explain the meaning of Scripture and of the church's formulations, patristic theologians boldly and imaginatively used the philosophical *lingua franca* of their day. Theirs was the task of remythologization, and we find them constantly endeavoring to explain Scripture in the terms available to their society without ever confusing interpretation with the text interpreted.

If theology and exegesis are as closely united as we have suggested, it follows that to write the history of interpretation in the ancient church would be to describe the history of doctrine. The theological views of a given writer are in the long run his exegetical principles. And while all could agree in principle with Irenaeus that the Rule of faith (or the Nicene Creed) explained how Scripture was to be ordered, there were significant differences with respect to how the faith of the church was to be understood. In the earlier period (before 200) the debate was not merely about a valid theological understanding of the Bible but also about which books were canonical. For example, the Gnostics and the Montanists both appealed to texts in John's Gospel as warrants for their views. Some of their opponents sought to exclude not only the heretical beliefs but also the writings that supplied a basis for them. As late as the end of the second century in Rome there were those otherwise orthodox who rejected the authority of the Johannine literature. Nevertheless, for most of the patristic period debates centered upon the interpretation of the Christian Bible. Several examples of these debates will suffice to explain the way in which competing theological views stood at the heart of the ancient church's attempts to explain its sacred writings.

In order to place these examples in some sort of context, however, it is necessary to begin by making a few general observations about the history of doctrine in the first five centuries. The first point to make is that in broad terms the theological framework articulated by Irenaeus remains a constant throughout the period. Christian theology revolves around the Christian story that traces human progress from creation to the incarnation and to its consummation in the age to come. The story moves from the immaturity or the unstable perfection of Adam in paradise to the maturity or stable perfection of the resurrection life in the heavenly city. Though the story has suffered a sea change in Origen's treatment of it, even he reproduces its main lines. Granted this point, the next one to make is that theological controversies focus upon defining Christ, the hero of the story. Since for ancient Christianity, with the probable exception of Augustine, piety was Christocentric, it was important to define Christ as the object of Christian worship. The councils of Nicaea (325) and Constantinople (381) found a way of describing Christ as divine without abandoning an insistence upon monotheism. And the councils of Ephesus (431) and Chalcedon (451) produced a compromise formula that required any account of Christ to insist on his perfect divine nature, his perfect human nature, and their undivided and unconfused union. For our purpose we need only remember that theology revolves around defining Christ. Other theological themes such as the meaning of salvation, grace, freedom, faith, and human nature were subordinated to the Trinitarian and Christological discussions.

We may take the first example from the Monarchian controversy at the beginning of the third century. The Monarchians, as their name suggests, insisted that there could be but a single God and a single divine rule. This meant that they opposed the Word theology of the early church because it appeared to teach two gods. We know something of the Monarchian teachings that Noetus brought to Rome in the first quarter of the third century through Hippolytus' refutation of his opinions. Noetus' monotheism was largely based upon scriptural proof texts, including the obvious passages from the Hebrew Scriptures that appeared to teach the existence of a single God (e.g., Ex. 3:6; 20:3; Isa. 44:6). According to Noetus, the passages that spoke of God's Word must be regarded as merely employing a figure of speech, a way of speaking of one of the modes in which the one God appears. Noetus' most interesting proof text is John 10:30: "I and the Father are one." He supposed that the verse proves the identity of Father and Son and denies that the Word can be thought to be a distinct person. Hippolytus' refutation depends upon noting that the verb in the scriptural text is in the plural. "He did not say, 'I and the Father *am one*, but *are one*'" (*Ante-Nicene Fathers* [*ANF*] 5, p. 226). Thus, the true interpretation must be found in a Trinitarian view that insists simultaneously upon the unity of the Godhead and the distinction of the divine persons from one another. We need scarcely say that the problem of interpretation arises directly from the theological dispute. Moreover, we are dealing with little more than the appeal to a proof text, even though Hippolytus read the text the way a lawyer might read the small print in a contract.

The early stages of the Arian controversy will supply us with a second set of examples. The Arians held that Christ was the first of God's creatures, a sort of gigantic archangel. They found many proofs of their view in Scripture. Proverbs 8:22 ("The Lord created me as the beginning of his ways") in the Septuagint clearly defined Wisdom, identified with Christ, as a creature. Psalm 45, understood to refer to Christ, says (v. 7): "You love righteousness and hate wickedness. Therefore God, your God, has anointed you with the oil of gladness above your fellows." Again the implication that Christ is a creature seemed to the Arians self-evident. Hebrews 3:2 says that Christ was "faithful to him who *made* [RSV: appointed] him." In addition to texts that directly or indirectly defined Christ as a creature, the Arians had no difficulty finding texts that attributed change to Christ. Luke's references to Christ's growth (Luke 2:40, 52) implied his creaturely status; and all the references in the Gospels to Christ's hunger, thirst, weariness, suffering, and death were given the same reference. If Christ is described as capable of the changes that characterize human existence, his nature must be mutable and he cannot be divine.

The fragmentary character of what remains of the Arian writings prevents us from examining their interpretation of these and similar passages in detail. But we do possess lengthy interpretations of them by the orthodox fathers, who were obliged to refute the Arian readings. Athanasius in his treatise *Against the Arians* establishes one basic framework by which to reinterpret the texts in an orthodox sense. He argues that the interpreter must take account of "the moment, the person, and the subject" in examining any scriptural passages (*Against the Arians* 1.55). What he really means by this is that sometimes Scripture refers to the consubstantial and eternal Word of God quite apart from the incarnation, while sometimes it speaks of the Word incarnate. In other words, some attributes are to be predicated of the Word by nature; others, only in virtue of the economy. "Economic" attribution is real, but does not affect the nature of the Word. When the prince becomes a pauper, his filthy clothes are really his; but they do not alter his identity or nature as the prince. Similarly, when the Word of God became incarnate, he truly lived a human life, suffered, and died; but none of this affected his identity or nature as the eternal Word of God. Athanasius notes, as well, that scriptural statements about Christ that are qualified in some way usually refer to the incarnate Word and not to the Word in his divine nature (*Against the Arians* 2.60). For example, Prov. 8:22 explains the purpose of the "creation" of the Word by adding the phrase "as the beginning of his ways." Thus, the verse can refer to the incarnation as establishing the foundation of the *new* creation. In contrast, Prov. 8:25 (LXX) says, "Before all hills, he *begot* me"; and this unqualified statement must refer to the eternal generation of the Word from God the Father. Once we grant Athanasius' distinction between two times in the Word's existence and two modes of predication, we can appreciate his refutation of the Arian exegesis. As we shall see in a moment, a completely different approach to the Arian exegesis was taken in Antioch, and these differing approaches lie behind the Christological controversies of fifth century. Suffice it to say that it is Athanasius' Christology of the Word of God appropriating humanity and making it his own that ultimately governs his interpretation of the problematic texts.

We may turn next to one aspect of Theodore's exegesis, where attention shifts from the Trinitarian question of Christ's relation to the Father to the Christological question of the relation of Christ's divinity to his humanity. Like Athanasius, he was obliged to deal with the Arian interpretations we have already mentioned. For Athanasius as for the Arians, all references to Christ in Scripture (e.g., "Jesus," "Son of Man," "Son of God," "Son of David," "Word") were applied to the eternal Word of God, and Athanasius avoided the Arian conclusion by arguing that attribution could be "economic" as well as "natural." Thus, a single subject (the Word of God) is spoken of in two different ways. For Theodore this way of refuting the Arians is ruled out of court because it presupposes a natural and substantial union of divinity with humanity that either reduces God the Word to mutable creaturehood or renders the humanity of Christ docetic. This assumption probably derives from the Antiochene approach to defining Christ that prevailed before the Arian controversy, but it is sharpened and made more explicit by the Trinitarian debate. As well, Theodore was concerned to refute Apollinaris, who taught an extreme form of the Athanasian Christology. Theodore's refutation of the Arians, then, proceeds by distinguishing two subjects in Christ rather than two modes of attribution. Scripture sometimes refers to the Word of God; sometimes, to the Man assumed by the Word in the incarnation. Nonetheless, though Scripture when analyzed always distinguishes the divine from the human subject, it refers to Christ as a single *prosōpon*. And it is this Christology that Theodore employs against the Apollinarians and that represents the main lines of the Antiochene view of Christ.

Theodore's interpretation of Ps. 45, one of the Arian proof texts, will best explain the points that have just been made. Throughout his commentary on Psalms he argues that each psalm must be given a single and unified *prosōpon*. The technical term means "mask" and may best be understood by noting that in middle Platonism one of the major questions concerned which of the characters in the Platonic dialogues were the spokesmen for Plato himself. For example, Timaeus is one of the *dramatis personae* (Greek *prosōpa*) in the dialogue that bears his name, and he represents Plato's views. Similarly, Theodore argues that in the psalms David adopts the *personae*, or *prosōpa*, of various figures in Israel's history, thus predicting what will happen. In Ps. 45 he adopts the *prosōpon* of Christ and so predicts the incarnation. Nevertheless, within this prediction David is careful to preserve the distinction of Christ's two natures. Verse 6 ("Your divine throne endures for ever and ever") can only refer to the eternal Word of God. In contrast, v. 7 ("You love righteousness and hate wickedness. Therefore God, your God, has anointed you with the oil of gladness above your fellows") obviously refers to the man "anointed" by God when the Word of God assumed him. Thus, David "marvelously separates for us the natures, and indicates the union of *prosōpon*" (*Commentary on the Psalms* 45). Having identified the *prosōpon* of the psalm in this way, Theodore goes on to suggest that it be regarded as a parable of the love between Christ and the church.

By comparing Theodore's interpretation of Heb. 2:10 with Athanasius' and Cyril's we can sharpen an understanding of the way Christological issues shaped exegesis. The verse reads: "For it was fitting that he, for whom and through whom [RSV: by whom] all things exist, in bringing many sons to glory, should make the pioneer of their salvation perfect through suffering." The exegetical issue is the references of the subject and the object of the sentence. Athanasius understands the verse to mean "God the Father perfects the Incarnate Word through suffering" (*PG* 25.572). Theodore rejects this interpretation for two reasons. First, since the subject is the one *through* whom *(dia)* all things exist, we must identify "he" with God the Son rather than with God the Father. The universe was made *by (hypo)* the Father *through (dia)* the Son. Second, we cannot attribute suffering to the Word, and so the "pioneer" must be the man. For Theodore, Heb. 2:10 means "the Word of God perfects the Man through suffering" (*Catechetical Homilies* 8.8–9; *On the Incarnation* 12, H. B. Swete, *Theodore of Mopsuestia's Commentaries . . .* , Vol. 2 [1882], pp. 303f., *Commentary on Hebrews*, *PG* 66.957). Cyril is obliged to agree with Theodore's first point but rejects his second. For him, the verse means "the Word of God perfects himself through suffering" (*Sources chrétiennes* 97, p. 463). A parallel may be found in John 17:19, where the incarnate Word says, "And for their sake *I consecrate myself,* that they also may be consecrated in truth." Differing theologies explain the differing interpretations.

One illustration of this point may be found in differing interpretations of Christ's priesthood. Hebrews, of course, supplies the fathers of the church with a biblical basis for understanding Christ's function in this way, but it also leaves a number of difficult questions open. What is the relationship of this priest to the God who "made" him (Heb. 3:2), especially when he is defined as God's Son "through whom also he created the world" (Heb. 1:2). Moreover, Christ like all priests must be "chosen from among men" (Heb. 5:1). Yet he must at the same time be "called by God" (Heb. 5:4), and this divine call to be "a priest for ever after the order of Melchisedek" is equated with God's appointment in Ps. 2:7, "Thou art my Son, today I have begotten thee," a verse more often than not associated by the fathers with God the Father's eternal generation of the second person of the Trinity. A careful reading of Hebrews raises not only the question of Christ's relationship to God but also the dilemma of how the agent of creation can experience suffering and death. Attempts to solve these problems correlate with the development of doctrine in the early church. Origen, for example, understands Christ's priesthood as a way of talking about the mediatorial function of the eternal Word of God. Thus, it is the Word who is priest; and he exercises that priesthood both apart from and in the incarnation. With the Arian controversy in the early fourth century, however, came a rejection of this mediatorial view of the Word, since such a view might imply the Arian belief that the Word's subordination to the Father required him to be a creature. As a consequence, Christ's priesthood came to be limited to the incarnation; and attention shifted to the relationship of the lofty and the lowly aspects of the incarnate Lord. For the Alexandrian fathers it is the Word incarnate who becomes the priest and exercises that priesthood by offering himself on the cross and by entering the true tabernacle of heaven itself once he has perfected his own sanctification in the resurrection. The priest is, when all is said and done, God the Word himself, who has condescended to become our Savior by coming among us. In contrast, the Antiochene fathers argue that since this priest was "chosen from among men" (Heb. 5:1) and "learned obedience through what he suffered" (Heb. 5:8), he can only be identified as the Man assumed by God the Word. For the Antiochenes, it is the human Jesus who is priest, and the mystery of the incarnation is not so much how God became one of us as how a perfectly human obedience and suffering brings us God. It is obvious that these interpretations reflect the technical theologies that developed in the ancient church, but we must insist that they also reflect close readings of the biblical text and honest attempts to resolve its difficulties. We can also suggest that the developing interpretations are not so much reapplications of the text to changed circumstances as efforts to bring the vision of Christ's priesthood found in the text into sharper focus.

The Moral and Spiritual Meaning of Scripture

Scriptural interpretation in the early church functioned in contexts quite apart from doctrinal controversy. Needless to say, the Bible was constantly used as a warrant for theological views even when those views were not controversial, and the Christian message of salvation was constantly proclaimed by the use of Scripture. We must, however, turn immediately to a rather different function of interpretation. The Bible supplied a warrant for convictions about how Christians should live their lives and was, more than that, an important resource in enabling the moral and spiritual progress of believers. Again, we shall be able to do no more than give examples of ways in which Christians understood this function. We must beware, however, of distinguishing the moral and spiritual use of

Scripture too sharply from the theological use. In our time we have become accustomed to thinking of theology and the study of Scripture as academic disciplines that have no necessary bearing on how people live their lives. The early Christians, however, saw the church as the context for both disciplines and were convinced that theory and practice belonged together. In other words, while the fathers always interpreted Scripture theologically, they were concerned to show how their theology could be translated into the Christian life with its moral and spiritual dimensions.

The point can be illustrated from the Prologue to Origen's *Commentary on Song of Songs* (*Classics of Western Spirituality* [*CWS*], p. 218). Spiritual growth and maturity are required of those who seek to understand this book. Origen appeals to the Jewish custom of reserving Song of Songs, the creation account of Genesis, Ezekiel's throne vision, and his account of the restored Temple to those fully trained in interpreting Scripture. Christians should accept this rule and reserve Song of Songs for those who have attained "a perfect and mature age." Origen's conviction may be related to his understanding of the dialectic between contemplation and action or the life of virtue. Moral purification is what enables the contemplation of divine truths. The further Christians have progressed in the virtuous life, the more fully they are able to pray and to perceive the mysterious spiritual meaning of Scripture. Interpreting Scripture is a spiritual task. Equally, the mature understanding of Scripture provides solid food for the Christian and enables further moral and spiritual growth. Virtue leads to vision, and vision empowers virtue. A dialectic is established between contemplation and action; and in terms of the function of Scripture, it is virtue that opens its meaning, while it is the apprehension of Scripture's meaning that gives the believer the power to live the Christian life. Origen's view is typical and sets the context in which we may consider the moral and spiritual function of biblical interpretation, that is, the way in which Scripture shapes and guides the Christian life.

In his *Conferences* (14.13), Cassian (early fifth century) has Abbot Nesteros argue that Scripture "ought to be constantly poured into our ears or should ever proceed from our lips. . . . And so it will come to pass that not only every purpose and thought of your heart, but also the wanderings and rovings of your imagination will become to you a holy and unceasing pondering of the Divine law." What he means, of course, is that Scripture will so purify the memory that the moral and spiritual life will be rightly directed. Cassian is thinking of the monastic offices and of the monk's constant prayers, which drew largely upon the treasures of Scripture. But the same point can be made more broadly of the public reading of Scripture in Christian worship. The liturgical use of Scripture was not understood primarily in terms of edification and instruction. Instead, it was designed to shape Christian lives by the constant reminder of the message of salvation and of the response required by that message.

One way in which the church fathers used Scriptures to define Christian moral teaching was to assemble proof texts for various precepts of that teaching. A good example may be found in the third book of Cyprian of Carthage's *Testimonies*, written in the middle of the third century. One hundred and twenty precepts are given, each supported by biblical proof texts that are cited without further comment. Some of these precepts are moral injunctions; for example, "Anger must be overcome, lest it constrain us to sin" as is proved by Prov. 16:32; 12:16; Eph. 4:26; and Matt. 5:21–22 (*Testimonies* 3.8, *ANF* 5, p. 535). Others are designed to explain the world's rejection of Christians and the value of suffering and martyrdom. Martyrdom brings benefits, as is demonstrated by Prov. 14:25; Wisd. 5:1–9; and many other texts, including Matt. 5:10; 10:28, 32–33 (*Testimonies* 3.16, *ANF* 5, p. 537). Still others have to do with Christian beliefs that touch upon believers' attitudes toward life—for example, that "God is patient for this end, that we may repent of our sin and be reformed" (*Testimonies* 3.35, *ANF* 5, p. 544). The same sort of pattern may be found more than a century later in Basil the Great's *Shorter Rules*, where precepts for the monastic life are presented with supporting biblical texts. Much of the homiletical literature of the early church depends upon using the stock moral teaching of the church together with its scriptural warrants. Chrysostom toward the end of the fourth century constantly gives his hearers moral advice based on his understanding of Scripture and exhorts them to "inquire from the Scriptures" to learn what true riches are and how they should live their lives (*Homily* 13 on 2 Corinthians).

Athanasius' *Life of Antony* takes us beyond the mere proof texting of Christian moral teaching, and we may use its evidence as a basis for discussing other ways in which Scripture functions to enable the Christian life. Athanasius wrote his work shortly after Antony's death in 356 and during his exile with the monks in the Thebaid south of Alexandria. His purpose may well have been to cement an alliance between the patriarchate of Alexandria and the monks, enlisting their aid against the Arians by extolling one of their most venerated leaders. Nevertheless, the book also served another purpose by describing the exceptional life of the hermit Antony so that others would be persuaded to follow his example. Augustine's reading of a Latin translation of the *Life of Antony* in Milan was one of the major factors leading to his conversion in 386. Scripture plays a role throughout Antony's life. Orphaned when he was eighteen or twenty, Antony was left responsible for the family property and for his young sister. Less than six months after his parents' deaths he went to church pondering the story in Acts 4–5 of how the Christians in Jerusalem sold their goods and gave the proceeds to the apostles for distribution to the poor. No sooner had he entered the church when he heard in the Gospel, which was being read, Christ's words to the rich man: "If you would be perfect, go, sell what you possess and give to the poor, and you will have treasure in heaven" (Matt. 19:21). The pattern was repeated the next time Antony went to church. This time the Gospel command was, "Do not be anxious about tomorrow" (cf. Matt. 6:25).

Antony understood the commands of the Gospel in an oracular fashion and applied them to himself. After providing for his sister and disposing of his property he began his career as a hermit, moving first to the edge of the village, then to the tombs some distance away, and finally to an abandoned fortress in the desert (*Life of Antony* 103). It is clear from the way Athanasius tells the story that Scripture *did* something. It is not merely that Antony heard precepts that he chose to follow. Instead, he found in the liturgical reading of the Gospel a divine grace operating that moved his will and granted him his vocation. Augustine's conversion happened in much the same way. When in the garden in Milan he heard the child's chant, "Take it and read!" he immediately turned to the book of Paul's letters he had been studying. He had remembered the story of Antony, and when he opened the Scriptures at random he found the words, "Not in reveling and drunkenness, not in debauchery and licentiousness, not in quarreling and jealousy. But put on the Lord Jesus Christ, and make no provision for the flesh, to gratify its desires" (Rom. 13:13–14; *Confessions* 8.12). In both these cases the oracular character of Scripture supplies the gracious enabling power that changed the lives of those to whom Scripture spoke.

In a less dramatic way Scripture continued to guide Antony in his new life. He learned from it how the devil operates and what disciplines are necessary to win the victory over him (*Life of Antony* 7). Later he taught "the discipline he had learned from the Scriptures" to many others (*Life of Antony* 46). His instructions made special reference to Paul's words, "Do not let the sun go down on your anger" (Eph. 4:26; *Life of Antony* 55). Scripture became for him a kind of handbook for the monastic life. The same point of view may be found elsewhere in patristic writings. For example, Gregory of Nyssa's *Life of Moses* takes the story of Moses as a basis for a lengthy allegory, spelling out in some detail the central aspects of the Christian life as Nyssa understood them. Moses' birth stands for the free choice that initiates the Christian life. His meeting with Aaron means that after Christians have begun to make progress in the life of virtue, God's assistance comes to them in the form of the guardian angels. The vision of the burning bush is the second stage of the Christian life in which the vanity of the created order is perceived by intellectually contemplating it, and Moses' entrance into the dark cloud is the third and final stage in which one is united with Christ in love and enabled to make perpetual progress toward the infinite good. The three stages are, as well, symbolized by Solomon's three books. Proverbs teaches ethics; Ecclesiastes, physics and the intellectual contemplation of the created universe; Song of Songs, the perfect union in love of the believer and Christ. Much more could be said, but the major point to make is that Nyssa takes the idea of the *Life of Antony* that Scripture supplies a handbook for living the Christian life and elaborates it by applying his allegorical method to the biblical narratives of Moses' life.

Returning to the *Life of Antony*, we find one last function of Scripture. Biblical texts become weapons in Antony's battle with Satan. When demons attacked him in the form of warriors or beasts, Antony dispelled them by praying and by chanting Scripture, particularly the psalms (*Life of Antony* 39–40). A more elaborate and sophisticated explanation of this function of Scripture may be found in Athanasius' *Letter to Marcellinus on the Interpretation of the Psalms.* The letter, which is really a small treatise, begins with a discussion of the excellence of the psalms. They summarize the themes found elsewhere in Scripture and set them to music. Still more, they contain "even the emotions of each soul. . . . Therefore anyone who wishes boundlessly to receive and understand from it [the book of Psalms], so as to mold himself, it is written there" (*Letter to Marcellinus* 10, *CWS*, p. 108). A little later Athanasius says:

> If the point needs to be put more forcefully, let us say that the entire Holy Scripture is a teacher of virtues and of the truths of the faith, while the Book of Psalms possesses somehow the perfect image for the soul's course of life. (*Letter to Marcellinus* 14, *CWS*, p. 112)

What Athanasius means is that the psalms provide more than a guide to life; they give Christians divine power in every circumstance of their lives. For example, "If you should see the foe attacking . . . recite Psalm 38." Athanasius' instructions help explain

Antony's use of Scripture as weapons against the devil, and they enlarge the use of Scripture in this way by considering a wide variety of human circumstances in which Scripture supplies assistance.

It was George Herbert in the early seventeenth century who said that the true interpretation of Scripture may be found in the lives of Christians:

> Such are thy secrets, which my life makes good,
> And comments on thee: for in ev'ry thing
> Thy words do find me out, and parallels bring,
> And in another make me understand.

But Herbert's view is far from novel. The fathers of the early church would have agreed. For them, Scripture yielded a theological vision when rightly interpreted. And theological disputes in the early church were largely arguments about how rightly to describe that vision and to define the hero of the story that comprised the vision. Nevertheless, the theological vision did not exist for its own sake. It was meant to be translated into renewed human lives. Consequently, the moral and spiritual function of scriptural interpretation not only must be tied to theology but also must be regarded as the ultimate purpose of the theologian's task.

Interpretation for Its Own Sake?

We have argued that scriptural interpretation in the early church is always directly or indirectly theological, and it may therefore seem paradoxical to insist that the fathers were interested in interpretation for its own sake. It is true that the interpretations we find in homilies and theological treatises differ in no way from those we find in biblical commentaries. Moreover, patristic commentaries are frequently concerned to refute what are regarded as heretical interpretations of Scripture and to expound the text in terms of what the writers consider orthodox. We must remember, however, that our distinction between exegesis conceived historically and hermeneutics understood as a theological and homiletical task was not one made by the fathers. No contrast was drawn between the historical and the theological meaning of Scripture; the *historia* was the obvious narrative meaning of the text and must not be confused with the modern use of "history" as a way of talking about the reconstruction of what really happened by using the texts as historical evidence. The *historia*, as well, had theological significance; and the distinction between the narrative meaning and the spiritual meaning (*theoria*) for both the allegorists and the typologists was that between obvious meanings that were in part theological and the deeper and more mysterious theological meanings to be gained by meditation on the text. Consequently, a concern for orthodoxy by no means excludes a concern for fair-minded interpretation from the point of view of the fathers.

The point may be illustrated by one general consideration and by appealing to two comments made by biblical commentators in the early church. Generally speaking, it is instructive that the biblical commentary emerged as a literary genre as early as the time of Heracleon and Origen, the first part of the third century. The analogy is not a strict one, but we may compare the Christian distinction between theological treatises and biblical commentaries to the rabbinic distinction between the Talmud and the midrashim. Just as the Talmud organized discussion around points of the oral law, so Christian theological treatises took various theological themes as their subject. Yet in both cases Scripture is integral to the task at hand. Similarly, the midrashim and Christian biblical commentaries both make their point of departure the scriptural text taken in order. Yet both are concerned to interpret the text in the light of the fundamental religious convictions held by church or synagogue.

With this in mind, we may look briefly at Origen's letter to Gregory the Wonderworker in which he states the presuppositions of scriptural study (*ANF* 10, pp. 295ff.). Origen draws a parallel between the philosophical schools of his time and the school he had established in Alexandria. After turning over the direction of the catechetical school to his pupil Heraclas, Origen established himself as the master of a school for Christians who were "more perfect" and had the leisure to investigate the deeper truths of their faith. His scriptural commentaries were the fruit of this enterprise. In his letter Origen urges Gregory to study the divine Scriptures. "For we require to study the divine writings deeply, lest we should speak of them faster than we think." Gregory is to "knock" at the Scriptures (Matt. 7:7) in the expectation that God will open their meaning if he approaches them prayerfully. Origen transfers the insatiable quest for truth which characterized Platonism to the Christian study of Scripture. And however much that quest enables Christians to grow spiritually, it is one that, from another point of view, must be engaged in for its own sake.

We find a somewhat different understanding of the purpose of biblical commentaries in Theodore's preface to his *Commentary on John* (ed. Vosté, pp. 1ff.). He promises that he will not linger over passages that are obvious and easy to understand. Unlike the preacher who can permit himself to treat easy and difficult passages alike, the commentator must focus his energy on the problematic ones. Sometimes the difficulty involves the heretical misuse of texts, and Theodore explicitly mentions the commentary of Asterius the Sophist, an Arian. But sometimes the difficulties are simply that. Many of them have to do with reconciling John and the Synoptics and with understanding apparently insignificant details of John's narrative. Theodore's concern to reconcile the four Gospels is, of course, designed to show that the narrative meaning of John can be trusted; but it is difficult to see that any explicit theological purpose is served. And his comments on peculiar details in the Gospel are always commonsense explanations. For example, the reference to "much grass" at the feeding of the five thousand (John 6:10) simply provokes the comment that it was spring "when the earth is usually adorned with growing grass, especially in a place hotter than others" (ed. Vosté, p. 94). Theodore must have seen a Palestinian spring.

One major reason that Scripture may be interpreted for its own sake is that the Rule of faith is a negative rather than a positive principle. That is, it excludes incorrect interpretations but does not require a correct one. Of a given passage there may be many interpretations that are valid because they do not contradict the Rule of faith, but we cannot be sure of its true meaning. In their differing ways both Origen and Theodore recognize this and so leave room for interpretation as an ongoing task. And both recognize the validity of differing interpretations in specific instances. Theodoret's commentaries are particularly instructive, since even though he was committed to the Antiochene Christology, he often recognizes the validity of Alexandrian interpretations of crucial texts.[11] Unity of belief in the early church is never confused with uniformity of belief or with assent to a definite list of theological propositions. And by the same token, the unity of valid scriptural interpretation does not require uniformity.

The point just made represents a central theme in Augustine's treatise *On Christian Doctrine*. The work, finished in 426 or 427, considers the nature of Christian culture and education but focuses upon understanding and teaching Scripture. Two themes are tied together to make the basic argument. First, a distinction must be made between use and enjoyment. Enjoyment involves treating something as ultimate, and so only the Trinity may be enjoyed, while everything else must be "used," that is, treated as means to the greater end of enjoying God. Second, signs are to be distinguished from what they signify and are to be classified as natural or conventional. Conventional signs, in turn, may be either clear or ambiguous. Since Scripture is to be understood as a collection of signs, the interpreter's basic decision must be whether or not a given passage is ambiguous and therefore figurative. The details of Augustine's argument need not detain us, but it will be seen that the signs of Scripture function properly when they rightly direct our attention to the Trinity, which can alone be enjoyed.

Augustine brings part of his argument to a conclusion by saying:

> The sum of all we have said since we began to speak of things thus comes to this: it is to be understood that the plentitude and the end of the Law and of all the sacred Scriptures is the love of a Being which is to be enjoyed and of a being that can share that enjoyment with us, since there is no need for a precept that anyone should love himself. (*On Christian Doctrine* 1.35.39)

What Augustine means is that the fundamental touchstone for validity in interpreting Scripture is the rule of charity, the love of God and of our neighbor. Any interpretation that conforms to this rule is valid even though it may be incorrect. A metaphor clarifies what he means. The Christian is on a journey, and the only thing that really matters is progress on the way. Consequently, if someone "is deceived in an interpretation which builds up charity, which is the end of the commandments, he is deceived in the same way as a man who leaves a road by mistake but passes through a field to the same place toward which the road itself leads" (*On Christian Doctrine* 1. 36.41). While Augustine recognizes the Rule of faith as a necessary criterion for valid interpretation, he insists that the only sufficient criterion is the rule of charity. The close connection between right belief, right understanding, and right living is obvious.

We may conclude by suggesting that the chief characteristics of patristic exegesis are its orientation toward theology, its insistence on the unity of theology and life, of vision and virtue, and its flexibility. From one point of view, the Rule of faith was limited as a unifying framework for interpreting Scripture. It did not settle the question of method, nor did it solve problems of detail in the theological, moral, and spiritual exposition of the Bible. But from another point of view, what seem to be limitations are precisely what enable the task of interpretation. Built into the patristic understanding of exegesis is the conviction that the Christian's theological vision continues to grow and change, just as the Christian life is a pilgrimage and progress toward a destiny only dimly perceived. The framework of interpretation, then, does not so much solve the problem of what Scripture means as supply the context in which the quest for that meaning may take place. Origen puts it this way:

> But in all these speculations let our understanding have sufficient coherence with the rule of piety, and let us think of the Holy Spirit's words not as something that shines as a speech fashioned by frail human eloquence, but as it is written, "All the king's glory is within" (Ps. 44:14 LXX—45:13). . . . For no matter how far a person advances in his investigation and makes progress by a keener zeal, even if the grace of God is within him and enlightens his mind (cf. Eph. 1:18), he cannot arrive at the perfect end of the truths he seeks. No mind that is created has the ability to understand completely by any manner of means, but as it finds some small part of the answers that are sought, it sees other questions to be asked. And if it arrives at those answers, it will again see beyond them to many more questions that they imply must be asked. (*On First Principles* 4.3.14, *CWS*, pp. 202f.)

Epilogue

Not so very long ago, before the fragments were disassembled, it was possible to see in the Yale Art Gallery the reassembled remains of the mithraeum and the early Christian baptistery from Dura-Europos, preserved from the third century c.e. by their chance incorporation in expanded ramparts for the city of the eastern border of the Roman empire. And, although the original remains had been left in the Middle East, one could also imagine the Jewish synagogue of Dura. Three architectural fragments conveyed at least a shadowy impression of three religions as they existed more than a millennium and a half ago. What struck the eye and the imagination was that the three were more like one another than like anything from another period of history. Something like this strikes the student of early Judaism and Christianity. Jews and Christians understood and interpreted their Bibles more like one another than either anticipated the standard approach of the modern historical-critical method. However much Jewish and Christian communities have preserved the religious use of Scripture for themselves, to one degree or another they have been affected by the rise of a modern "scientific" approach to Scripture. Both the common mind-set of ancient Jews and Christians and the striking difference between that mind-set and the modern historical-critical approach find illustration in two sets of considerations.

First, neither Jews nor Christians in the ancient world were preoccupied with method. To be sure, there were methods. Conventions of interpretation came to be thought of as rules for interpretation in Israel. And the debate between typology and allegorism among Christians had a methodological dimension. But what was decisive for both traditions was not method but a set of attitudes. Both insisted that every detail of Scripture mattered, and both read the texts almost microscopically. Moreover, both insisted upon the harmony of Scripture. At one level, this meant that the task of interpretation was to resolve apparent contradictions and to bring to light the underlying unity of the sacred text. At a deeper level, this implied a strong sense of a canon, a special collection of books that bore unified testimony to religious convictions. The same divine purpose found expression in the different books whether they were narratives of history, compilations of wisdom, or hymns by which to worship God. And for the Christians the same became true for what was eventually called by them the Old Testament as well as for the apostolic writings making up the New Testament. The canons of Scripture possessed by both traditions were seamless wholes. Finally, these two attitudes drove toward the fundamental conviction that Scripture was intimately bound up with the life of a religious community.

If Jews and Christians in late antiquity agreed that a set of fundamental attitudes mattered more than method, they also agreed that the historical dimension of Scripture, at least as we have come to define history, was not at the heart of biblical interpretation. It is not that history was unimportant. No one could read the accounts that have been given in this book without realizing that history does matter enormously. Israel constantly remembered its past, and the church largely defined itself by the history of Jesus. The point is that neither tradition treated Scripture as historical evidence. Unlike the historical-critical method, they were not interested in reconstructing what had happened once upon a time. On the contrary, what had happened was important because of its bearing upon the present. The meaning of history and not history as such found pride of place.

Moving beyond the contrast with the modern historical-critical method, we can characterize early Jewish and Christian interpretation more positively by speaking of three areas in which both broad agreement and yet important differences are to be found—the differences reflecting still more basic divisions between Judaism and Christianity themselves. First, both traditions saw their respective Bibles as collections fashioned out of the religious experience of a people, in which history itself held a sacred message, the unfolding of God's will. For Jews, this meant the nation's experience over an extended period of time: the patriarchs, the exodus, the conquest, the monarchy, the Babylonian exile, and the return. The task itself of assembling this past into a sacred library took place only gradually, and involved a continuous adaptation of the past to the present. Early Christianity was heir to this same sacred history and inherited its Scripture, but the attention of early Christians was of course focused on Christ's life and fate, and the relationship of these to the

Great Past; this in turn generated new texts and eventually new Scripture, indeed, a new reading of the whole. Christianity formed its sacred library relatively rapidly, in no more than a century and a half. If its Scripture too represents an adaptation of hallowed traditions and texts to a new reality, the adaptation was thus both less gradual, and more single-minded in its focus.

A second point of broad agreement balanced by a crucial difference is the idea of revelation that underlies the work of interpretation. For Jews, God had revealed his word through his prophets and sages—and most prominently (indeed, in some accounts, exclusively) in the revelation at Sinai. The Torah, the written substance of that revelation, was thus the very essence of divine speech, and its interpretation was to be ever refined by succeeding generations of teachers, for "all is in it"—rules of conduct, ethical models, the past, the present, and the future. For Christians, on the other hand, God had spoken ultimately, and uniquely, in the life and teachings of Jesus. To be sure, the mainstream development of the church never wished to divorce this central concern from God's other teachings or to sever Christ's story from the story of Israel. But we cannot mistake the centrality of Christ to Christianity. In this sense, Christians were less a "people of the book" than the Jews, for the Christian revelation was located in Christ and only secondarily in the Scripture that bore witness to him. This division between the two religions appears in the context of broad agreements, but it remains a crucial difference nonetheless.

A final point is the manner in which both Jews and Christians saw the task of interpretation as that of bringing Scripture to bear upon the present and upon the religious life of their respective communities. This, as we have seen, had several dimensions: the reinterpretation of ancient prophecy as bearing on Judaism's messianic hopes, or, among Christians, as confirming the belief in Jesus as the Messiah, is one way in which ancient texts took on new meaning. But more generally, Scripture itself was now conceived to be a great corpus of timeless truths which made it forever relevant to the community, the Great Book of Teaching. And here again there is a difference. For Jews, the nature of these truths touched many things: history, halakha, hopes for the future—all these, and more, were part of what Scripture taught. For Christians, though there was a similar diversity, the truths were in one way or another related to Christ, who as the one in the form of God was Truth. In a way, this returns us to the difference highlighted in the previous paragraph, between Judaism's focus on Torah versus Christianity's on Christ—for each community's notion of timeless truth was affected thereby.

It is instructive that the figure of Wisdom, portrayed in Prov. 8:22ff. as God's agent of creation and revelation, was equated in Ecclesiasticus (Ben Sira) with the Torah but was identified by Christians as early as Paul with Christ. From the same point of departure we thus find two paths, strikingly similar in many of their presuppositions and methods, but finally divergent.

Notes

Chapter 1: The Rise of a Christian Bible

1. Irenaeus knows Hebrews and the *Shepherd of Hermas* but does not regard these writings as apostolic and authoritative.

2. E. Hennecke, *New Testament Apocrypha*, ed. W. Schneemelcher, ET ed. R. McN. Wilson, 2 vols. (London/Philadelphia: Lutterworth Press/Westminster Press, 1963 and 1965).

3. James M. Robinson, ed., *The Nag Hammadi Library in English* (San Francisco: Harper & Row, 1977).

4. See Jean Daniélou, *Théologie de judéo-chrétianisme* (Tournai: Desclée et Fils, 1958).

5. See Helmut Koester, *Synoptische Überlieferungen bei den apostolischen Vätern* (Berlin: Texte und Untersuchungen 65, 1957).

6. Cited in Eusebius, *Ecclesiastical History* 3.39.4.

7. Cited in Johannes Quasten, *Patrology*, Vol. 1 (Westminster, Md.: Newman Press, 1950), p. 172.

8. Justin Martyr, *Dialogue with Trypho* 80. Cf. *Dialogue* 47, where he recognizes the difference but also the legitimacy of Jewish Christians.

9. Eusebius, *Ecclesiastical History* 4.22. Cf. Marcel Simon, *Jewish Sects at the Time of Jesus* (Philadelphia: Fortress Press, 1967).

10. Cited in Eusebius, *Ecclesiastical History* 4.22.4.

11. Eusebius, *Ecclesiastical History* 5.21 and 8.1 (persecution and the devil); 2.13 and 4.7, 24 (heresy and the devil); 2.6 and 3.5–7 (punishment of the Jews).

12. See R. A. Greer, "The Dog and the Mushrooms: Irenaeus' View of the Valentinians Assessed," in *The Rediscovery of Gnosticism*, Vol. 1: *The School of Valentine*, ed. Bentley Layton (Leiden: E. J. Brill, 1980), pp. 146–175.

13. Irenaeus, *Against Heresies* 2.30.14 and 1.29.1.

14. Eusebius, *Ecclesiastical History* 1.1.

15. See Marcel Simon, *Verus Israel* (Paris: Éditions E. de Boccard, 1964).

16. Suetonius, *Life of Claudius* 25.

17. Justin Martyr, *Dialogue with Trypho* 16.

18. Irenaeus, *Against Heresies* 3.24.

19. Ibid., 3.4.
20. See p. 110 above.
21. Irenaeus, *Against Heresies* 1.8.

Chapter 2: Christian Transformations of the Hebrew Scriptures

1. See C. H. Dodd, *The Apostolic Preaching and Its Development* (1936; London: Hodder & Stoughton, 1963), and Barnabas Lindars, *New Testament Apologetic* (London/Philadelphia: SCM Press/Westminster Press, 1961).

2. See John Piper, *"Love Your Enemies": Jesus' Love Command in the Synoptic Gospels and the Early Christian Paraenesis* (Cambridge: Cambridge University Press, 1979).

3. The passage in Isaiah begins at 52:13 and ends with 53:12. Isaiah 53:12 is cited in Luke 22:37 as a prophecy fulfilled by Jesus' arrest and execution. Paul reflects his knowledge of the apologetic by citing Isa. 52:15 (Rom. 15:21) and 53:1 (Rom. 10:16), but he adapts the apologetic to his argument that the Jews have rejected their own Messiah, who has been accepted by the Gentiles. Isaiah 65:2 ("All day long I have held out my hands to a disobedient and contrary people") is given the same function in Rom. 10:21. John 12:38 cites Isa. 53:1 to show that the Jews have failed "to believe our report." The reference in the prophetic verse to "the arm of the Lord" certainly implies the cross, but like Paul, John uses it in his argument with the Jews. Isaiah 53:4 is cited by Matt. 8:17 as a prophecy of Jesus' healing work, and we can compare his use of Isa. 42:1–4 (Matt. 12:18–21) as a prediction of Jesus' withdrawal from public view. Other possible allusions to Isaiah 53 may be found in passages such as 1 Peter 2:22 and the eucharistic words of Jesus (Mark 14:24: "blood . . . poured out for many"; cf. Isa. 53:12: "poured out his soul to death . . . bore the sin of many").

4. In the Synoptic passion narratives the psalms are not explicitly cited, but they inform the way the story is told. The soldiers divide Jesus' garments (Ps. 22:18/Mark 15:24 and parallels). Those who pass by mock him and wag their heads (Ps. 22:7/Mark 15:29 and parallel). Their derisory words in Matt. 27:43 are taken from Ps. 22:8 and Jesus' cry of dereliction (Mark 15:34‖Matt. 27:46) is a citation of the first verse of Ps. 22. In John's Gospel the psalm is explicitly cited. The division of Jesus' garments and the casting of lots for his seamless robe fulfill Ps. 22:18 (John 19:24), and Jesus' thirst may fulfill Ps. 22:15 as well as Ps. 69:21 (John 19:28–29). Psalm 69 is thus drawn into the picture and may lie behind verses in the Synoptic account (Mark 15:23‖Matt. 27:34; Mark 15:36‖Matt. 27:48). John 15:25 cites Ps. 69:4 (cf. Ps. 35:19) as fulfilled by the Jews' hating Jesus "without cause." Psalm 69:9, according to John 2:17, is fulfilled by Jesus' "zeal" for the Temple when he cleanses it. Paul uses Ps. 69:9 (Rom. 15:3) to show that Christ did not please himself, and Ps. 69:22–23 (Rom. 11:9–10) to prove

the Jews' blindness in rejecting Christ. We begin to find shifts in the application of the psalms. Hebrews 2:12 cites Ps. 22:22 to prove Christ's unity with his "brethren." Acts 1:20 refers to Ps. 69:25, and Ps. 109:8 to the fate of Judas. As well, allusions to Ps. 22 and 69 may be found in Rev. 19:5–6; 20:12–15; and similar passages.

5. Cf. Sirach 44:16–19 (and the whole of 44–50); 1 Maccabees 2; 4 Macc. 16:20–23; Wisdom 10; *The Fathers According to Rabbi Nathan*, ed. and tr. Judah Goldin (New Haven: Yale University Press, 1955), pp. 155ff.; *The Song at the Sea*, ed. and tr. Judah Goldin (New Haven: Yale University Press, 1971), pp. 156ff.; Cicero, *On the Nature of the Gods* 68–88; Mary Rose D'Angelo, *Moses in the Letter to the Hebrews*, Society of Biblical Literature Dissertation Series 42 (Missoula, Mont.: Scholars Press, 1979), ch. 1.

6. For Abraham, the title "friend" proves his excellence, and the actual proof text (Isa. 41:8) is not cited. The other testimony texts are Job 1:1; Num. 12:7; and Ps. 89:20. The texts proving their humility are Gen. 18:27; Job 14:4–5; Ex. 3:11; 4:10; and Ps. 51:1–17.

7. Cf. Pierre Prigent, *Les testimonia dans le Chréstianisme primitif: 1' Épître de Barnabé i–xvi et ses sources* (Paris: Études Bibliques, 1961); L. W. Barnard, *Studies in the Apostolic Fathers and Their Background* (Oxford: Blackwell, 1966), ch. 9; Lindars, *New Testament Apologetic*.

8. Cf. Robert Kraft, *The Didache and Barnabas*, Vol. 3 of *The Apostolic Fathers* (New York: Thomas Nelson & Sons, 1965), pp. 84–85.

9. In *Barnabas* 2, Isa. 1:1–13; Jer. 7:22f.; Zech. 8:17; and Ps. 51:19 are listed to prove that God "needs neither sacrifices nor burnt-offerings nor oblations." Cf. Rabbi Johanan ben Zakkai's view that "acts of loving-kindness" make up for the loss of the Temple (*The Fathers According to Rabbi Nathan*, p. 34); see Justin's use of Isaiah 1 in *First Apology* 37 and 47 and Irenaeus, *Against Heresies* 4.17. One peculiar feature of the last of these citations deserves comment. Psalm 51:19 is elaborated by adding the phrase "A smell of sweet savour to the Lord is a heart that glorifies its maker" to the psalm's statement "Sacrifice to the Lord is a broken heart." The same elaborated citation is found in Clement of Alexandria, *Tutor* 3.12. A note in Codex Constantinopolitanus attributes the added phrase to the *Apocalypse of Adam*. But another explanation suggests itself. In the added phrase, "A smell of sweet savour to the Lord" correlates with "Sacrifice to the Lord," while "A heart that glorifies its maker" correlates with "A broken heart." It looks as though the added phrase interprets the verse from the psalm member by member; Barnabas seems to be citing the verse *and* its interpretation as if both were Scripture.

10. Cf. Justin, *Dialogue with Trypho* 114.5.

11. See Jean Daniélou, *Études d'exégèse judéo-chrétienne* (Paris: Beauchesne et ses Fils, 1966), ch. 8.

12. Novatian, *On the Trinity* 26; Cyprian, *Testimonies* 1.21.

13. Cf. Cyprian, *Testimonies* 1.16–17; Justin, *Dialogue with Trypho* 34, 76, 100, 126; Irenaeus, *Against Heresies* 3.21; *Christian Sibyllines* (E. Hennecke

and W. Schneemelcher, eds., *New Testament Apocrypha* [Philadelphia: West-minster Press, 1966], Vol. 2, p. 710).

14. *The Fathers According to Rabbi Nathan,* p. 23.

15. Cf. *Barnabas* 9, where several of the texts that Justin cites are used, and Irenaeus, *Against Heresies* 4.15–16.

16. Cf. Rom. 10:18.

17. See *Apocryphon of John, Hypostasis of the Archons, On the Origin of the World, Paraphrase of Shem.*

18. Robinson, *Nag Hammadi Library,* pp. 335–336. Similar assessments of the creator God are found in every kind of Christian gnosticism. See *Nag Hammadi Library,* pp. 105–107, 153–158, 165, 331, 411–412. We can add the Sethian Ophites (Irenaeus, ed. Harvey 1.226), Basilides (Hippolytus, *ANF,* p. 106), and Ptolemey (Irenaeus, ed. Harvey 1.47).

19. Cf. *Barnabas* 12; Clement, *Stromata* 6.132.4. But note the omission of the altered version of Isa. 45:1.

20. Cf. Athenagoras, *ANF,* p. 133. *Dialogue with Trypho* 129 cites Gen. 19:24; Gen. 3:22; and Prov. 8:22ff.

21. Cf. *Dialogue with Trypho* 120, where the LXX reading "Till he come for whom this is laid up" instead of Trypho's reading "Till the things laid up for Him come" is accepted.

22. Justin argues this last point in a number of places, using a variety of proof texts: Isa. 54:1 (*First Apology* 53; cf. *2 Clement* 2); Micah 4:1ff. (*Dialogue* 109); Zech. 2:10–13 and 3:1–2 (*Dialogue* 115–116); Malachi 1:10–12 (*Dialogue* 117, 28, 41); Isa. 61:12; 65:1; Gen. 26:4; 28:14; 49:10 (*Dialogue* 119ff.); and Isa. 42:1–4 (*Dialogue* 123). Christians are the true Israel, and the Jews have been rejected by God, as the destruction of Jerusalem proves.

Chapter 3: A Framework for Interpreting a Christian Bible

1. See Helmut Koester, "One Jesus and Four Primitive Gospels," in James M. Robinson and Helmut Koester, *Trajectories Through Early Christianity* (Philadelphia: Fortress Press, 1971).

2. See Nils A. Dahl, "The Crucified Messiah," in *The Crucified Messiah and Other Essays* (Minneapolis: Augsburg Publishing House, 1974).

3. See Willi Marxsen, *Mark the Evangelist,* tr. James Boyce, Donald Juel, William Poehlmann with Roy A. Harrisville (Nashville: Abingdon Press, 1960).

4. See W. D. Davies, *The Setting of the Sermon on the Mount* (Cambridge: Cambridge University Press, 1964), and M. Jack Suggs, *Wisdom, Christology and the Law in Matthew's Gospel* (Cambridge, Mass.: Harvard University Press, 1970).

5. H. E. Tödt, *The Son of Man in the Synoptic Tradition* (ET, London/Philadelphia: SCM Press/Westminster Press, 1965).

6. See Norman Perrin, *A Modern Pilgrimage in New Testament Christology* (Philadelphia: Fortress Press, 1974).

Chapter 4: Applying the Framework

1. See *The Cambridge History of the Bible*, Vol. 1: *From the Beginnings to Jerome*, ed. P. R. Ackroyd and C. F. Evans (Cambridge: Cambridge University Press, 1970), ch. 5.

2. See Robert M. Grant, *The Earliest Lives of Jesus* (New York: Harper & Brothers, 1961).

3. E.g., 2 Cor. 4:18 (*Ex. to Martyrdom* 44; Prologue to *Commentary on Song of Songs*, CWS, p. 236).

4. See 1 Cor. 3:1–3; Heb. 5:12–14; Rom. 14:2; Origen, *On Prayer* 27.5; Prologue to *Commentary on Song of Songs*, CWS, p. 218.

5. Cf. Cassian, *Conferences* 14. 8 (*Nicene and Post-Nicene Fathers*, pp. 437ff.), where he divides the spiritual sense into "tropological, allegorical, analogical," the distinction common in the Middle Ages.

6. See my discussion in R. A. Greer, *The Captain of Our Salvation* (Tübingen: J. C. B. Mohr [Paul Siebeck], 1973), pp. 8–24.

7. See R. V. Sellers, *Eustathius of Antioch and His Place in the Early History of Christian Doctrine* (Cambridge: Cambridge University Press, 1928), pp. 75–81.

8. The passage is translated in Maurice F. Wiles and Mark Santer, eds., *Documents in Early Christian Thought* (Cambridge: Cambridge University Press, 1975), pp. 151–154.

9. See Maurice F. Wiles, *The Spiritual Gospel: The Interpretations of the Fourth Gospel in the Early Church* (Cambridge: Cambridge University Press, 1960), pp. 13–21.

10. See *The Cambridge History of the Bible*, Vol. 1, p. 538.

11. See Greer, *The Captain of Our Salvation*, pp. 291–305.

Index
of Scriptural Citations